DEEP Clearing

Releasing the Power of Your Mind

"A complete guide for practitioners and laymen
on how to integrate mind, heart and body
in personal development work."
3rd Revised Edition

By
Rolf Dane

Publisher: AbilityOne Press
Copenhagen, Denmark

Publisher: AbilityOne Press, www.Ability1Group.org
Ability One Group offers seminars and professional training in DEEP Clearing. Contact us via our website for more information.

Copyright © 2015-2019 by Rolf Dane, all rights reserved.
Author's website: www.RolfDane.com
email: Rolf_Dane@Yahoo.com

Print version, 3rd edition ISBN: 978-87-999547-3-5
EAN: 9788799954735

Table of Content

Foreword by Dr. Keith Scott-Mumby..A-1
Foreword by Heidrun Beer..A-6
Foreword by the author..A-9
Introduction...A-10

PART 1: Clearing Work - Basic Theory

Chapter 1: Life Cycles — 3
The Actual Life Cycle 4 | Life Cycle and Clearing 5 | Scientific Evidence 7 | Other Techniques 7 | Life Cycles and Work 7 |

Chapter 2: Intention and Attention — 9
Intention 9 | Attention 9 | Money 10 | Live Attention/Intention Vs Machines 11 | Incomplete Cycles 11 | Freeing of Attention Units 11 | Other Techniques 12 |

Chapter 3: Live Communication — 15
The Elements of Communication 15 | TYPES OF COMMUNICATIONS 16: Social Conversation 17 | Having an Argument 17 | Public Speaking 17 | Interested – Interesting 18 | Talking Around an Issue 18 | Exchanging Views 18 | Admiration 18 | Two Rules for Good Communication 19 | Trauma and Communication 19 | Manners in Alien Encounters 20 | Interviews 20 | Communication and Life 21 | THE COMMUNICATION DRILLS 21-22 | Exploring the CDs 23 | Assertive communication 24 | Emphatic Listening 24 |

Chapter 4: The Scale of Affinity — 25
Human Character and Temperament 25 | The Classic Temperaments 25 | The Scale of Affinity 26 | The Basic Scale 27 | The Expanded Scale 28 | Sub-zero Affinity Levels 29 | The Body and the Affinity Scale 29 | Affinity and Emotion 30 | The Affinity Scale and Behavior 31 | How to Find a Person's Affinity Level 32 | Raising Somebody's Affinity 32 | The Affinity Scale and Clearing 32 | Summary 33 |

Chapter 5: How Real is Reality? — 35
Subjective Reality 36 | Realities 37 | Physical Universe and Agreement 38 | The Zero Point 39 | Clearing Work and Reality 39 | Footnote on "The Big Bang" 40 |

Chapter 6: The Triad of Relationships and Understanding — 43
Communication is Key 43 | Human Relationships 43 | Learning 45 | Culture, Civilization and the Triad 46 | The Triads in Clearing Work 47 | Handling Upsets 48 |

Chapter 7: Be – Do – Have, Modes of Existence — 49
Be-Do-Have in Organizing 51 | BEING in Clearing Work 51 | Ability to DO and Clearing 53 | Ability to HAVE 54 |

Chapter 8: Spirit – Mind – Body 55

The Spirit 55 | The Mind 55 | The Mind and its Parts 56 |
The Conscious or Rational Mind 56 | The Subconscious Mind and Bypass Reactions 57 |
The Repressed Mind 57 | Logic and Bypass Reactions 58 | Network of Incidents 59 |
Formation of the Bypass Mechanism 60 | The Body-Function Systems 61 |
The Body 61 | Placebo and Nocebo Effect 62 | Clearing and Health 62 |
Another Model 63 | The Aura or Energy Body 63 | Head, Heart and Hand 64 |
Three Parts of the Brain 64 | Belief and Results 65 | The DEEP Package |

Chapter 9: Life as a Game 67

Opposition Games 67 | Other Opposition Games 68 | More Games 68 |
Competitive Games 68 | Man against the Environment 69 | Elements of Life 69 |
The Games of Mr. Jones 70 | Work and Games 70 | Complementary Games 71 |
There Must Be a Game! 71 | No-Games-Conditions 72 | Freedom and Games 73 |
Choosing of Games 73 | Levels of Engagement 74 | Games and Happiness 75 |
Games and problems 75 | Games and Roles 76 | Games and Clearing Work 77 |

Part 2: DEEP Theory

Chapter 10: Emotional Charge 79

Emotions are Energy and Communication 79 | Emotional Charge 80 |
The Biomonitor 81| Inspecting the Poles 82 | DEEP—the Acronym 83 |
DEEP Element > < DEEP Element 85 | Intention as Cause 86 | Outside Repression 86 |
"I Love My Story" 86 | Releasing the Power of Your Mind 88 |

Chapter 11: Viewpoints, Identities, Characters 89

Points of View and the Mind 89 |
Points of View in DEEP Incident Clearing 90 | The Other Viewpoint 91 |
Is the Client Prepared? 92 | DEEP Character Clearing and Viewpoints 92 |
DEEP Subject Clearing 93 | DEEP Body Clearing, Basic Version 94 |
DEEP Viewpoint Clearing 94 | Dialogue or "Hello-OK" 94 |
Attached Entities 95 | Other Beings and Viewpoints 95 |
Some History and Thoughts 96 | Identities and Living 96 |

Chapter 12: The DEEP Package 97

Recordings of the Mind 98 | Physical Matter 99 | Body: Effort, Impulse, Kinesthesia,
Sensation 99 | Emotions, Feelingsn100 | Thought, Decision 101 | The Shock Moment 102 |
Examples of Dictates and Self-limiting Thoughts in Shock Moments 102 |
Polarity or Points of View 102 | Relative Importance of Decision, Emotion, Effort, Polarity 103 |
Knowingness and Forgiveness 103 | Repeat and Tell 103 | "Life is a Pinball Machine" 104 |

Chapter 13: Some Questions and Answers 105

Part 3: DEEP Clearing – The Main Actions

Chapter 14: The Clearer's Professional Conduct 109

Chapter 15: The DEEP Toolbox 113

Control, Duplication and Completing Cycles 113 | Four Basic Rules 114 | The Tools 115 |
Children 120 | Different Types 120 |

Chapter 16: Repeat & Tell — 127
How 'Repeat & Tell' works 127 | Curious, positive interest 128 |
The Sorting Out Step 128 | Finding the DEEP Element and integrating it 128 |
What Works and does not Work 130 | Repeat & Tell as Communication 130 |
Some Tips 132 | Incidents, subjects, characters 132 |
Description of the DEEP Elements 133 | Impulses as Non-physical Actions 134 |
The Elements of the DEEP Package 134 | Body sensations 134 |
Action, Movement (physical experience) 135 | Emotions and Feelings 136 |
Thoughts, Decisions (dogmas, dictates) 137 |
A Sequence of the DEEP Elements 139 | Rounding Off 140 |

Chapter 17: DEEP Subject Clearing (DSC) — 141
Unblocking 141 | DEEP Subject Clearing (DSC) 142 |
Adding a DEEP Step to other Clearing Techniques 143 |

Chapter 18: DEEP Body Clearing (DBC) — 145
New Biology 145 | DEEP Body Clearing by Steps 145 | Transparent Body 147 |

Chapter 19: Deep Incident Clearing — 149
Defining the Complaint 150 | The Main Difference from Earlier Techniques 150 |
Main Spheres of Interest 151 | General Principles of DIC 151 |
Reviewing an Incident 152 | Locating DEEP Packages 152 |
Polarities and Points of View 153 | The Shock Moment 153 |
DEEP INCIDENT CLEARING BY STEPS 153 | Assessing for the Item 153 |
DEEP Mode 155 | Discharging the DEEP Packages 155 |
Other Points of View 156 | God and Bystanders 156 | How much is enough? 157 |
Going Earlier 157 | Flattening DEEP Elements 157 |
Ending Sessions 158 | Exploring Earlier Lives 158 | The Flows 159 | Fresh Reality 159 |
DIC Light 160 | Being Ready for Session 160 | Session Venues 160 |

Chapter 20: DEEP Viewpoint Clearing — 161
DVC Procedure with explanations 162 | New Vitality Lists 164 | DVC versus DCC 164 |

3. Chapter 21: DEEP Character Clearing – Basic Concepts — 165
The Super Problems Action 166 |

Chapter 22: Happiness and DEEP — 167
Harmony of Thought, Emotion and Action 167 |
Happiness versus Misery 167 | Paving the Way 167 | DEEP and Happiness 168 |

Appendix
The Expanded Affinity Scale 169 | DEEP Subject Clearing, Short Form 170 |
Deep Incident Clearing, Short Form 171 | DIC Light 172 | DEEP Body Clearing, Short Form 173 |
DEEP Viewpoint Clearing, Short Form 174 | New vitality lists 175-180 |
Dreams and DEEP 181 | Making Programs for DEEP Clearing Work 182 |
Several Layers of Case 182 | Model Programs for DEEP Clearing WORK 184 |

Glossary for DEEP — 185

Foreword by Professor
Keith Scott-Mumby, MD

As the very first student on the planet to study and learn the mechanics of a brilliant new science of mind and method, I feel a strong sense of privilege in being asked to write a foreword to this book, by the principal researcher who developed and instigated the new techniques.

Once in a while something turns up which is truly revolutionary; different from anything which has gone before and in every sense a "new" approach to matters. Sadly there have been few such developments in the field of the mind. Probably the most pivotal breakthrough of all time was the recognition of the power of the *subconscious mind*, so named by French psychiatrist Pierre Janet and later, rather unfairly, attributed to Sigmund Freud.

Certainly Freud has a place in history, justly deserved. His seminal 1895 work *Studies in Hysteria*, written jointly with Josef Breuer, showed that the subconscious mind was very powerful and capable of influencing thoughts, emotions and behavior, while remaining out of view to the patient or client. It was truly *sub*-conscious. Together, Freud and Breuer took Janet's original insights and developed a whole new specialty that laid the foundations for modern psychiatry and clinical psychology.

For a time, what became known as psychoanalysis held the center stage and practitioners were getting remarkable transformations and recoveries, using the simple technique of getting the client to talk about his or her problems. Indeed, the method was to be long known as "the talking cure", with a slight sneer of disapproval from those who considered it trivial.

By the 1960s we had reached the point where almost every medical affliction, other than fever and malnutrition, was seen to be a result of dysfunctionality in the mind. Doctors began to believe that everything was "psychosomatic" in origin, a word which means mind-body. Gradually, the use of this word morphed into something more sinister: that a person was weak or inadequate and imagined their symptoms, which were not actually real.

Things might have continued along those lines but for the rise of the current chemical view of mind states: the idea that every feeling—good or bad—is the result of a lack or imbalance in neurotransmitter molecules in the brain. Even happiness today is deemed to be a result of having sufficient quantities of serotonin and dopamine. This chemical model has resulted in a shift of emphasis in studying mind function away from the impact of a person's life experiences towards the idea that everything is caused by biochemical dysfunction.

It's a sterile (and dangerous) model, that has led medicine astray for decades and resulted in legions of individuals swallowing "happy pills" in the mistaken belief that their uncomfortable and unwanted feelings are the result of some deficiency state or excess. I need hardly point out the parallels between this chemical dream and the current recreational drug craze.

Somewhere along the way, the old idea that a person thought what they thought, felt what they felt and behaved as they did, because their experiences in life had led them in that direction, has disappeared in a welter of pharmacological marketing and hype. The sad truth is that this biochemical model is not working. People are not happier by taking antidepressants. Instead, the person's helplessness is being reinforced and made more inescapable.

A few struggling counselors, with no effective model on which to base their help, struggled on with the notion that life experience was important and formative. But without adequate understanding of how unpleasant memories translate into unwanted feelings and behaviors, their efforts can be seen as ill-advised and often unhelpful, merely grinding the client deeper into their misery by repetition and endless discussion.

That was the condition of well-meaning help... until recently.

Now we have DEEP! This is a breakthrough technology that I rate as second only to the discovery of the subconscious mind and its powerful automaticity. It takes the story very significantly forward. Through the DEEP method we learn exactly how experience is internalized and why the accompanying "charge" (black energy) is able to take executive control of a person's mind.

The answer, it turns out, is really rather simple. Although the result of negative experiences is unwanted and disempowering thoughts, those thoughts are NOT the cause of the problem! The trouble comes about due to the mechanical impact of those same experiences; the force, the effort, if you like. It is this force or psychic violence which pins unpleasant emotions into place and leads to disturbing and unwelcome thoughts.

To merely process or try to eliminate those "bad thoughts" is hardly ever effective because the underlying mechanism holding them in place is not addressed at all. Rolf Dane and his research partner Heidrun Beer have together evolved a method of removing what I just referred to as the psychic violence. This releases the negative emotions and then... bingo!... as if by magic, all the unwanted thoughts come tumbling out, like an unblocked water channel and they quickly vanish from view, never to disturb the client again.

The person is utterly transformed by their release from the grip of the subconscious mind. So much so that in my personal writings I am referring to this new method as Transformational Mind Dynamics, or TMD for short. It really is all about the dynamics within the mind and it really is transformational when things from the past really do start to move and then crumble and fade!

I have experienced it, seen it at work and learned to do this for myself, so I am talking to you here from direct experience, not mere theory. I am very pleased to have learned this new approach; it has totally transformed how I deal with a dysfunctional human being.

And you know what is so great about this? It's very, very easy to do.

New Language

There is a whole fresh language which we need to chart this new territory. Many of the concepts Dane and Beer found crucial have not been described before, or at best only dimly grasped and the correct importance not given to them.

DEEP itself is a witty acronym, derived from decisions, emotions, energy or effort (kinetics) and personalities or poles. It really goes deep into the psyche. The basic mechanism is that the energy or force buries emotions and makes their origins difficult to trace; emotions in turn hold in place self-limiting or destructive thoughts. The latter appears to be what the person is suffering from but in fact thoughts are insubstantial and, in theory, should not twist and damage a person's life and living.

It's the force which holds everything in place. And that—importantly—includes psychic force or mental energy. We have all had the experience of trying to "will" something to happen or get somebody to do something (or not do something). This is psychic energy that can twist and hurt and, as Dane and Beer have shown, it can be just as damaging as physical impact.

Another key concept uncovered by these redoubtable researchers is that of threads or pathways running in the mind, with numerous "nodes" or significant intersections. You probably always suspected it: that certain events radiate their bad effects outwards and stir up other similar events, making you feel generally uncomfortable or challenged. It's rather like the effect of musical resonance—if you stand near a piano and continue to talk, the instrument will begin to vibrate and make whispering sounds, copying the tones of your voice.

This concept of multiple connections is a surprising revolution.

Freud rightly taught us that earlier is better. Incidents he said run in "chains" of similar, connected events. Running incidents from a chain reduces its impact by getting charge off; unburdening he called it. We call these threads because they are more of a tangle than chains implies. Plus, they can be untangled and broken quite easily, if you have the right technique!

But key was to find the basic or "root" on the thread—the earliest event—and erase that. Then the whole thread would "blow". It is rather like pulling up the root of a plant; it will rapidly wither and die. We teach all our starting clients this approach.

But now we can carry the story much further forward and get better results faster. The DEEP approach is not about bouncing along a thread and digging earlier, rather it's about thoroughly reducing the effect of each life encounter, eradicating the force, effort, emotion, thoughts and postulates surrounding the event that happened.

In fact we are not really concerned with "the story" at all. That's been the major distraction introduced by Freud and taken up by New Age counselors and "therapists". We have become so accustomed to listening to the client/patient telling us what happened, that we have come to believe that the case is all about what happened. That's just not true. It's about the force of what happened, and the reaction to what happened, trapping encysted emotions, and building up layers of self-defeating thoughts and decisions on top of the unpleasant experience.

We bleed off the force, which releases the emotions, which frees up thinking and allows better decisions. The future is changed, because we emerge changed, refreshed, with new awareness and new postulates to guide our future.

When I use the term force I'm not just confining this to people punching each other or slapping into the car dashboard during an automobile accident. I chiefly mean psychic force or effort. In our mind, when interacting with others, we try to control the mechanics of that interaction, by intending the person to do something we want or, conversely, trying to avoid something we don't want. The two principal directions of energy are pulling towards (tractor beam) and trying to push away (pressor beam).

For example, if you've ever been part of a relationship breakup, you will be aware one partner is mentally thrusting the other away while the unfortunate party is clinging, that is, using the tractor (pull) strategy.

But there may be an effort to hold still, to shake something loose or simply endure. We call these energy vibrations the "kinetics" of a situation. These are the truly dynamic elements of the mental landscape; hence the term Transformational Mind Dynamics.

The Key Context

I have no wish to diminish the skills and methodology of Dane and Beer when I point out the historical context of their remarkable discoveries. In truth, Freud and Breuer in *Studies on Hysteria* very clearly described the importance of engaging with the dynamics of the case, the energy, the effort or force. It turns out to be pivotal.

One of their cases—the mother of a sick child, which had at last fallen asleep—was so intent on keeping still (the effort to not move) it became a subsequent psychosis. Endless tellings of the event made no impact. Only lifting off the intense effort she made to hold herself still relieved the problem. Note: the release of the effort is done wordlessly.

In another case, a highly intelligent man was present while his brother had an ankylosed hip-joint extended under an anesthetic. At the instant at which the joint gave way with a crack, he felt a violent pain in his own hip-joint, which persisted for nearly a year. Yet again, the problem was not solved with merely talking about it, but by contacting and "re-living" the violent force contained in this unusual memory.

Freud and Breuer are at pains to point out that the impactful psychical process which originally took place must be repeated (re-experienced) as vividly as possible. The physical stimulus—the force—must be brought back to its *status nascendi* (moment of birth) and made to re-appear once again with the fullest intensity and then vanish forever.

DEEP processing is, to my knowledge, the only certain and fully developed method of achieving this desirable effect. Otherwise, recovery takes place only occasionally and only by chance.

Other People Involved

But this isn't just about the self viewpoint. Dane and Beer have evolved a very comprehensive technique that also takes care of the feelings and reactions of other people involved along with us in our activities.

"No man is an island," poet John Donne (1572–1631) famously said. "Never send to know for whom the bell tolls; it tolls for thee…" It's your funeral, as well as the dead guy's burial. We are all in this together! So nothing happens to you that doesn't also happen to me, to your parents, to the local boys club, to the pooch. Everyone is in on it.

This is more than poetic whimsy however. If only people understood their actions send a flood of energy outwards from the epicenter, which affects the whole environment, perhaps they would behave better towards each other. In my book *Medicine Beyond* I recount the work of scientist Pierre Paul Sauvin, an electronics expert from New Jersey. He showed that plants wired to electronic detectors reacted briskly whenever he experimentally hurt himself. Also, at the precise moment he and his girlfriend were having orgasmic sex, in a forest eighty miles away, the plant reactions sent the needles off the dial!

We think in hushed tones what this tells about the wonder of plants. But consider also... What does it tell us about ourselves? That thoughts in our head and energies in our bodies radiate outwards for a hundred miles or more and can be felt by any sensitive detector! That includes other living creatures and human beings.

So not surprisingly, things which happen to us and because of us, affect the people around us. They are not just spectators; they are players too. We impacted them; but THEY IMPACT US. It's rather like an echo; it's our voice that shouts but the echo comes right back to us. And the sound bounces around the environment a good deal, before it finally fades.

It's astonishing that other schools of growth and development don't take these multiple-personality dynamics more seriously.

In DEEP practice, we have our willing client take up the viewpoint of others, starting with the antagonist or opposition. What did the rapist feel at the moment he was carrying out the brutal assault? What in God's name was she thinking of when she walked out the door? Why did Mom always talk to me that way?

The strange thing is, we seem to know! If you occupy the viewpoint of the domineering husband, the inept boss at work, the chump who stole your first girlfriend, and find his emotions, his effort and what disastrous thought computation he was struggling with, suddenly you are released and cleansed from something you didn't even think belonged to you! It's wonderful to behold.

By having the client see the events of their lives through the eyes of others and with the others' feelings, we gain a far deeper insight into the meaning of what we jokingly call life.

It builds compassion. It builds wisdom. We grow immensely in stature as we finally learn tolerance and forgiveness. We come at last to understand, as John Donne said so beautifully, that we are all in this together!

The thing is, the trouble may even start with another individual and we walk into it and get stuck there, like a fly trapped by a sticky ribbon. The case of the man who took on his brother's hip pain is a graphic example of this mechanism.

I wish Rolf Dane and Heidrun Beer every success in their activities and further research. For the reader, I cannot commend this new science of mind and living highly enough. It's something I always dreamed would be "out there", even as an inquiring medical student! Now at last, it's real...

This is a fine and fascinating book, written extremely well. This is itself is remarkable, since English is not Rolf's native language.

Keith Scott-Mumby
MD, MB ChB, HMD, PhD

Foreword by Heidrun Beer
"Why DEEP is a Stroke of Genius"

It is February 2019, and we are coming up on the 10th anniversary of the birth of our DEEP modality. Like very few other methods, if any, DEEP is truly the "baby" of two people - Rolf Dane and myself. It is a true and real co-creation: neither of us would have done it alone.

I specifically remember one crucial moment in 2011, where I was still in Austria and Rolf and I were chatting on Skype. Somehow that talk felt way too private, too casual and relaxed to me; I missed the usual passionate, nearly driven sounding reports about progress in Rolf's research projects. So I asked him: "How is it going with the Karma Buster project?" Karma Buster was an early name for what would become DEEP in the then future. We had done some pilot sessions on it earlier and had proceeded to testing other methods. Rolf hesitated for a moment and then said: "Oh, I have nearly forgotten about that!" Upon which I screamed "Nooooooo!" My voice was so loud that he could have heard me without a headset - that scream went across the whole distance from Austria to Denmark - at least that's how it felt!

At this pivotal moment it was still undetermined whether DEEP as a Clearing modality would ever be "born" - I still shudder when I think what would have happened, or rather failed to happen, if I had been just a tiny little bit less observant. The path to not only using DEEP as a new method but also adding it as an extra tool to methods that we had used earlier was not always smooth. We were trained to see these procedures as "sacred cows"; altering them was nearly a sacrilege. But we had also learned to pay attention to priorities - magnitudes of importance. I had to repeat my message many times to get the DEEP approach incorporated into everything we had used earlier. And as it turned out, we can use DEEP to fully discharge and integrate the areas other methods have uncovered but not fully resolved. It requires some courage to leave a well-beaten track and blaze new trails into what appears like a thicket when you first venture into it. But when it was finally done, suddenly it was totally logical and natural and elegant - as if it could not be any other way! Just how it always should have been - a joy to behold.

Rolf made steady progress. He first wrote the procedures and then combined them with chapters from an unpublished book he had written earlier, that contained some fundamentals about the mind upon which DEEP was built. This resulted in this groundbreaking book "DEEP Clearing". And he trained himself in video editing and created most of the videos that we have online today. I spent most of my time in Denmark and began to practice DEEP; I also built databases and websites. I developed training materials for our first students, and helped at fairs where we presented DEEP to the Danish public. Additionally I learned video editing myself and provided some DEEP training videos. But most essentially I kept bringing ideas to the table; and while some other authors become lone wolves after a while and develop an arrogant guru mentality, Rolf was always listening and we kept having a productive dialogue.

In some cases I saw a way to simplify the approach to a case issue, for instance with "self-serving computations", where one simple procedure now cuts through the whole Gordian knot of complexities that we had before. Sometimes I was able to add more precision - I skip the details here, since they are highly technical. But I also came up with concepts that turned into whole new chapters - things I had read in hundreds of books by authors outside of our own training, but also things that I originated myself. "Tractor efforts" (energetic motions of a pulling character) and "split characters" (sub-personalities or identities inside the same person) were among the concepts that I suggested and that became parts of DEEP very quickly, after they proved useful in sessions with a variety of clients.

Some of these changes were really dramatic and life changing. The same was true for the whole area of non-physical impulses and actions, which is highly charged for many very socially competent people, who keep most of their impulses inside and rarely or never act them out.

And the introduction of a concept that we now call the "Outside Observer" has led to a whole new dimension of insights in the sessions of numerous clients - somehow when they look at their situation from the outside (after it has been discharged), they develop a wisdom of understanding that is simply not there when they look from the inside, from their own point of view. In this step we honor an idea that is popular in modern spiritual movements: that possibly Earth is just a school and life is a series of lessons that have to be learned. If that is true, some traumatic incidents could well be "teaching movies", and simply discharging them is not enough - more importantly, their lesson must arrive in the individual's consciousness. That's why we ask the "Outside Observer" for lessons to be learned for each "actor". As soon as our client is certain that he has extracted all potential learning from an incident, that incident has served the purpose it may have had in his life plan (if it was not the result of the randomness of the universe), and can be let go of and move to the past.

Another thing that I found important but had been absent in our previous training was the existence of the physical body as an independent life form, a point of view that can contrast sharply with the spiritual being who inhabits that body. I had developed methods to deal with that before I met Rolf, and later tested them on him with good results, so it was natural that we incorporated that as DEEP Body Clearing. Dialogue or "talks" between the spirit and his body became a tool that made a great difference for many clients who had never before been aware that there could be a conflict, or that such a conflict could negatively affect them. This "DEEP Body Clearing" tool proved its value especially once, when Rolf himself had an accident where he cut his wrist - his hand had a lot of unfriendly things to tell him after he had been stitched back together in the hospital! And once that charge was released, the doctors were surprised how fast he was healing.

Yet another subject that was close to my heart was the consciousness field of families, groups, nations, cultures or a whole planet - what Rupert Sheldrake calls a "morphic field", but could also be understood as a "group mind". I had written about that subject before and found it important to include it in DEEP, especially since some of my clients had conflicts not with individual enemies but with a whole culture's mindset. So in order to properly dissolve their charge, these cultures had to be seen and addressed as an opposing point of view. In other cases they act as amplifiers, or in other words, they reinforce rather than oppose certain non-optimum traits that a client is struggling with. That too needs to be looked at. It took me a while to "sell" all these concepts to Rolf - but as before, the successes I had in actual sessions with actual clients were better sales points than anything I could say, so today we have group minds in the advanced levels of DEEP training, and when a client comes with such an issue, our trainees are prepared for it.

There is another special pet subject of mine: the spirit world and its inhabitants. We found an elegant solution to that in DEEP: we now simply treat it as additional viewpoints populating the client's world. I can perceive that some of these invisible people are actually in contact with us Earthlings - namely deceased loved ones, former drug addicts who seek out earth dwelling drug addicts to get their fix by drawing perceptions from their still living bodies, and a class of people who are assisting us in our Earth lives - called by many names, like "guardian angels" or "spirit guides" or even "screenwriters"... To me all these spirits either have pressing issues, or advice to give, or there is the proverbial "unfinished business" to handle between them and our client. There is an urgency to their yet undelivered messages which sometimes has kept building over years or even decades. Ultimately that can lead to mountains of charge on both sides.

The solution we came up with, as mentioned, was that any viewpoint that influences the client, and the client can perceive, can be taken up as such. It can be it a known person, a spirit, a group mind, etc. If the client can perceive it as a live entity, communication can be established and clearing can take place. In practice this has benefitted the client and possibly the entity as well.

The successful handling of major charge in an actual client is always the factor that convinces Rolf. I kept telling him about these session encounters, where I improvised by applying our then standard DEEP methods to the unexpected guests in my sessions. Demonstrating the key quality of a Clearer, which is LISTENING, Rolf finally realized that here too was a case area for which we had to prepare our students, because "Ooops, I have not learned how to handle that" is not really a good answer to give a client who is just about to explode with charge in a session! So now we simply handle such encounters as additional viewpoints affecting the client. Rolf himself benefitted from that. He had a very emotional encounter with his own deceased mother in one of our early sessions, which led to tremendous relief. It was not the deciding factor, but made it more real to Rolf that if he got something out of making good with his mother, some of our clients might also benefit from that! Not everybody sees spirits or their guardian angels, but to those clients who have these perceptions and for whom they are natural, we can happily say that we can deal with that too, not just with ordinary human-level trauma and stress. *The approach is to define and address them as viewpoints that influence the client.*

So the unifying concept, which in my opinion makes DEEP a stroke of genius (I may be too modest here...) is that **we see all these points of view simply as units of consciousness**. Whether you clash with your boss, your wife, your own body, some wispy demon with a green face and red horns, or the harsh group mind of your company or church - we always use the same DEEP methods to dissolve the charge on both sides. We have the tools to clean up the connections with your lost loved ones and your spirit helpers, and to break your bond with body-less drug addicts who may be driving you to excesses and are taking unfair advantage of you. And if internal conflicts tear you to pieces, we again help you to define your colliding own "parts" as units of consciousness, separate them from one another with great precision, and again use the same DEEP methods to reconcile the conflict between them. It's your own self in the center, "split units" (sub-personalities) below, "merge units" (group minds) above, and other individual selves interacting with you at your own level. Whether they have a body or not, they are all units of consciousness with an urge to survive and to thrive, and they all respond to the same methods of clearing away negative energy.

So now, finally, all the energies, entities and influences the client is subject to can be addressed. DEEP has turned into a complete and real and well tested Clearing modality. The combination of its powerful basic simplicity with a flexibility and versatility that nobody else has, turns it into what could be called a universal approach. In the whole field of consciousness work, I see nothing that could shake or surpass the validity of DEEP Clearing, even though some people may remain attached to more specialized and less complete methods, simply because they resonate with them - we have no objections against that and wish them the best of luck. With or without their agreement, Rolf's and my "baby" has grown up, it stands on its own two legs now, we are releasing it into the world, and if that world is ready for it, it can help countless people on their path of personal growth and evolution.

May you grow big and old and do much good, my dear child!

Heidrun Beer,
February, 2019

Author's Foreword

DEEP Clearing is the result of 10 years of clinical work with clients around the world. Much of the groundbreaking research in counseling and self-development was done in sessions conducted via the internet.

During my long career in counseling and self-development, going back to 1970, I have worked with many different techniques and methods in order to achieve personal freedom and a high level of sanity and ability for my clients. I have found inspiration in many of these techniques. What DEEP adds to this is a new understanding of emotional charge, how it comes about and how it is handled in practical work. With this more workable understanding and definition of charge, existing techniques can be put to work and produce stellar results where it before DEEP was a hit and miss proposition.

I want to thank Heidrun Beer for all her help and enthusiasm in joining the efforts of researching the various techniques, procedures and methods that comprise DEEP Clearing. Without her help it wouldn't have happened. She has contributed with important ideas and many hours of research counseling with clients. It all started when she volunteered as "guinea pig" for my new ideas in 2009. Since 2011 we have joined forces and today she is active as DEEP Clearing Specialist and responsible for training new DEEP Clearers.

There are many others I want to thank and acknowledge. I want to thank Professor Keith Scott-Mumby, MD, for embracing this new modality by taking the training and inspiring us in many ways. Likewise I want to thank Per Schiøttz, a veteran counselor and ability coach for his valuable input in many discussions and his back up in applying this new approach to clients.

I want to thank Marian Volkman and Jim Halsey for training in Traumatic Incident Reduction and Applied Metapsychology. I treasure this training and the insights it brought.

I also want to thank Robert Ducharme, the developer of R3X, an advanced incident clearing technique. I took much inspiration from his groundbreaking ideas and techniques.

There are of course countless others I should mention. I can mention many brave clients who have volunteered but want to remain anonymous.

In the second edition we added important material. Chapter 16, Repeat and Tell is new as is Chapter 20, DEEP Viewpoint Clearing. The Appendix has also been expanded with material of very practical nature. The new appendix contains the New Vitality Lists, instructions in how to make longer action programs in DEEP and a section with short versions of the techniques that are helpful as 'cheat sheets' in session.

Rolf Dane, December 23, 2016

Update, 2019, 3rd Edition

In the 2019 edition we have mainly updated some procedures so they reflect the 3 years of experience we have gained since 2016. We have corrected minor errors and typos and smoothed out the language here and there. We have expanded and revised the glossary. Otherwise it's the same book. We are planning to offer it in PDF and Kindle versions free of charge, simply to get the word out and get DEEP in broader use.

Rolf Dane
Copenhagen,
February 7, 2019

Introduction

The present book is divided up in three parts plus a useful appendix.

Part one covers the background of DEEP Clearing. This is what we have called Clearing Work or Clearing Technology in general. The sources of clearing work are many. Part One reflects our own understanding as it has developed over the years. Part One gives the philosophical foundation that we operate from and have operated from for years—also prior to DEEP Clearing. Principles like the life cycle; attention and intention; the importance of communication; the triad of relationships and understanding; the connection between spirit, mind, body; and life and living understood on the basis of games theory – all are basic concepts we have found valuable in our work and they are part of DEEP Clearing as well.

Part two covers our own research and results and some principles that are new in therapy and self-improvement. The reader will find a new understanding of emotional charge, the importance of points of view in resolving issues and cases. The chapter on the DEEP Package is central to this book and the DEEP Clearing method.

D.E.E.P. stands for Decision, Emotion, Effort, Point of view/Polarity. These are the elements we address in issues and cases. Decisions and thoughts; Emotions and feelings; Efforts, including action, motion, habits and body sensations are the layers all issues consist of. The layers parallel the age-old model of man as consisting of head, heart and hand; of the mental, emotional and physical sides of our lives and behavior. Each layer has to be addressed separately in each issue to ensure that the techniques are effective and swift.

However, any issue that persists has a pole and a counter-pole. It takes a plus and minus pole to generate electricity. It takes conflicting points of view to generate resistive emotional charge. How this works in the mind and in resistive issues is covered in theory in part two.

Part Three gives exact instructions in how to apply these principles in practice. We cover three main actions: How to clear up just about any subject with *DEEP Subject Clearing*. Anything from "fear of spiders", and "trouble with the children", to "stress" and "the tense climate at work" can be addressed successfully. There are complete instructions on how to address traumatic or stressful incidents with *DEEP Incident Clearing*. There are exact instructions in *DEEP Body Clearing*, a technique that improves the client's physical well-being by freeing up the life force and make it flow more freely to the benefit of the client's general health. Finally there is a chapter on DEEP Viewpoint Clearing, a very useful technique, especially for advanced clients.

In part one we use traditional terminology. The one receiving service is called "client". The one delivering the service is the "practitioner". Various systems often have their own words for "client" and "practitioner" and DEEP Clearing is no exception. In part two and three we introduce our own terms of "introspector" for client and "clearer" for practitioner. Any new terms found in the book, by the way, is defined in the extensive glossary in the appendix.

We hope you will find the information in this book of practical value. It is a complete guide in how to apply DEEP Clearing to clients and cases. Regardless of the technical and theoretical content, the book is written in an easy-to-understand style and provided with many illustrations.

Appendix: In the second and now third edition the appendix contains much material of practical importance. You will find the New Vitality Lists, instructions in how to make longer action programs in DEEP and a section with short versions of the techniques that are helpful as 'cheat sheets' in session.

Rolf Dane

A-10

PART 1: Clearing Work Basic Theory

Chapter 1: Life Cycles

One of the most fundamental principles in life that Clearing builds on is the concept of Life Cycles. You can see time as an endless stream of events that continuously overlap each other and thus time never stops. A Cycle, within this continuum, is one clearly defined event with a starting point and an end. Events, actions, the four seasons, manufacturing processes, life spans, a piece of music, etc. all follow this principle.

The concept of the Life Cycle is not a new principle in philosophy—by far. The Vedas, the ancient Indian books of wisdom, describe this Life Cycle well. The Vedas state it this way: from chaos comes birth. After birth growth follows. At some point full growth is achieved. Now decay sets in. This decay ends in death. After death there is, again, chaos.

We see this scenario play out with all living organisms. They get born and gradually grow into adulthood. Once full maturity has been reached it's a matter of time. At some point old age starts to set in; first as reduced mobility; later as aches, pains and illness; eventually as severe malfunction and death. Larger entities, such as groups or nations, go through a Life Cycle as well. "The Decline and Fall of the Roman Empire", Gibbon's famous book from the 1700s, is about the Life Cycle of Ancient Rome—and especially how the Empire came to an end. The main difference between the life span or cycle of a fly and an empire, in this context, is really only the time span covered—and of course the scale of events.

When we look at manufactured things, they start with materials scattered in nature or in a workshop. They get put together by the manufacturer, who brings about 'birth' by putting order into the chaos. After a manufactured object is 'born' it usually gets shipped and delivered, brand new, and then put to use. A certain amount of maintenance will extend the object's life. At some point it cannot be repaired or it is not cost effective to repair it. The object is allowed to decay. Eventually it is discarded and thus joins "chaos" once again.

Natural phenomena, such as a storm or the formation of mountains, go through Life Cycles as well. Mountains are pushed up from the deep of the earth. Finally they reach a peak. Now the water, weather, and plants start breaking them down. Eventually the mountains are leveled, becoming completely broken down once again. This Cycle takes millions of years.

What we are describing here is the Life Cycle, the life span or cycle, with examples. Depending on whether we deal with living or dead entities, man-made or natural creations, physical objects or ideas and projects, etc. the language we use will change; but all created and perceivable things and phenomena follow a cycle with a starting point, a development, a peak, a decay and an end. Since we have to choose language, we will here describe it as: Create, Survive, Destroy. The question to ask here is: Is the Life Cycle as Create, Survive, Destroy what is actually taking place or is it an appearance? *A close analysis reveals: The Life Cycle as Create, Survive, Destroy is only an Appearance.* An Appearance is how something seems to be; how it looks on the surface. It is different from how something actually is when we look closely at it and analyze how something actually functions. It is important to understand how something works if we want to gain control over it. This is the most important lesson we have been taught by natural science and engineering.

As we have said, the Life Cycle is apparently *Create, Survive, Destroy*. We believe that to be true because that is how it looks. It is also based on how we think about it, on our considerations. We expect this to happen and thus that is what we see and perceive. A person can grow old quickly or slowly. How quickly a person ages has a lot to do with his/her expectations and attitude towards life. In clearing it will be seen that each phase of Create, Survive, Destroy is an appearance; a sum total of considerations and agreements imposed by the community and society. It's what we expect to happen and thus it happens.

The above analysis is an example of a principle that actually can be put to the test. The test we use is primarily clearing procedures of one individual at a time. By using the traditional understanding of the Life Cycle in clearing work, can we make anyone well or more intelligent? Does it work in a practical engineering way of thinking? The answer is No! This, yet again, tells us that we are dealing with an appearance. It only *appears* to be true. Once we fully understand a phenomenon we should gain more control over it and not just "go with the flow" of our fears and peers.

The Actual Life Cycle

The true understanding of the Life Cycle is what is called the *Actual Life Cycle*. This is an understanding that enables us to do something practical with our knowledge and have control and a positive effect when applying it. Our interest and goal is to make people better. Let's see how it works out:

The Actual Life Cycle is as follows: *(1) Create, (2) Continuous-create, (3) Create/Counter-create, (4) No Creation, (5) Nothingness.* Here, all the phases are expressed in terms of *Creation.*

(1) Create: is the initial bringing into being. This can be through manufacturing, construction, decision or postulate, conception and birth.

(2) Continuous-create: to maintain things in the stream of time they have to be continuously created. This is Survive in the Apparent Life Cycle. For a car to "survive" as a means of transportation, we have to continuously maintain it through filling up on gas, making oil changes, cleaning it inside out, taking care of repairs, etc. It's a continuous process of Create. The same is true for a home, for fitness and good health, a job, and just about anything else. The moment we stop this continuous process of Creation decay of its condition will set in quite rapidly.

(3) Create/Counter-create: this means to create something against an existing creation; or to create one thing and then create something against it. In other words, we created, say, a figure in clay; then we got bored with it and took our fist and flattened the whole thing with a blow. The blow was the Counter-creation. We created an effect and a flat blob of clay, if you will, but in terms of the original figure in clay it was a total Counter-creation.

(4) No Creation: This means absence of any Creation; there is no creative activity taking place but the object remains and is in continuous decay.

One of the characteristics of No Creation is that the persons concerned haven't made up their minds. The Cycle is in a state of *"Limbo"*. They haven't simply ended the Life Cycle and put it behind them. One can end the cycle by completing something and declare it for complete. If the cycle was a mistake or has no desirable conclusion, one "ends it" by disengaging from it and making this clear to self and others.

(5) Nothingness: This is the ultimate no creation. There is no concern about Creation/No Creation anymore; the whole thing is filed in the past, or it hasn't yet occurred to anyone. Contrary to the limbo of No-Creation, no attention is paid to it or tied up. Started Cycles should be brought to this state as no further energy or attention is tied up. One has a fully completed Life Cycle and can move on.

As you see, the phases 1-5 can all be understood in terms of creative activity. Intensity and direction may change but they are all based on Creation.

In the Apparent Life Cycle we have Destruction. Our analysis has revealed that destruction is better expressed as Counter-creation. It's a creation hitting smack against something that was already there, the original Creation.

Example: Let's say we have an abandoned house. It was created or built at some point in time. Somebody bought it, maintained it, cleaned it, heated it in the winter, paid the taxes and mortgage on it, etc., etc. There was a Continuous-create taking place. At some point the owner had to move to another city for some reason. The house was put up for sale but nobody bought it. Finally a builder and developer bought it from the bank that at some point became the unwilling owner of the house. The developer wants to build retail stores on the lot. He is an active and creative businessman. The first thing he has to do is to tear down the old decayed house. He has to Counter-create using wrecking balls and heavy machinery. His Counter-create is motivated by his plans of putting stores there. The destruction he undertakes is simply a Counter-create to the original structure and its function. If the old owner were still around he would obviously see it as destruction. Maybe the neighbors would share his views and sentiments. This, obviously, has to do with points of view and agreements. But when we include point of view and agreements we are clearly talking about an Apparency, not an Actuality.

Actual Life Cycle

*1. Create=
Initial creation*

*2. Survive=Continuos-create
(maintenance)*

*3. Destroy:
counter-create*

*4. No Creation:
attention trap;
cycle in limbo*

*5. Nothingness:
no attention paid.
Totally neutral.*

There are two types of destruction. There is the Counter-creation the builder did in order to make room for a new building. The other type is the slow decay that sets in after the owner moved away. There was simply a complete absence of Create and the building went into a slow but sure decay. The building "ceased to exist", you could say, as far as the original owner was concerned. More likely, it became his worst nightmare since he didn't know how to put up with the situation. Both types of destruction are here defined in terms of creation: Counter-creation (3 above) and No Creation (4 above). Nothingness (5 above) is a neutral condition that doesn't occur until either (3) or (4) is utterly completed. All this supports that the Actual Life Cycle in each phase can be accurately defined in terms of Creation.

Life Cycle and Clearing

The above discussion may seem elementary to the point of being meaningless. When we start to apply this theory to the mind and clearing work, however, we discover that it really *works!* As a matter of fact, when we start to use all the good applications this theory can be put to we discover it's dynamite! What we want to bring about is improvement of conditions. Our goal is to improve the individual's mental outlook and state of mind, his physical well-being, as well as his abilities, his efficiency, and his relationships. The datum of the Actual Life Cycle is helpful and necessary across the boards in these ambitious goals. The most pervasive truths may seem elementary and are easily overlooked for the same reason. The Actual Life Cycle is such a basic and elementary truth. It is solid rock you can build a skyscraper on!

The traditional idea is that we have to destroy unwanted things by force. But as long as we hold on to that idea and try to apply it to the mind we have chaos. There is creating and knowing one is creating. But there is also creating and NOT knowing one is creating. There are such phenomena as *automatic actions*. We perform many actions every day that we are not aware of. Yet, when we inspect them it is obvious that they are actions under *our* control and of *our* creation. Driving a car or a bicycle are good examples. It takes careful instruction and learning but at some point it becomes second nature and we pay little or no attention to all the small skills and actions that go into it. We are in the moment completely unaware of all these small automatic actions and the fact that we are performing them.

Although these patterns of action were created in the past, we are also creating them in the present or they wouldn't take place.

In clearing work we are interested in removing unwanted conditions. It can typically be patterns, impulses, emotions, and even inexplicable pains that now are bothering the client. To stay with driving a car as our example, it could be nervous reactions and fears that make driving difficult, risky or painful. That's what we call bypass reactions, involuntary reactions where repressed material takes over and dictates our reactions and behavior. It is influences from the subconscious mind. The driver cannot clearly perceive the present due to pressing worries and disturbances rooted in his past. He created these fears, concerns, or pains at some point in his past. His doctor may tell our client to take a painkiller or some pill to "calm his nervous system". That's an example of Counter-create in our terminology. "Have a pain? Take a pill to block it out!"

In clearing work we go in another direction. We want to restore the original healthy condition. There are no side-effects to worry about. There is no lowered alertness or reduced presence of mind. To restore the original healthy condition, we have to find the Counter-create that now makes our client unwell and unhappy. This is typically done by guiding the client into his past to find the exact moment when the person created this discomfort that now disturbs his driving. Say, he gets a sharp pain in his knee each time he drives his car. In session, the practitioner will skillfully guide the client to find the incident when this pain was first "created". The pain was typically caused by an injury or a blow that happened under similar circumstances. For the sake of our example, we can say our client had a car accident 5 years ago. He injured his knee and was unable to drive for weeks. It is obviously not normal language to say that a pain caused by a blow or hard bump to the knee was his own creation. But the

curious thing is, and it bears out in clearing work, that even though there was a clear physical cause to the injury, there was also an anticipation of the pain on the part of the driver. He "created" the pain in anticipation of the collision. This was in a split second before the actual impact. Some of the pain he "created" in response to his body hurting. He, as a spiritual Being, copied the body's pain. Weeks or months after all physical causes of the pain are healed, he is still creating part of this pain. It may only be an echo. It may only be when he is driving his car. But what we learn from reviewing this injury in session is that he is actually creating it in present time each time he gets this pain. Again, our skillful practitioner knows what she is looking for and how to restore the original healthy condition. With certain precision techniques the practitioner has the client re-experience the accident moment by moment. The client will typically be in some discomfort, agony and pain while this is taking place in session. He is, as a matter of fact, guided to re-create the whole spectrum of emotions, pains and sensations of the accident. He "created" this whole spectrum unknowingly in the accident and he re-created it, again unknowingly, each time he went driving in his car. In the session the practitioner is capable of getting the client to *knowingly,* and with full presence of mind, to create it, to take a good look at it to a point where the driver in fact decides not to hold onto the Counter-creation anymore. In the technique we are describing here, there will be an exact point where the client can let the whole thing go. He will find odd decisions he made during the accident and if the practitioner has done a good job, the most central thought or decision the pain is tied to is resolved and all the discomfort and fear blows away. It is gone for good. It could be, "Oh, this is going to hurt!" "Oh Dear, I am going to die!" "My knee hurts like mad!" It can be any number of such "stupid" statements that is the theme and anchor statement of the whole Counter-create.

The technique loosely described above is called incident clearing or incident running. Incidents of interest are typically physical traumas: something that contains physical harm, pain and lowered awareness, ranging from losing presence of mind to deep unconsciousness.

The same technique can be adapted to grieving clients. People who lose loved ones are entitled to grieve. They are also entitled, at some point, to go on living their lives and return to normal. You can address their devastating loss as an incident, an emotional trauma with no physical pain but plenty of sorrow and grief and fear of the future and what it will bring. By reviewing it in session, the client will get closure and not re-live the nightmare forever. Incident Clearing has likewise been applied to war veterans, victims of violent crime, and sexual abuse. In each case the client got *closure*. By this we here mean that the Counter-create, that made the client's life difficult or unbearable, got uncovered and knowingly re-created in every smallest detail. By doing so it was possible to *close it off* as well. That particular Life

Cycle or event cycle got completed once and for all. The client could now walk away from it as a Nothingness that no longer demanded constant attention on a conscious or subconscious level.

Scientific Evidence

The session results are the only proof we offer here. The session results may be "scientifically incorrect" or unacceptable to skeptics. A critique you often hear from academia, is that only "anecdotal evidence" is offered for the validity of the theories and results of clearing work. Academia wants controlled experiments with statistical material. It wants explanations that agree with the prevailing schools of thought of psychology, sociology, neurology and medicine. Critics call for "objective evidence". They want to exclude any testimonials as they consider this anecdotal evidence.

But did you know that not one single diagnosis in the main handbook of psychiatry (The Diagnostic and Statistical Manual IV and V) has any objective scientific test? That's right. Not one single so-called mental disease has any diagnostic test, via blood, x-rays or any other significant measurement that will establish the condition as proven. In other words, psychiatric diagnoses are based on opinion. Medicine is likewise full of accepted cures that have no scientific evidence to build on, like taking out an inflamed appendix. This technique has never been subject to any kind of "proof". It's just something doctors do and have always done.

Since our goal is to improve how our clients feel, experience and understand things from their points of view, to exclude testimonials does not come naturally. What comes naturally is to ask the clients if they feel any better; if their fears and pains are gone; if they feel more capable of living and succeeding. We are taking an engineer's approach to the "mysteries of the mind". Once the bridge is up and is holding, we are satisfied. Once the problem is fixed, we move on. Yet, in scientific terms we do offer an experiment that can be replicated (copied and repeated) in distant laboratories. The practitioner and the procedure are the only variables introduced into a controlled environment, the session. The practitioner is not allowed to influence the client's opinion or thought process except by means of administering the clearing work techniques to the client. The practitioner works under very strict guidelines, the Clearer's Professional Code. It is, indeed, a controlled environment. The beneficial results are also being replicated time and again with individuals with widely different backgrounds in terms of education, belief system and culture; in terms of complaints they want handled and language used in expressing their complaints. The proof we offer, then, is to experience clearing for oneself or get trained as a practitioner and be the firsthand observer in the "laboratory" of the session environment.

Other Techniques

There are many different techniques and procedures available in clearing. Incident Clearing is an example of one such technique. Another approach that is workable is to have the client knowingly re-create a condition that he unknowingly is creating. This principle is used as part of DEEP Clearing. It can also be used in instructions or as a self-applied remedy. One can with this simple technique get rid of puzzling or unwanted habits or UN-learn repeated errors. Let's say a young driver, learning to drive a car with stick shift gear, keeps putting it in the wrong gear. A smart instructor will ask the youngster to pull over and stop. Then he will ask his student to intentionally put the stick shift in the wrong position. He will have his student repeat this wrong action a couple of times. Then he will have his student put it in the right position. Soon the student driver will be able to put the stick shift in the wrong gear or right gear at will. The driver's attention has been freed up from this little detail and she can move on to learning the next detail of good and safe driving. What happened was that the student gained full control over the wrong action. She could start, change and stop it at will. Therefore the driver could also decide not to create it. It is now a "Nothingness" (see (5) above), no longer needing or absorbing the attention. The example reveals the relationship between Life Cycles and good control (competence). Good control consists of the ability to start, change and stop the thing in question at will, be it a car, a process or one's body, etc. Good control is the essence of competence and it leads to completed cycles.

Life Cycles and Work

In doing work it is important to complete your Cycles. Once a cycle is complete, you have a product of some kind. It can be filed away, sold, exchanged or used as part of a bigger project. It's a *completed* unit that is used for something else. You may have the problem of how to use it, sell it, etc. But that's a *new* cycle. You don't have to revisit the completed one. Your attention is determinately off that cycle.

Now you can use the free attention to tackle other jobs and tasks, including how to use your already completed product.

I have often used this know-how on myself and with clients. If I feel stressed and lack energy, I pause and then I start to make a list of projects and things I have going. The mails I haven't answered; the things I promised to get out of the way; the repairs in the house that I postponed, etc. Sometimes it is a shock just to see how long such a list is. But just putting these incomplete cycles down on paper gives me some relief. Then I can sort the cycles and maybe discard some of them and others just take minutes to get out of the way. Then there are some real important ones that take some more time. But just having the list and getting started on the list is one big cycle that sweeps my mind clean, so to speak, gives new energy. My mood improves. My energy level goes up little by little each time I can cross off an item on the list.

I do the same with clients if they come in looking overworked and maybe frustrated from work. I help the person to write up all his/her incomplete cycles that is on their mind: unpaid bills, neglected chores, dropped contacts and correspondence, incomplete projects, etc. We include all the jobs that got swept under the rug. We make a to-do-list of all the incomplete cycles we can think of. We organize the list in a logical fashion. The rest is homework. Once this is well on its way, the client experiences renewed joy and energy. If you simply feel tired at some point during the day, despite enough sleep, look at what cycles went wrong or weren't completed. Either complete them or, if impossible, note them down for later completion. Some cycles simply need to be discarded. Decide with determination to end the cycle and check it off your list.

Chapter 2: Intention and Attention

We want to return to the importance of the Cycle of Action in relation to clearing work in a moment. Before we do that, we have to introduce some other elements of thought and awareness the practitioner is working with continuously. Those are *Attention* and *Intention*.

In medicine there are vital signs. When you want to see a doctor, someone will first check your temperature, blood-pressure, heart rate and respiration rate—your vital signs. When we talk Intention and Attention they are as important to the practitioner as breathing and heartbeat are to our physical health. Both Intention and Attention are in the realm of thought and awareness and closely related "vital signs".

Intention: can be defined as causative thought. The dictionary defines it as: "That which one is resolved to do; purpose". It is causative and an outflow. It is mainly concerned with the future.

Intention is an idea, thought or decision in the mind of the beholder, to cause a certain effect or to perform a certain act. Synonyms would be "Having something in mind", "Putting one's mind to it", "To insist", "To wish for something", "Decide" and "To will something to happen". 'Intention' is not an action; it's non-physical in nature. It does, however, precede physical action. It has to be present from the very start to the finish to *ensure* that a cycle of action is carried to its successful completion.

We can compare Intention to the planning and supervision of a project. An architect, for instance, will work out in great detail on paper how she wants to go about building a house. She will spend months working out all the details of a project before any action, in terms of actual building, is ever begun. When the plans are done, she has to constantly make sure they are carried out correctly. If she is a skilled and experienced architect the physical building of the house will apparently go smoothly, on-schedule and on-budget, to its successful completion. But the truth is that she constantly has to overcome difficulties, problems and shortcomings for that to happen. She overcomes them by executing her *intention*.

The law talks about "Criminal Intent" with much understanding. The intention behind a certain unfortunate act is carefully evaluated. Did the defendant want and plan it to happen? Or did it happen by accident? In the first case the law talks about a premeditated crime and the defendant is convicted as a criminal. In the second case the unfortunate act was accidental and the defendant is partly forgiven and given a lighter sentence. He is seen as partly being the victim of the unfortunate event.

Attention has to do with being able to focus on something. It's focused or fixed interest; it's directed or held interest. It could also be defined as receptive thought. The dictionary defines it as: "Giving one's mind to something, mental concentration, notice." *Attentive* is defined as: "Giving one's mind to what is going on; thoughtful of others, especially in meeting their needs or wishes." It's an inflow. It is mainly concerned with the present.

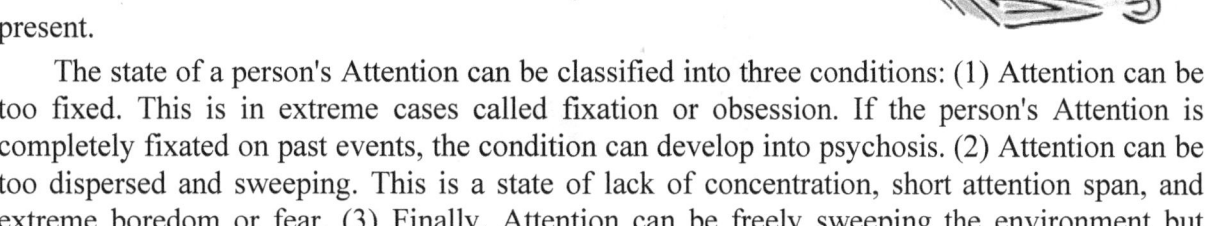

The state of a person's Attention can be classified into three conditions: (1) Attention can be too fixed. This is in extreme cases called fixation or obsession. If the person's Attention is completely fixated on past events, the condition can develop into psychosis. (2) Attention can be too dispersed and sweeping. This is a state of lack of concentration, short attention span, and extreme boredom or fear. (3) Finally, Attention can be freely sweeping the environment but under the person's control. The person is inspecting things of interest, one thing after the other. This shows a healthy, often relaxed state of mind. The person is alert and fully aware of his environment. He is in "present time".

As one can see from the definitions, Intention and Attention are closely related. A little simplified, Intention can be seen as causative and out-flowing; Attention as receptive and inflowing. In any given activity you will see them both present. The Intention is the execution side; Attention is the inspection and perception side. Attention is used to get data and to estimate and verify results and determine any further efforts needed. In the example with the architect above, you can easily see how closely they have to interact in order for the cycle of action to go forward to a successful completion. They are as close as positive and negative electricity. They work as a pair of equally important vital signs.

Attention units: In Clearing we define something called Attention Units. It could be considered a thought energy unit of awareness existing in the mind. They exist in varying numbers from person to person. The more Attention Units a person has available, the better off and alive he/she is. Attention Units are what we use when we enjoy life, when we think, and when we do a piece of work.

You may ask, how do you measure an Attention Unit? The answer is that Attention Units, by themselves, are not physically measurable by direct means. The concept helps us, however, to understand how our attention, piece by piece, can be absorbed by events and problems of the present, past, and future. This happens one unit at a time. In this manner Attention Units can be caught up in incidents of the past and be locked up in these events. A person, who is 'not there' mentally, has most of his Attention Units locked up. The reason Attention Units get locked up or absorbed by problems and events is that something is unresolved; a Cycle of Action of some kind was still ongoing, possibly in a loop, the same little sequence over and over; possibly a limited number of scenarios are reviewed mentally time and again. Typically, it's a variation of the limbo of No-creation discussed in the previous chapter.

Money

In society the idea of Attention Units is very real and quantifiable; it is called Money! A person who attracts a lot of favorable attention, such as a Hollywood star, will attract big money. A certain community project that keeps attracting attention will receive ample public funds. Dramatic disasters with innocent victims usually attract international attention as well as funds. The more news coverage a disaster gets the more aid the disaster attracts. Despotic rulers will spend money on wars, palaces and monuments; not on eradicating illiteracy and poverty that attract little attention. The advertising industry is all about attracting favorable attention to the featured products. They know the money will follow. The thing that most profoundly catches a person's attention is, however, bad health. A sick person will spend fortunes to regain his or her good health.

In a democratic election you could compare each vote with an Attention Unit. Only here, it's a contest of popularity. Unpopular politicians with unpopular programs do not attract votes; they are simply ignored and thus not elected.

> **Live Attention/Intention Vs Machines**
>
> *Once I helped a young mother bringing her three year old daughter to the hospital for a health check. This was while I still lived in the USA. The local doctor had listened to the girl's heart, using a stethoscope, and had found that there could be a problem with irregular heartbeat. The local doctor ordered a hospital examination. We brought the little girl in and she went through all kinds of tests. The girl was placed in a big machine and the machine produced all kinds of graphs and numbers. She was wired up to another machine and more numbers and graphs were produced under the supervision of a stern looking machine operator. He was looking at the machine and all its output and never at the young patient. The tests went on for hours and the mother and the girl got more and more nervous and so did I. Finally we met an oriental doctor, working on this Midwest American hospital. Apparently he had grown up in a different, less machine oriented culture. He took his stethoscope and placed it on the girl's heart and listened intensely, with attention and intention, to the heart beat. Then he said, "the heart beat is OK. It's regular and normal." It took less than a minute. We felt relieved. The oriental doctor had saved the day by applying some live attention and intention to the situation. We never picked up all the graphs and figures. They were unnecessary in the presence of human contact. It just illustrates that human contact with attention and intention makes us feel taken care of while the impersonal machines make us feel lost and ignored.*

Incomplete Cycles

We now return to our discussion of Life Cycles, of Cycles of Action. A cycle of action gets started with an Intention. It can be a banal little thing, such as turning on the light in a dark room, or it can be a major life goal such as choosing a career. In each case there is an intention, a purpose or goal the person has in mind that needs to be done and usually be brought to a smooth completion. Unfortunately, not all cycles of action are as smooth as turning on the light. We may wish for things that, when considered, seem worthwhile and doable, but soon turn out to be way over our heads and riddled with obstacles. It may be missing information, lack of resources, unforeseen problems, hidden enemies and dangers, etc. What seemed a walk in the park turns out to become our worst nightmare. Sometimes we wish for things out of anger, frustration, lack of foresight, etc., that we really don't want to happen. "I wish I were dead!", "My life is over after my spouse's death!", "I wish that driver had an accident!", "I wish I had no money so I didn't have to pay taxes!" When we wish for something that we soon after regret, the natural human reaction is to counter-create it in the hope of being able to undo it. "Regret" is an emotion that accompanies a certain type of counter-create.

Any cycle begun, whether well planned or not, demands a certain amount of attention. At first we give it willingly and full of expectations. But a tiny percentage of the totality of cycles started goes wrong in one way or the other. We suddenly discover that our attention has become stuck; our attention has been absorbed and trapped. Sometimes we don't even recall the cycle very well. It all turned out so bad that we tried to simply forget about the whole thing. Sometimes we do succeed in forgetting, but we didn't succeed in getting the cycle undone or brought to the neutral Nothingness.

Freeing of Attention Units

The cycles of action that were completed as intended gave us a good feeling and we soon left them behind. If we had to go through hell and high waters to complete a certain cycle the feeling is that of victory when we finally succeed. It's the small percentage of cycles that somehow failed or stopped in their tracks that are the trouble makers. They absorb attention as we haven't completely given up on them. This may be a conscious or more likely a suppressed and subconscious effort. The more important these cycles were to us the more attention units we invested in them, and we need to free this the absorbed attention.

The failed cycles, in countless variations, are what the practitioner encounters time and again in session. Knowing the general anatomy of the situation, the practitioner can systematically and rather elegantly begin to sort things out. The goal is not to make the client forget all about it. The practitioner wants to enable the client to inspect the cycle at hand closely, find the intention that started it and in this manner enable the client, once and for all, to discard and un-create this cycle that robbed him/her of

Attention Units. To be able to do that, the practitioner has to establish a very safe session environment. The practitioner gently lends the client analytical power and support. The practitioner uses *attention and intention*. This increases the client's ability to confront. Then the practitioner expertly *guides the client's free attention* to areas where Attention Units are caught up. This is done with communication and a technical knowledge of how the mind works. The practitioner may have to skillfully guide the client through numerous past failures and upsets. The client may at times feel much negative emotion, such as regret, apathy, grief, fear, and anger. But if the practitioner gently insists the client will get through it. The *perfect* "un-create" is accomplished once the client realizes the original intention that set it all in motion. Having uncovered that and the circumstances when it was conceived, he/she can often simply change his/her mind about it and the situation is ended.

In DEEP Clearing we go one step further, however. We have found that thoughts, emotions and efforts associated with the incident or issue have to be addressed individually and discharged one by one. Even though the intention was the mover, was the agent that initiated it all, we have to clean up all important aspects that it caused in relationships and in mind heart and body. By doing this, by addressing thought, emotion and effort the client cleans up all the important aspects of the issue.

Once the build-up of emotional charge and failed efforts is removed, the client can often in a flash see the whole thing, including the thoughts and decisions embedded in the issue and let it all go. The issue can literally evaporate accompanied by the client's laughter. When this happens, the practitioner will end off. The session has accomplished the main objective it was going for: to unstick the frozen Attention Units. Once they are unstuck the cycle of action unsticks as well and will complete itself mentally or simply appear to evaporate from the client's mind.

The above describes some basics principle in clearing. In practice we use a great number of different clearing techniques. They do, however, all use review of experiences and issues and finding the thoughts, emotions and efforts that originally accompanied the experiences. The thought elements would include the original decisions and intentions and typically a string of related decisions used to try to solve or cope with the situation. The emotional part is the emotions originally invested in the issue. The effort part is the record of all the work, motion and effort that went into dealing with the issue and how the body reacted. A complete handling may also include points of view and the intentions, emotions and efforts adopted from others. In all these techniques the objective is to unstick the frozen or trapped Attention Units. Once that is accomplished the issue can, if obsolete, be brought to its conclusion mentally. If the issue is still ongoing, the client will now feel energized and can do something about it in life.

Other Techniques

There are other techniques, such as enabling the client to freely create cycles of action at will. For instance in dealing with problems, the practitioner can work with the client's ability to create similar problems or worse problems than the ones he is burdened with. This enables the client to let go of old problems and the decisions, etc. underlying them.

This approach can also be used outside session with some workability. Some energetic people do it instinctively. If they suffer a major loss or setback they throw all their energy into their work to take their minds off the misery. Since work in our terminology is Continuous create, doing so through one's work has some workability based on the principles described.

> *When I was young and still had to work other jobs besides delivering clearing, I once had a painful breakup with my then girlfriend. Rather than give in to the emotional turmoil I felt, I decided to simply put all my energy into my work. At the time I made my living as a contractor, fixing up and selling condo apartments with my brother. I remember installing a kitchen in a certain apartment here in Copenhagen the day after the bad news. I was in a horrible mood. But working, I felt a clean energy building up within – just by putting my heart and energy into the physical work. Somehow it dispelled the heavy feelings in my heart and beyond. When I contacted my maybe former girlfriend and told her how I was working hard I could feel that the upset that existed between us had changed markedly. We could talk and we succeeded in settling our differences and get back together. If I had just given in to the emotional turmoil I don't think I would have had the necessary positive energy to talk with her constructively.*

The Attention Units, once freed can be used for planning and enjoying the present and future. The person is more "in present time". In Clearing there are hundreds of techniques and procedures available that all aim at freeing attention from failed and incomplete cycles. In this way we can increase the available number of Attention Units. This causes the client to be more aware of self and others, be brighter and more intelligent in general. It helps the client improve relationships, as he/she now can pay more attention to friends and associates and better see their points of view.

Chapter 3: Live Communication

"Communication" as a group of industries is a multi-billion business. These industries cover mail, printed media, telephony, including mobile phones, internet, radio and TV broadcasting, and more. Despite the billions spent on technical developments every year there are basic simplicities that receive little attention. The communications industries offer a choice of media through which communication can take place. They concentrate on the physical transmission of print, spoken words, pictures and sound. They ensure this transmission is successful and leave the rest to the users. They pay little or no attention to live communication. As technical systems develop the volume of communication seems to go up and up with no end in sight. In the last many years, new social media, such as Facebook and Twitter, have entered the scene and gotten multi-millions of subscribers. It's obvious we human Beings love to communicate.

What we are most interested in here is *Live Communication*. We are interested in how and why communication works in human interaction. One practical reason for this interest is that live communication is the active ingredient in clearing. Thus any improvements that can be gained in live communication means better results in clearing work. The practitioner has to continuously work on this. The clearing practitioner has to perfect what is called the Communication Exchange. The Communication Exchange is a specialized cycle of action—delivering a message from one human being to another. Once the message is delivered and understood by the recipient, the cycle is complete. One cycle is obviously just a fragment of the whole conversation or exchange of ideas. It's the smallest complete unit of conversation and communication. But as such it's where we should start before getting into more complex situations.

When we talk of clearing work, the practitioner's use of communication is very disciplined and specialized. During a session the clearer does not engage in any social conversation or discussion. The practitioner's role is better understood as a handler of the *client's* attention and communication. The clearer gives the client center stage. He/she does that by being an excellent listener and showing the client

undivided attention. Anything the client says is given unflinching interest. The clearer is acting as a listener against whom the client can discharge. The clearer is continuously working on establishing a safe and distraction-free atmosphere in which the client can contemplate and work out his/her completely personal issues. Once the client has fully engaged in contemplating them and then telling about them, he/she is said to be *fully engaged*. To be able to bring about this fully engaged state of mind is vital. Not until this engagement is achieved is clearing occurring for real. Once full engagement is established, the practitioner can concentrate on administering the right technique and guide the client toward self-realization. The clearer can help the client contact and discharge emotional and confusing issues. This is all very disciplined on the part of the practitioner. The only casual thing about it is how it looks and feels to the client.

The Elements of Communication

What, then, are the characteristics of live communication? What are the principles that determine whether a communication becomes successful or not? Some people always end up arguing. Others never get to the point. Yet others are so boring in their communication no one bothers to listen. Some people are unable to hear a sentence to its end and interrupt all the time. Obviously, there is something here that directly affects our endeavors in life, our relationships and our ability to succeed.

Basically, Communication is the delivery of a message from one person to another. The basic analysis of live communication is expressed in what we call the Elements of Communication.

Sender (speaker)   **Receiver** (listener)
Intention/attention   *Attention*/intention

Message   **Duplication/ Understanding**

The Elements of Communication are: Sender, Distance, Receiver and using Intention and Attention to achieve Duplication and Understanding.

Taking turns at speaking and listening is called Exchange of Communications.

Here we have 'Intention' and 'Attention', our two important vital signs of life. We talk about a 'Sender'. That is the person speaking. There is a distance to overcome. Then there is 'Receiver'; that is the person listening to the communication. In a live communication the Sender must have Intention for the communication to be successful. The Sender must pay Attention to the listener's location and condition.

'Attention' is of course also part of being a good listener, capable of receiving a communication. The listener as well, needs to have an intention to listen and to understand. The action of communicating has to result in *Understanding*. The Understanding part is unique to a *live* communication. There are in other words three ingredients that make communication live: *intention, attention, and understanding*.

'Duplication' (see illustration) means that the message actually arrives; a duplicate is being recreated at Effect. It does not say what the receipt point does with it.

The communications industries concentrate on making Duplication possible over a distance and that is certainly an important point to establish. Let us take a fax machine as an example. The sender will  place a printed page onto his machine. The page will be transformed into electronic signals. These signals are then transmitted via a telephone line to the recipient. When the signals hit the receiving fax machine the signals will again be translated into a printed page on a piece of paper. The recipient will see a page being printed before her eyes. It can be a near perfect copy of the original document. The recipient can, of course, overlook the fact that she has received the fax. The fax can make her upset or jubilant; or it can be in a foreign language she can't make any sense out of. But the fax received is certainly a duplicate – almost as good as if the sender had been next to the receiver and simply handed her the original.

When it comes to Intention, Attention and Understanding, they cannot be transmitted electronically. There can be such a thorough understanding between sender and receiver that it still works. But it depends utterly on the mindset of the two parties. It's completely in the realm of awareness and thought. So is finding a message (consideration) to communicate. You may object and say: "I get my daily newspaper and it is full of reports and stories on what is going on." You are, of course, right. Content oriented media employ reporters, writers, and photographers, who are aware Beings, who originate the content of these media articles.

TYPES OF COMMUNICATIONS

Below are some practical situations to illustrate uses of communication. One reason we go over this is to make clear how social situations are different from the session situation. Although the basic elements of communication remain the same, the style of communication used in session is only occasionally appropriate in life. The basic skills *are* very relevant but we have to understand how to apply them to life to become an all-round effective communicator.

Social Conversation

In social conversation we have two or more persons talking with each other. This is a favorite pastime for human Beings. At a typical dinner party we have light, flowing conversation. No subject is pushed very hard. The subject changes frequently in a type of free association phenomenon. Subject A reminds a guest of subject B and the whole conversation drifts to subject B, then to C, etc. Only pleasant subjects are, as a rule, taken up. An old etiquette rule is, "Never discuss politics and religion at the table". This rule is in place to avoid heated discussions and arguments. The elements of communication are in play back and forth and crossways; Duplication and Understanding sometimes happen, often they do not. The whole exercise seems to be motivated by a wish to belong, maybe show off and impress; sometimes to establish new contacts for later use.

Having an Argument

When two people argue without resolution the Duplication and Understanding is not working. The Distance between the two seems to become greater and greater. Besides physical distance, such as sudden departure, we also use it as distance in points of view. A good conversation leads to better understanding and shared points of view. The successful Duplication and Understanding of each cycle bring that about. When two people argue, the intent is often to exchange insults and verbal blows. Arguments often happen between people who don't want to listen to each other. The lack of Duplication builds up over time and explodes. During the argument, while the one is talking, the "listener" is often only thinking up the next insult to fire off. Some claim that a good argument can clean the air. This may be true, but not the typical outcome. With a mediator between the parties there may be enough Duplication and Understanding taking place to work out the differences. It takes discipline imposed by a sharp moderator for this to work well.

Public Speaking

Lecturers, educators, politicians, senior members of organizations, and activists for causes all have to speak loud and clear to be effective. They constantly have to monitor their audience (pay attention) to make sure they are getting their message across. The best of speakers can play a large audience as if it were one person. Yet, they know that this is done by speaking to each single individual in the group. Sender-Distance-Receiver with Duplication and Understanding times a hundred. To accomplish that they have to address different members or segments of the room on a rotating basis. They have to look boldly at the "monster" and not get caught up in or  hide behind notes. They can mix in humor and anecdotes to establish better contact and rapport. They have to adjust their vocabulary so it can be understood and yet be respected as valid information. They scan their audience to see if a majority can follow what they are saying. Yawning, looking around, private conversations, walk-outs, etc. in the audience are, of course, all signs of warning. The speaker should have a clear idea of what Effect he wants to create. In some situations the speaker wants an emotional Effect to rally the troops. In other situations he wants to convince the listeners with logical arguments. Or he may simply want to make sure that the audience gets some facts 100% right, as in education. The speaker has to have a single mind about getting his intention and message across. The speaker can use gestures to underscore points. He can use a blackboard, pictures, video, etc. to keep the audience interested and entertained. He has to be interesting and interested at the same time.

Interested – Interesting

To be a good communicator one has to understand the difference between Interested and Interesting. *Interesting* means, one seeks to attract attention to self. Actors use that. They put on a costume; use their bodies and gestures to express themselves and the role they play. The best members of this profession have it totally under their control. They can change from Interesting to Interested in a second. Some actors are, however, stuck in being Interesting and their art suffer.

Interested means that the communicator has her attention on the other person or the audience. She does not try to attract undue attention to her person, but tries to emphasize her message. She can follow her communication across the distance and ensure it arrives as intended. Thus she seems more comfortable about being at cause. This is a healthier state of mind, but it is not an absolute.

You will however find when a communicator is stuck in being only Interesting, just being attractive, being a class clown, showing off as a lecturer by using big words the audience doesn't understand, etc. that the communications skills need a lot of work.

A good communicator has to know the difference between Interested and Interesting and use this knowledge as a tool. All communication is a give and take; inflow following outflow; attention following intention. A proper understanding of Interested and Interesting is part of that.

Talking Around an Issue

In interviews you often hear politicians talk on and on and you can't really make good sense of it. That happens when they choose to talk around an issue. The interviewer asked some straightforward question, "Are you for the new school project?" The politician instantly begins to talk about education, earlier building projects and the kids in his district, etc. but nothing about the planned school. What is going on? Doesn't he get it? What you see in action is an actual technique that is taught to politicians. They are taught to show, by gesture and facial expressions, that they have understood the question and want to answer it. The politician talks, apparently, on the subject because he talks about the children, building schools, etc. in each sentence. *But he doesn't answer the question asked!* What the politician counts on is that at least 51% percent of the audience still thinks he is a great speaker that knows what he is talking about. You may not like this technique since it's a misuse of the principles of communication. The elements would be something like: Sender, -D-i-s-t-a-n-c-e-, Receiver, Misduplication, Deception. It is, however, a technique widely used in public and social life and thus of interest and possible occasional use.

Exchanging Views

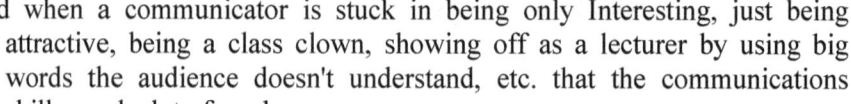

In stark contrast to the above is constructive exchange of views. That's what happens between best-of-friends and what makes such friendships priceless. You can say "anything" to your best friend and he or she will understand instantly or continue the conversation until he/she does. Likewise, you will understand anything your best friend says to you and respond in a caring and compassionate manner. In this type of relationship the interest is very high. The Duplication is almost telepathic. They can talk over the phone from each side of the planet and still feel they are right next to each other. The "Distance" has become non-material and disappeared. You can have different constellations, such as parent-child; husband-wife; equal "buddies", etc. Sometimes only one of them is the confidant, such as the mother in a mother-child relationship. Among peers, the ideal is that they are equal partners and take turns in their "confessions". The listener will tactfully, but rather freely, give his or her points of view, give advice, etc. In a later situation the roles are switched.

Admiration

There also exists one other quality in such a relationship: Admiration. Admiration could be defined as 'loving Attention'. The dictionary says, 'delighted contemplation of something worthy or beautiful'. In Clearing we see Admiration as the very substance of a communication line. It is that thing which the receiver usually considers most desirable. Admiration can be understood as a particle which resolves and unites all types of energy. Admiration specifically resolves and pacifies force. Admiration works like an effective solvent of conflicts and force.

Admiration is powerful stuff! Try this experiment: next time you are with a misbehaved child, give the child full attention while it is doing its misbehavior. You keep it up and ask a few questions to understand what is going on. You will find the point the child is trying to make. Acknowledge that with praise and admiration. "Oh, so you were trying to find out if cats drink wine. How smart you are." You will see an instant change in behavior. The bad behavior seems to evaporate and the child will start to laugh. That is an example of admiration being the solvent of force. It works with adults too.

Marriages, where there exist genuine mutual admiration, seem to be able to withstand almost anything in terms of "for better and for worse, through sickness and health"—the ups and downs of their marriage and external changes. In the traditional model for marriage, the "woman behind the man" would take care of home and children and admire her husband in all that he does. It is too one-sided in a modern world—yet it was workable when the woman was willing to take on that limited role.

Two Rules for Good Communication

Only a selected few of the people we know are our best-of-friends or confidants. How do we effectively communicate with estranged family members, co-workers, customers, bosses, classmates, teachers, etc.? These two rules can serve as a guide:

1. Be able to experience anything.
2. Cause only those things which others can experience easily.

1. In terms of communication, rule one says that you should be able to duplicate and understand anything communicated to you. You keep your composure, make sure you fully understand the situation, and give it an unbiased look. In violation of this rule would be: getting upset, respond with prejudice, instant attack on the speaker, "killing the messenger", reacting automatically rather than considering.

2. The other side of the coin is how you select subjects for discussion; or how you choose your words, how you respond to unfamiliar or strange opinions and views. Rule two tells you to consider the other person's world and values. It says to express yourself in a manner that can be accepted and understood by the recipient.

The very purpose of true communication is Duplication and Understanding. In exchange of communications it goes both ways. If the above rules have become second nature, you are on solid ground as a good communicator.

These rules apply to clearing work in the following manner: The clearer should listen carefully to the client and ask for clarification when needed. The clearer should never jump to conclusions but give the client time, space and opportunity to fully explain matters, when needed.

The clearer should make sure never to overwhelm or force the client against his/her will. The clearer may have to explain in detail the procedure and what he/she is going to do. Clear up definitions and theory with the client, etc. But unless the client willingly gives consent, the action isn't started – for that simple reason that only a smooth cooperation between clearer and client will ever be beneficial. More so because it is the client that has to do the hard work. So the clearer has to be very good at adjusting to a client in terms of pace, intensity, explanations, and exchange of flows in general. Being able to adjust in this manner to the individual client is the difference between a beginner and a top professional clearer.

Trauma and Communication

There is one additional and important thing to say about rule number one, "Be able to experience anything." What happens in the mind when a person is unwilling to experience something terrible that is happening to him or her is that the person gets overwhelmed. The person gets stuck with an incomplete cycle of experience and perception. This is a trauma. The individual becomes traumatized. Let's say we have a young woman who gets mugged and sexually assaulted. She will, of course, fight against this and "counter-create", as explained under Cycle of Action. We are not suggesting that she shouldn't. We are merely trying to explain the actual anatomy of a trauma, which gives us the key to unlocking it.

The woman, when assaulted, will be the victim of the assailant's efforts to overpower her by the emotions he expresses, and the intentions and actions he tries to execute. Against those the woman will put her own counter-efforts, counter-emotions, and counter-intentions. This is, technically speaking, a counter-create. The terrible things she had to go through will be suppressed and repressed. At some point she was overwhelmed and stopped resisting. She gave up on exerting control over what happened to her. This incident, this cycle of action, now seems to have a life of its own. The woman will have terrible flash-backs, have nightmares about it and physical and mental scars that easily get triggered and don't seem to heal.

Should she be so fortunate to find a Clearing practitioner there is still hope. No reason to fill her with medicine to totally numb her mind so it is unable to mentally counter-create. The practitioner will know what to do. The clearer knows the client's ability "to experience anything" in the area is severely hampered. The practitioner has to approach it gently and may use a number of light techniques to unburden the trauma and make the client better able to fully view what happened. This initial step may take many sessions, but at some point the client is up to the full task at hand. What eventually will resolve the trauma is when the client is capable to re-experience everything and anything that happened "that terrible evening." The incident will now be fully reviewed in session. The whole incident is being uncovered piece by piece.

The best illustration of this review is flashback techniques seen in movies. The whole incident is knowingly being replayed in session as if were happening right now. The client will be able to re-experience it in great detail. The assailant's efforts, emotions, and intentions; and her own counter-efforts, counter-emotions, and counter-intentions. The whole incident will 'discharge' thanks to the practitioner's ability to show unflinching interest and support; thanks to the practitioner's ability to be there for the client and enable her to discharge the content of the incident against another person. Once this is successfully completed, the client will no longer have automatic flashbacks or nightmares. The cycle of perception is now truly completed. The practitioner enabled the client to "experience anything" that happened. This also enabled the client to recreate and then un-create the incident as it existed in her mind, heart and body. All the practitioner used is under the heading of communication and the elements of communication. That's a good illustration of why communication is called an universal solvent.

Manners in Alien Encounters

If you like to travel you probably have an appetite for meeting people with totally different backgrounds and cultures than yours. You may run into people that don't speak any language you understand. These peoples probably have their own social rituals and etiquette that seem bizarre and impossible to follow. How can you interact without having to study their ways for years?

There are two ground rules that apply to such situations:
   1. Grant importance to the persons you communicate with. This is done by paying attention, showing interest, and giving importance to what they say and do.
   2. Use a good communication cycle. This includes making sure you are understood as well as understanding them.

Use drawings and sign language if verbal communication is near impossible. You should acknowledge what they say to show that the communication has arrived. You should be willing to look them in the eyes. It may be unacceptable in some cultures to "keep starring people in their eyes", but at least you should have the ability to do so and use it at initial contact.

In business school they sometimes teach students to look at the other person at a point where the neck meets the shoulders, "the knot of their ties". You have to convey that you "focus your interest" on them and on what they say. That's the operating definition of attention. If you look away, or make your eyes wander a lot, you are expressing lack of interest and focus. Some will say shifty eyes equal sly intentions and unreliable character.

The granting of importance plus a good communication cycle seem to be the fundamental operating laws of good manners. They are so fundamental so they transcend differences in social class, race, culture, religious beliefs, language barriers, age, etc.

Interviews

When you see skilled in-depth interviews on TV you will see a communication cycle not too different to the one the clearing practitioner uses in session. The interviewer asks questions to make the interviewed person shine and express his/her points of view clearly.

There are some important differences that disqualify it. A TV interview is ultimately made for the viewers, not the interviewee. Therefore, the interviewer does not acknowledge as that would slow things down. The interviewer sometimes uses silent nodding. He may also interrupt to move things forward, thus leaving the interviewee with things unsaid. Also, the interviewee is addressing the message to the audience via the interviewer.

There are other types of interviews on TV that don't deserve the name. After all, "interview" means "to view within". In the news you see 'sound bites', one-liners that are picked out of a context to illustrate the *reporter's* message. You see inexperienced or self-important interviewers use the opportunity, when interviewing others, to express their *own* views at great length or start an argument. That is, by the way, an example of being interest*ing* rather than interest*ed* as an interviewer. You see hostile interviews where trick questions are used, such as "Do you still beat your wife?" Both 'Yes' and 'No' make the interviewee look bad.

Communication and Life

We said above in this chapter that the use of communication in session is very disciplined and specialized. Learning this type of communication was an important part of my early training as a practitioner. What happened to me, and many of my fellow students however, was that I got so "good at it", so specialized, that it hampered my natural social skills. I became a good listener but was afraid of taking part in just about any controversial discussion. I wouldn't give my frank opinion even to friends. I thought it was a "sin" to attract undue attention to a point where I became invisible in groups.

This backfired in life. To make some extra money, I worked for a couple of years as a freelance web designer and copy writer in advertising. I was part of many brain storming sessions to find new ideas to ad campaigns and websites. First when I adopted a totally different style of communication, where I had to throw out wild ideas and entertain the participants, was I able to get heard and taken seriously. I wrote this chapter to put an end to stiff and silly habits. See also the section 'Assertive Communication' at the end of this chapter. Assertive communication is a formal subject, taught in workshops, that supplements the communication drills when it comes to real life situations.

THE COMMUNICATION DRILLS

With this as a warning, the communication drills below are still some of the most important elements in training as a practitioner. Learn them well. But do me and yourself the favor of not giving up on the social forms of communication described in this chapter when you are in a different setting than a formal session.

Acquiring the specialized communications skills is an important part of training as a practitioner, as said. This training is centered on the Communication Drills (CDs). Each drill takes up one little skill. At the end of a training program they are all put together. Selective use of the Communication Drills helps in all the above types of communication, but the CDs are designed with clearing work in mind. Below is a short description of the basic drills.

The One-Routines consist of three drills, 1a, 1b, 1c that enable the student to hold his /her ground and maintain focus. They teach the student *session presence*, to remain calm and receptive even under trying circumstances and for a considerable length of time.

Communication Drill 1a: Being There

Two students sit *with closed eyes* across from each other, about 1 meter apart. They do this drill to be able to be there, comfortably in front of another person. "Being there" and holding a position is the first prerequisite for communication.

Communication Drill 1b: Unflinching Interest

Once the student is comfortable about being there, Unflinching Interest can be started. The two students sit across from each other with open eyes. They have to be able to maintain attention and interest in the person across from them. This is done for as long as it takes, until the student practitioners can maintain it for two hours straight. They are not allowed to move, blink excessively, yawn, dope off or anything else other than being there. They may have to do this training for days. It's done until they can demonstrate that they can sit calmly across from a client and look at that person with interest without having to do something else. They have to demonstrate they can concentrate on doing clearing work only for two hours straight.

Communication Drill 1c: Pushing Buttons

Once Unflinching Interest is completed, the students start on drill 1c, Pushing Buttons. One student shows unflinching interest. The other student, acting as instructor, tries to distract and crack up the student practitioner. This drill is rough, tough and a lot of fun. The purpose is to perfect the student practitioner's ability to show calm interest in a client under the most trying circumstances. The instructor will act out being a rough client, tell jokes, make fun of and be insulting to the student, make faces, etc., all in an attempt to throw the student practitioner off and get him/her to laugh, cough, flinch, blink, etc. In short, the instructor imitates a rough session and seeks out buttons to push on the student practitioner. At the end of the drill the student practitioner is capable of "experiencing anything" any client can throw at him/her with calm, unflinching interest and without breaking up or reacting.

Communication Drill 2: Delivering a Clearing Instruction

The student practitioner is drilled in delivering clearing instructions naturally and as live communications. It can be questions or instructions. The student reads the instruction from a list or a book. The student can pick any sentence, a question or a statement. The student has to make the sentence his/her own and then deliver it naturally and with intention as if it is something the student just thought of and really wants to get an answer to or a response to in return.

Communication Drill 3a: Full Acknowledgment

Once the student practitioner gets an answer or execution of a clearing instruction, the student always acknowledges the client. This is to let the client know that the clearer has heard what the client said and has understood it. That ends one cycle of communication. The student practitioner is not expressing agreement, disagreement or approval. In that respect the student has to remain neutral. The student is simply expressing that he/she heard and understood the client and is closing off that particular communication cycle with the acknowledgment

Communication Drill 3b: Half Acknowledgment

Half acknowledgments are used as encouragements and get a client to keep on talking. It can be "aha?", "yes?" and other noises that express interest and let the client know that he/she is being listened to and the practitioner wants to hear the rest of the story. Once the client has said it all, the student practitioner would use a full acknowledgment (CD-3a) to end cycle on the full communication.

Communication Drill 4: Repeated Instruction

The Repeated Instruction Drill consists of one instruction or question (sometimes a set of instructions/questions) given over and over to the client in order to penetrate any social and occlusion mechanisms of the mind. By repeating a meaningful question or instruction, the client will dig deep into the subconscious mind for hidden, forgotten, and sometimes surprising answers. This is, of course, done with the client's full consent under the rules of the clearer's professional code (chapter 14). This type of clearing action can have a profound effect on the client's ability to get to the "root of the problem" by penetrating all these defense mechanisms and occlusions.

In CD-4 the student practitioner drills the delivery of a repeated question or instruction. The student has to do it freshly; each instruction/question has to appear new and unasked. Usually one question is used, such as "Is the world round?" or "How is your dog?" Only one question is used over and over at a time. Each answer is acknowledged and that cycle is completed. The instructor introduces detours and 'Pushing Buttons' to test the student's resolve in getting the original question answered. Once answered and acknowledged, the next instruction is "brand new" and yet the same question is used without any variation. A good acknowledgment is required as that completes the previous cycle and the slate is wiped clean.

Communication Drill 5: Handling Pop-Up Remarks

A Pop-Up remark is a client statement that falls outside simply answering the clearing instruction. The practitioner has to drill handling a variety of Pop-Ups so he/she can handle them with skill. The student has to let the client know that the student has understood what the client is saying, yet not be thrown off or lose sight of what he/she is working on. (1) The student can have the client clarify the statement; (2) the student handles anything that needs attention; (3) the student acknowledges the client (4) and returns the client to the regular clearing technique. To complete the cycles of action in clearing is considered very important. Each major clearing action is designed to lead to its End Point, including relief, feeling great about the subject, and having a new realization. Yet, anything outside the questions or instructions that the client brings up starts another little cycle that the practitioner has to pay attention to and handle expertly before returning the client to the main set of questions. Attempts to only distract or annoy the practitioner are listened to and acknowledged but are, of course, given less importance than genuine concerns or new insights.

Exploring the CDs

Let us briefly describe how the CDs work in practice. Due to the CD-1 drills (presence), the practitioner is capable to fully concentrate on the client with attention and interest, regardless of what the client brings up or any emotional reactions the client may have. It has often been seen that a poorly trained practitioner that flinched, giggled, looked startled, or had any other small reaction, while the client was looking inward or describing something sensitive, would immediately distract the client and put him/her on guard. That would end the session in the sense that the client now had to use social defenses and half of his attention to deal with the practitioner. The client has to feel safe enough to completely shut off all these small defenses and use all his free attention units to look at and work on the issues. Once the answer to a question or instruction is found, the client has to feel safe in telling it exactly as it appears to him/her. Telling it results in a small discharge. It's almost an electrical phenomenon. The practitioner's acknowledgment is, however, necessary for this discharge to be stable. It completes the cycle and you could say it grounds the client. The "electrical circuit" has run its course. The next such communication cycle, including the client's answer and the acknowledgment, will discharge the next little piece of a confusion or disturbing emotion or thought that is being stirred up under controlled conditions by the practitioner using the technique.

You could also compare the session situation with cave exploration. The client wants to go down into a dangerous cave, the home of a fierce dragon. The client can only do that if he/she has an experienced partner that can hold the rope that will get him/her safely down and safely up again. There is no room for social conversation, jokes, personal remarks, etc. Now, the practitioner is not only such an expert rope-holder. The clearer is at the same time the client's guide and handler. The clearer knows that all of the client's attention has to be on where he is going. The clearer has to anticipate the slightest of slips and any danger in front of the client. The better the clearer is at that, the less he/she will get noticed. Thus the practitioner has to be *interested*, not interesting. They become a perfect cave exploration team that victoriously can explore and conquer any cave and overcome any dragon living in the deep. The CD-1 drills (presence) hold the rope. The CD-2 drill (clear instructions with intention) enables the client to look into the dark. The CD-4 drill (repeated instruction) enables the client to penetrate the dark without turning around in terror. The CD-3a drill (good acknowledgement) ensures the client's secure footing, one completed step at a time. The CD-5 drill (pop-ups) takes care of all the unforeseen dangers and distractions, small and large, that are bound to appear; CD-5 quickly takes care of them. The end point of the whole activity is to slay the dragon, get the client back to the surface safely and celebrate the successful outcome.

Assertive communication

The formal subject of Assertive Communication is in the author's opinion a necessary supplement to the communication drills when it comes to real life situations. In the CDs the clearer steps aside and leaves center stage to the client. The client is given an in depth interview without interruptions. In real life that would leave you, the interviewer, as an attentive listener but not as a participant. Learning what's called Assertive Communication will give you the formal skills to overcome that effectively.

According to Wikipedia; "**Being assertive** is a core communication skill. Being Assertive means that you express yourself effectively and stand up for your point of view while also respecting the rights and beliefs of others. Being assertive can also help boost your self-esteem and earn others' respect." Synonyms for Assertive are words like: confident, positive, bold, self-assured, self-confident, etc.

An Assertive communication workshop will teach you to recognize the rights of self and others. You recognize and respect their boundaries and your own. In practice you abstain from accusations and other aggressive communications. But you may insist on your own views, using CD-4 (repeated statement) if you will. You recognize other people's views by using CD-3, Acknowledgement. When it comes to conflicts you don't attack the other party with accusations. You stay on "your own side of the net" (as in tennis); you use "I" statements, like: "I feel that this is not necessary" instead of accusations like "You always ask too much of me!" Important here is also to keep cool, calm and collected and this is taught in CD-1 (presence). Assertive communication aligns well with the affinity scale (next chapter). You should stay away from communicating in anger and hostility by using higher levels of affinity, like interest. You don't abstain from communicating your needs and grievances—as often happens in fear or apathy. You state them boldly but without accusations. Instead of a 'them-or-us' situation you seek to establish cooperation and mutual respect and a pleasant tone. When you combine the skills learned in the CDs with Assertive Communications skills you are very well equipped to be successful in life and hold high positions. Look up Assertive Communication on the net or in the library and you will find the literature.

Emphatic Listening

In a therapy called Focusing (and in a number of other modalities) they teach what is called Emphatic or Active Listening. The practitioner repeats back what the client says, maybe in an implicit or paraphrased form. This demonstrates duplication and understanding. This system was originally developed by Carl Rogers and published in 1951. It has workability as part of Assertive Communication and also in conflict resolution. We find that using this form of communication throughout in clearing work, too often leads to misunderstandings and expressing practitioner's opinions (evaluations). It takes a master to use this technique without fallouts.

In clearing work we use really paying attention to the person and acknowledging what the person says. Occasionally the practitioner can say it back in some form; "I understand you experienced a feeling of fear and terror;" "You really tried to help–I understand that"—or the like. In clearing work we accept it as an optional tool used now and then – not as a rule. If the client seems to feel not fully understood, appears frantic about being duplicated, repeating things as described has a place. Use it sparingly – and do not repeat it all like a parrot. In my book that can be quite tedious for both parties and sometimes upsetting to the client.

Chapter 4: The Scale of Affinity

The Scale of Affinity is primarily a map of human emotions. It arranges well known emotions in a certain logical sequence and thus expresses something important about their nature. Understanding this scale makes it easier to deal with people in daily life and to understand "where someone is coming from". Any given person can be plotted on this scale in two ways: you can find a person's immediate level of affinity and emotion. This gives you an idea of the person's present state of mind, their feelings, and it gives you the key to how to deal with the situation. A person can, for example, momentarily be happy, interested, bored, disgusted, afraid, disappointed, or sad. A person also has a more permanent emotional level, usually known as temperament or disposition. A person's disposition can, for example, be upbeat and enthusiastic, have a temper that easily flares up, be grouchy, be a continuous pessimist, or always worry about things. The higher a person generally is on this scale the better off the person is in life. To be successful a person also needs experience and savvy, of course. That is not measured by this scale. What the scale measures directly is then the energy- and vitality-level of the Being. In that respect the scale measures a vital sign of great importance.

Human Character and Temperament

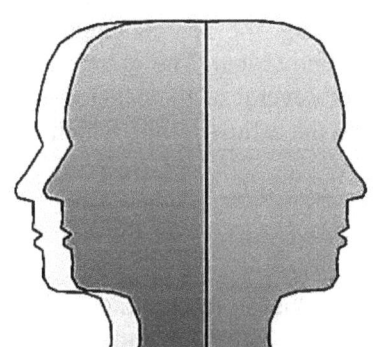

Human character and temperament are fascinating subjects. In popular weekly magazines you can routinely find self-tests consisting of questionnaires asking for your reactions in critical moments and daily life situations. At the end of such a test you add up your points and find out if you are an introvert or extrovert; an optimist or pessimist; if you are a leader or a follower; if you are the ideal lover/spouse or not, etc. Astrology is popular as well. In astrology you find that each birth sign is assigned certain personal characteristics. The theory is that a person born under a certain constellation of stars will have certain basic character traits that determine important aspects of their disposition and lives. The exact moment of someone's birth is thus the key datum used to predict their behavior and destiny.

For obvious reasons, understanding human character and trying to predict someone's future reactions and behavior have fascinated us throughout the centuries. Psychological literature is full of books on this subject. Each major school of psychology seems to have made valid observations and provided us with a system of viewing our fellow man and understanding individual characters. Yet, these systems seem to keep coming, the newest one invalidating previous schools of thought. Obviously, there are many ways of viewing the same set of problems of human character, temperament and behavior.

The Classic Temperaments

Hippocrates 460-377 B.C.

The best known system through history is **the four classic temperaments**. In classical Greek medicine, human character was divided into four categories. According to the original theory, each temperament was caused by the dominance of one particular body fluid out of four (blood, yellow bile, black bile, phlegm). The temperaments were also associated with the four classical elements of, air, fire, earth and water. Each temperament was compared to an annual season.

Hippocrates, the father of medicine, was the first one to describe these four temperaments in the literature. Aristotle wrote about them as well. In the 2nd century A.D. Claudius Galen, a Greek-Roman doctor and medical authority, brought the four temperaments back to the forefront of psychological thinking. The theory persisted well into medieval times. After the theory of the four body fluids was given up, the four temperaments still persisted as a significant system of categorizing human character. You will find it in use to this day even though the "scientific competition" between systems these days is much tougher. Below is a typical description of these four temperaments. They are always listed in this order:

Sanguine: "A person who is sanguine is generally optimistic, cheerful, even-tempered, confident, rational, popular, and fun-loving. A sanguine person can be day dreaming to the point of not accomplishing anything; be impulsive, acting on whims in an unpredictable fashion. This also describes the manic phase of a bipolar disorder (manioc-depressive). Dominant body fluid: Blood. The individual has the personality and temperament of *blood*. Element: air. Season: spring, wet and hot."

Choleric: "A person who is choleric is a doer and a leader. Many great charismatic, military and political figures are considered cholerics. On the negative side, they are easily angered, or bad tempered, easily irritated, even mean spirited, and over-controlling. In folk medicine, a baby referred to as "colic" is one who cries frequently and seems to be constantly angry. Dominant body fluid: yellow bile. Element: fire. Season: summer, dry and hot."

Melancholic: "a person who is thoughtful and reflective has a *melancholic* disposition. Often very kind and considerate, melancholics can be highly creative, as in poets and artists, but can become overly obsessed with the tragedy and cruelty in the world, thus becoming depressed. This temperament describes the depressed phase of a bipolar disorder (manioc-depressive).Dominant body fluid: black bile. Element: earth. Season: autumn, cold and dry."

Phlegmatic: "this personality is calm and unemotional. While phlegmatics generally are self-content and kind, their shy personality can often inhibit enthusiasm in others and make themselves lazy and resistant to change. They are very consistent, relaxed, and observant, making them good administrators and diplomats. Like the sanguine personality, the phlegmatic has many friends. But the phlegmatic is more reliable and compassionate; these characteristics typically make the phlegmatic a more dependable friend. Dominant body fluid: phlegm. Element: water. Season: winter, wet and cold."

As you can see, the order they are listed in is spring, summer, autumn, and winter, the progressing seasons of the year. This happens to be the Create-Survive-Destroy of the four seasons. Sometimes, different authors will express their personal preferences when describing the temperaments. The classification of a person is seen as a permanent labeling assigned to that individual. The system allows for mixtures of temperaments. Some people will display characteristics of several of the categories. All this serves as a good frame of reference and background for understanding the affinity scale, which is the subject of this chapter.

The Scale of Affinity

We see a person's "temperament" as a vital sign of the Being. It's the more chronic emotional state of a person. *Emotional energy* is, to a large extent, what is expressed in temperament and character – it is at least the energy that fuels them. Temperament and character are not seen as being totally permanent. It is seen as a set of characteristics subject to change over time. One person's position on this scale will tell a whole lot about the reactions you can expect. Likewise, a person's reactions, general outlook, and level of engagement in life are important factors to look at in order to find a person's correct position on this scale.

The basic scale is describing emotions very familiar to the reader. Yet, seeing these emotions as a scale is putting known phenomena in a completely new light of understanding and simplicity.

The scale has come about as a result of research in traumatic incidents. It plots the changes in the client when reviewing a traumatic incident many times. An example of incident running could be the experience as described in an earlier chapter of a young woman having been assaulted, where the clearer sends the client through the same incident again and again in order to get all the small details uncovered and re-experienced. The client, if similar to the woman, would typically first arrive in a state of regret, shame and blame. She could be in total apathy about life to a point where she "would rather be dead." Once the incident was fully contacted, she would re-experience the terror, the fear, the anger, the pain she originally experienced when the incident actually took place. The emotional discharge could change from one pass to the next. She would contact the original incident and discharge some emotion; next time through she might contact a different segment and discharge the emotion in that, etc. Doing this type of work with many different clients, male, female, young and old, and running many different types of incidents, a general pattern gradually reveals itself. The client's emotional attitude towards the incident will gradually improve. It would go from no hope and no future towards a gradually more optimistic attitude towards life and what the future would bring. A set of emotions that seems to follow each other in a set pattern or sequence, can be isolated as this improvement takes place. This sequence is what we call the Scale of Affinity.

The Basic Scale

The scale, first researched in incident running, applies to all walks of life and human behavior. It tells something important about the person's state of mind. Below you see excerpts. The full scale is in the appendix. (The full scale can be found in the appendix).

4.0 Enthusiasm	**1.2 No Sympathy (no compassion)**
3.3 Strong Interest	**1.15 Unexpressed Resentment**
3.0 Complacency, Contentedness	**1.0 Fear**
2.5 Boredom (indifference)	**0.9 Sympathy (feeling sorry for)**
2.0 Antagonism	**0.5 Grief**
1.8 Pain	**0.05 Apathy**
1.5 Anger	**0.0 Death (deep apathy)**

Examples of Levels on the Scale

4. Enthusiasm   2.5 Boredom   1.5 Anger   0.0 Deep Apathy

As you can see, the emotions listed here are all well-known and directly observable in individuals. Each line has been assigned a numerical value. The number expresses a degree of vitality and life-force expressed and felt by the individual. During a normal day you may find a person going through many different emotional tones, depending on who the person meets and what situations he/she faces. Good news and positive events will bring the person up the affinity scale. Bad news or negative events will take the individual down the scale. The individual will have a different emotional reaction to different spheres of life. Good friends, favorite interests and hobbies will put the person in a good mood. Detested jobs and chores and detested people will probably put the person at a much lower level.

You will, however, also find that any given individual will have a more **chronic level**. That is the affinity level that is characteristic for his/her general outlook on life. An individual with a low chronic level is less capable of coping with adversities in life, will be less forward looking and optimistic about the future. The circles and interests that comprise this person's world will usually be smaller and less open to growth. If you compare the chronic affinity levels with the four temperaments, you will see the two schools of thought are looking at the same thing. They may not have come to the exact same conclusions. But if you try to plot the four temperaments, you will have sanguine near the top, expressing enthusiasm and strong interest in life. Choleric would be found from contentedness through antagonism and anger to no sympathy. The melancholic temper seems to correspond to a band around fear, feeling sorry for, and especially grief. The phlegmatic temperament apparently expresses the emotion of apathy. But here we seem to have a misfit. What Hippocrates is describing, is a person that is cool, calm and collected, like a wise man, not necessarily a beaten down person.

The good news coming out of this research is that the emotional tone of an individual is not something that is genetically determined. The idea that we are born with a certain chronic tone that puts us in a certain category of individuals, or personality type, is false. It has clearly been demonstrated that the chronic tone of an individual can be changed. This can be done through clearing work as this activity is designed to raise a person's immediate and chronic affinity level.

That the affinity level of an individual isn't a permanent thing is actually easy to observe. It gradually changes throughout a person's life. It can be observed that children and young people usually are full of life and enthusiasm. If they are given a good education they are interested in, and live in a safe setting, their chronic tone will usually stay high. Eventually, as "life takes its toll" their tone will gradually go down. At some point they will settle in between 3.0 (contentedness) and 2.5 (boredom). This is still high. But as life goes on and if bad things happen they will eventually slide down the scale, step by step. As they get older, illness will gradually push them towards the bottom of the scale. When they die of old age you will see them "go out" at 0.0 (deepest apathy, death) of the scale.

In chapter 1 we described a life as a cycle of action; the affinity scale describes some important characteristics of this cycle. The apparent cycle of action was described as Create-Survive-Destroy. You will see the top of the affinity scale, enthusiasm and strong interest, are typical for Create. Complacency and boredom are typical for Survive. "Life is good as usual; let's not rock the boat." Antagonism and anger are clearly the emotions of Counter-create. As we go down, we see the individual losing out to the forces facing him or her, to the Counter-create of the environment and life. The loss of loved ones, worsening health, losing a job, an accident, and etc. – all comprises setbacks resulting in lowered affinity level. We get temporary or permanent setbacks resulting in emotions like fear, grief and apathy.

You may object and say that you feel much better now than you felt a few years ago. Let us use that objection to explain a point. Obviously life consists of many cycles of action. But let us look at one example. We have a job we have come to dislike. This is a slippery slope towards antagonism, anger, resentment, maybe insecurity (fear), and eventually the total lack of Create as in apathy. You probably caught it in time and made a career move. You gave yourself a new start at the top of the scale. You found your dream job and life was, again, interesting and full of creative challenges.

The same happens in friendships and all other relations of life. Unless we constantly create, we will eventually slide down the affinity scale in relation to each sphere of our existence. A new job or hobby, new friends, a new home or new possessions will all give us a renewed interest in life and to that degree a new start near the top of the scale. Getting over a disease will have the same positive effect. Falling in love is the classical boost from feeling miserable to living on cloud nine. We can, in other words, go up and down the scale considerably over time. We can actually do something about our chronic position. The things we do that are most dear and important to us can usually be understood as an attempt to get ourselves moved up this scale. It is good survival, if you will. A new start near the top of the scale certainly works in the direction of a longer and happier life.

The Expanded Scale

A number of versions of the affinity scale have been published over the years, including Frank A. Gerbode's Emotional Scale. Dr. David Hawkins, in his book "Power vs Force", has a similar scale, called 'Scale of Consciousness' that is worth a study. (The basic scale presented above follows Dr. Gerbode's.). The basic scale shows the band of human emotions that can be directly observed as facial expressions and body language. Below we use excerpts from the most extensive scale published, the expanded affinity scale.

There are many levels or tones above and below this well-known band. These speak more to how the person subjectively experiences life and his/her role in it. They speak to the condition of the spiritual Being. The expanded scale actually goes from +400.0 through 0.0 to -400.0. To mention some levels: at the top we have: 400.0 Sovereignty; at 40.0 Serenity of Being; at 30.0 Postulates; at 21.0 Games; at 20.0 Action; and at 8.0 Elation. Just below 0.0 we have: -0.2 Regret; -1.0 Blame; -1.3 Shame. At -40.0 we have Total Failure. At the very bottom we have -400.0 we have Spiritual Death.

Here are some comments on a few of them: "40.0, Serenity of Beingness" is a condition where we feel outside space and time. It may just be glimpses in a person's life where the person feels bigger than life and on top of the world and universe. "30.0, Postulates" is likewise ecstatic moments where we in a short span of time are capable of conceiving long range plans of utter importance. You may have discussed the bright future with your spouse-to-be and experienced this. What we decide in this state of mind just seems to happen. In "21.0, Games" the individual is utterly happy, competent and sure of self. Everything goes as planned; nothing can ever go wrong. Any danger is easily overcome or avoided. Life is truly a game we are sure of winning. "20.0, Action" is total dedication to a purpose, pulling all stops and overcoming all counter-intentions in the environment with determination and apparent ease. "8.0, Elation" is typically experienced after great accomplishments. In such cases it's the ultimate reward for work well done, for a major cycle of action completed. It's enthusiasm (4.0) times two. When a ball club wins the championship the fans will feel enthusiasm. They go out and celebrate all night. The coach, who worked so hard and had to overcome so many shortfalls to make it happen, will feel elation. It's the ultimate emotional reward for success; it's the emotion of genuine happiness.

Sub-zero Affinity Levels

Below "0.0 Death (Deepest Apathy)" we have "-0.2 Regret". It is an attempt to undo an action that is already done. The time is "out of order", forming a time-loop regarding the incident we feel regret about. In severe cases, regret causes flash-backs that can plague a person for years. The incident is constantly being replayed. At 1.0 we have "Blame": one can blame self or others for an act. This happens after something went utterly wrong. It doesn't fix anything; it really rubs the failure in and makes it into a terrible burden. It is, of course, an attempt to assign responsibility, often intentionally picking the wrong guy as a scapegoat. It is usually adding to the damage rather than fixing it. At -1.3 we have "Shame". We wish we were dead; we are so embarrassed and exposed. It's worse to be alive than dead.

The Body and the Affinity Scale

You may ask: "what does it mean that you can have an affinity level below death?"

What should be understood is that the band between "0.0 Death" and "4.0 Enthusiasm" has to do directly with the physiology of the body. These tones directly influence or control the body through the endocrine and nervous systems. The science behind this you can find in Canace Pert's book, "Molecules of Emotion". The emotions help direct the organism to avoid dangers and conquer pro-survival elements, such as food, shelter and companionship.

Above and below that band we have the "passions" of the Being; from the darkest to the most elated moments of life. Add to the "passions" the less dramatic robotic states which are only found below 0.0. These states of being are well described in literature and drama; from Shakespeare to romantic novels and crime stories. They include sickly jealousy, murderous rage and hate, extreme degradation, regret, shame, blame, etc. These affinity levels are below sanity. The dark side, the repressed content of the subconscious mind, has seized control—usually temporarily. These tones are usually only found in selected parts of a person's life and when the person is under extreme pressure. It is found in the best of us to a varying degree. We have all experienced these tones and passions in hard pressed situations.

The upper band above 4.0 includes elation and serenity of being. The expanded affinity scale – above and below the physiological band of 0-4 – thus maps such "passions" and robotic states of the Being. They do not have clear bodily expressions or physiological characteristics. Any such state will of course have a projection in the physiological band. "Controlling bodies" at -1.5 will thus project as "anger" that can be observed in the 0.0 to 4.0 band. One could call the band below 0.0 for "subjective negative tones" and the band above 4.0 for "subjective elated tones"

.

Another description of the below zero tones is: it is states below feeling any emotion, any responsibility or guilt about matters of importance. The person has become a zombie or robot of sorts; at some levels, a puppet in the grip of powers and passions stronger than self. Examples would be types of jealousy, revenge, being hysterical, or being fanatic. In other words, the person has ceased to operate based on reason or rational thought.

The full scale can be found in the appendices.

Affinity and Emotion

We have seen that the scale from 0.0 to 4.0 and a little beyond covers emotions. That is the emotional scale. The full scale is however correctly named the Affinity Scale. The difference between emotion and affinity requires an explanation. Emotion clearly has volume. A person can be a little angry or angry to a point of screaming their lungs out with the face turning purple. There is a difference in intensity or volume.

Emotion is expressed as facial expression and in body language. It is also felt in the body. That is no accident as it has a physiological function. When the person mentally experiences or generates a strong emotion it starts a biochemical process. It's a signal to the endocrine and nervous systems to go into action. Anger and antagonism are the emotions of physically attacking. Fear is the emotion of physically fleeing. Any such physical reaction is preceded by extra production of certain hormones, including adrenalin, called the fight and flight hormone. This hormonal production is ultimately triggered by the emotional state of the person. Strong sexual interest activates sexual hormones. A hungry man seeing food will be very interested and soon experience his digestive system being alerted and ready. This is ultimately triggered by the mind and the person himself. The yogis of India have demonstrated that such functions can be controlled by the conscious mind.

Although these functions to most people appear to be automatic, there is a clear influence caused by the mind. After all, the stimuli in the first place were usually only visual impressions or spoken words that had to be interpreted and understood by the person before any reaction took place. Emotions however influence the body and its physiology. Researchers like biologist Bruce Lipton and medical researcher Candace Pert have explained the science of this in popular books. Severe emotional upsets can cause heart attacks and other serious health problems. Losing a spouse to death can cause the survivor so much grief so he or she soon catches a serious disease and dies. On the other hand, receiving good news and having a healthy heartfelt laughter is sometimes the best medicine; not only for depression but for physical illness as well. The person feels it is worth living again and the physiology of the body responds.

Affinity, on the other hand, is a consideration. It is defined as "a consideration of distance" or "the willingness to occupy the same space as". People you love dearly you want close to you. You want to embrace them physically. People you hate you want far away from you. If you are in apathy you don't care one way or the other. It is, however, worth noticing that we can have more complex considerations about distance. We may want to be ready to move in or move out as a situation develops. Some relationships improve once more distance is introduced. Some people "love to hate" their enemies. They want them at hand – as having opponents, as in a game, is valuable to them. Considering "the right distance" to an individual or object in question is thus not as simple as 'closer' means higher affinity. Also, at the very top of the scale distance is no longer seen as a barrier. In stellar moments the person can reach out and embrace the whole world. The best definition, we find, is thus the open-ended "consideration of distance." A good workable understanding of affinity is, however, "willingness to occupy the same space as" where closer expresses higher affinity.

If we take a second look at the quoted description of the phlegmatic temperament, it mentions 'reliable and compassionate', 'dependable friend'; yet 'calm and unemotional'; makes 'good administrators and diplomats'. But also 'shy personality', 'inhibits enthusiasm in others' and 'lazy and resistant to change'. This is impossible to plot as one state on the affinity scale. It appears that several states, that look very much alike, have been grouped in one category. Serenity of beingness can to some look like mild interest, contentedness, boredom or apathy. These are harmonic affinity tones. They look alike but the amount of life-force present is very different. Let us take a practitioner with a solid background of doing the communication drills to perfect her communication skills: The first drill consists of remaining cool calm and collected regardless of what the client presents of startling stories. You will find that such a practitioner is capable of being perfectly calm under the most trying circumstances. She has to be reliable, compassionate, and dependable. Yet, she has to be capable of very high affinity in terms of being totally willing to let the client be himself in her immediate space and let him freely express any emotions, including enthusiasm. She has to be at strong interest or above, and *never* apathetic, to be effective. When we talk affinity it is not always what it looks like. You can't necessarily see the amount of life-force present. You can usually feel it and it sure reveals itself when observed and experienced over time.

Affinity at its highest level is space ("consideration of distance"). High affinity is pure beingness ("occupying space").

The Affinity Scale and Behavior

To determine a person's position on the emotional scale, going from 4.0 to 0.0, is relatively simple. It is explained in a section below. The question here is, what does the affinity level tell us about a person? How can it help us deal with people? As said above, the higher a person is on the scale, the more life-force or mental energy the person has available. That also means the person is more his/her own good self. The individual is closer to his/her optimum condition. So what is the optimum condition?

The optimum condition of a Being is: to feel happy; care about others (be ethical); be willing to see others' points of view; be friendly and likable; be capable of expressing feelings and points of view and interestedly listen to others expressing themselves; be persistent on worthwhile goals; inclined to tell the truth; wanting to take good care of possessions and own hygiene; be in good health; generally be in control of their life; be a good friend to have, etc.

Such an optimum condition may appear super-human and beyond what you can find in one individual. Yet, you see much of this expressed in young children. They may lack the language, the experience and skills, but they certainly, as a rule, do not lack the good intentions, the willingness to learn from mistakes, and the energy. Later in life you may find the same individuals, now in an advanced age, having gone down towards the bottom of the scale. At the bottom of the scale, then, the individuals will be all engrossed in their own problems, present and past, and have little energy left over to deal with the world at large. They may still function quite well, but mainly due to the skills, values and ideals they adopted early in life.

If you ask a number of persons when they felt "themselves", they will usually pick happy moments and times where they did something they could be proud of. When you compare such moments with the characteristics above, you will see a near match. The optimum characteristics, then, is the person's true self when he or she has her natural endowment of life-force, of attention units, available. The proof of this is not a matter of logical argument. It can be observed directly in clearing, the laboratory and proving ground for all statements and teachings of this book. Each person can have his/her "good old self" rehabilitated through clearing work. By resolving the issues he/she is engrossed in, past and present, known and subconscious ones, he/she will have his/her life-force rehabilitated and move up the scale.

It's not just a matter of age. You can find older people "young at heart and mind" as well as children that apparently think and act like old people. You will feel it is usually easier and less tasking to be together with people well up the scale. People do however tend to choose friends and relationships that seem to match their own chronic tone, their own temperament. They have more in common and think alike in many matters.

A good use of the affinity scale on this introductory level is simply to realize that people are different, yet basically have a good heart. With people lower on the scale, momentarily or more permanently, it may take a little more work and persistence to really get through to them. Realize that their state of mind isn't necessarily a reaction to you or what you are saying but more likely due to their own problems, prejudices, and unresolved issues. A person that at first is sad may suddenly get angry with you. Realize that anger (1.5) is much higher than grief (0.5). That means you have made progress; you are going in the right direction. Keep trying with a light heart and your communication will eventually get through. Also, when you yourself experience a mood low on the scale, take a quick look at what has gone on lately and see if you can spot why you suddenly are down. In clearing work recent and more serious issues are found and dealt with in a systematic manner in order to free trapped attention units and restore the individual's natural potential of life-force. As a result the person will move up the scale, feel more like his/her "good old self" and have renewed energy and vigor needed for succeeding in daily life.

There is another use of the affinity scale at this introductory level. If you have to choose between two equally qualified candidates, take their affinity level into consideration to break a tie. This can be used in hiring people, finding a plumber or carpenter, a lawyer or accountant. You may need day care for your child and you should take the affinity level of the people responsible into account. Usually, you may prefer the higher toned person. Some professions, however, require a certain affinity level to do it right. Accountants, money collectors, sports coaches, private investigators, defense lawyers, and foremen are not necessarily better when enthusiastic. Different professions take different temperaments to do well. If you can recognize where any given individual "is coming from" and make the best use of their abilities and inclinations, you have mastered maybe the most important lesson from studying the affinity scale. You will be comfortable in dealing with all kinds of people.

How to Find a Person's Affinity Level

The following little exercise is a simple method to quickly and quite accurately determine a person's affinity level in daily life. You simply test messages with different emotional content and see which one appeals to the person you are testing. In a normal conversation, you first drop great news and see how your partner reacts. "Did you hear that our team won last night?" Then you can talk about a cause most people are against (feel antagonistic about). "The new taxes are terrible." Go on to talk about something scary (fear). "Did you read about the murder?" You talk about something sad or dreadful (grief, apathy). "Did you hear that the school teacher died?"

You should use subjects that are equally real and relevant to the test-person to get a good comparison. You can, of course, use tones in between and explore each tone with a number of subjects. You simply notice the person's response to each. Where the reaction is most significant, that is where the person is on the scale. The person will usually start commenting on it while the other subjects seem of no interest.

Raising Somebody's Affinity

Once you have established a person's emotional state and affinity level you can, if needed, raise his/her tone by simple means. You use a step-by-step approach. This means you take one little step at a time in the direction that adds up to an overall improvement. This is a very effective tool in daily life. It ought to be called a professional technique. On the other hand it ought not to, because it is in the very fabric of human relationships. Once you have found a person's affinity level, you should address the person using a level 0.5-1.0 higher on the scale. If you learn how to use this technique smoothly, it will help you understand and handle all kinds of impossible situations. By using it knowingly in your daily life you will see your willingness to talk to and deal with all kinds of people improves. You can use it simply as a part of normal conversation, such as discussing the news. You will see angry people, impossible to get through to, suddenly crack up and laugh if you address them using an antagonistic affinity level. You don't have to attack the person; you can attack the government if that is appropriate.

Example: Let's say you find your friend, Sue, at the tone of grief (0.5) one day. Sue's dog, Fido, has run away. You can raise her tone by matching her emotional level. You stay on an emotional level 0.5-1.0 higher on the scale. That would be Sympathy (0.8) and Fear (1.0) up to Anger (1.5). You could express sympathy for her troubles, "Oh, that is terrible. You must feel awfully worried, Sue. It almost makes me cry too."

Then you can smoothly express fear about it, "I hope Fido keeps out of traffic..." This will get the person's attention. It is already starting to wake Sue up. You wouldn't stop there, of course. Then you could express anger towards something relevant, "Those drivers drive like maniacs around here. The other day....!" This is the way you get the person's attention and raise her from the original grief. She may be worried, upset, or angry about what you just said. But that is progress, going up the scale. So you have to keep up the action until the person is more cheerful, more ready to act. At some point: "Maybe we should go and look to see if he ran into the park on his own." Looking for Fido would at least be at 3.3, strong interest. She may not fully have made it up the scale yet but doing something about it helps. The situation will usually give you the script and the things to address as a meaningful conversation. Trying just to be 'enthusiastic' about things to cheer Sue up wouldn't work at all; such as, "I am sure Fido is OK, why don't we go and see this great new movie...!" It is too much of a jump for the person to consider and does not fit the situation at all. Using the described routine will do the job.

The Affinity Scale and Clearing

The affinity scale was first discovered in research sessions. It was found that the client's tone towards one particular incident would improve gradually in clearing work to a point where he/she could laugh the whole bad experience off. It was also found that a person's chronic affinity level, as a rule, consisted of the sum total of burdening experiences the client had been through. Different clients would however start out with different abilities to overcome the sum total of bad experiences life had dealt them.

Also, apparently same severity of an incident could knock one person out completely while another person would simply shrug it off. Our ability to face and overcome traumatic experiences in one area may be high; in another area very low. To fully understand the reasons for these differences a further study of the technology is recommended.

We can, however, point out two principally different types of techniques dealing with these problems. They both result in a raise of the client's affinity level. We have repeatedly used incident running in examples. The practitioner works with the client to find traumatic incidents. Once located, they are discharged for emotional content and sometimes physical pain. As a result there is a direct easing of the load of "old luggage" and bad experiences. There may be more or less unknown earlier similar experiences that will come into view and these incidents will, in turn, have to be reviewed. As a result of this work the person will feel much better about that part of life and in general go up the affinity scale.

Another approach that has proven very successful is principally different. Here the practitioner works directly with the ability of the client as an aware Being. By raising the client's ability to deal with adversities, problems and issues the client is capable of overcoming a lot of past experiences very efficiently without getting into all the small details. As a result the client can now discard a series of bad experiences and shortcomings in a short span of time. The client grows bigger and stronger, you could say. Some experiences still have to be dealt with "the old-fashioned way" by carefully reviewing them. A combination of these two methods in the course of a clearing program is therefore the strongest approach.

Summary

Emotions are three things:

1) Irrational reactions rooted in traumatic experiences. This is the source of irrational fears, inexplicable outbursts of anger, etc. The incidents can be found and discharged for negative emotional content by running them repeatedly.

2) Endocrine alerting and activation of the body, to be ready to meet situations on a rational level. To get the adrenalin pumping is an endocrine phenomenon. The glands pump the adrenalin into the blood stream to make the body ready to fight, flee or freeze. Fear is a quick withdrawal from danger and can, of course, be quite rational. The body is given additional endocrine or biochemical commands to bring that about.

3) The manifestation of life force. The higher the person is on the affinity scale the more life force is present.

Any individual will have an immediate emotional level as a reaction to the current situation. Likewise, the individual will have a chronic affinity level that usually is seen as an important part of the person's character and disposition. The chronic affinity level of an individual can be raised through clearing work. When the affinity of an individual is raised, the person will better be able to deal with adversities in life; the person will feel more energetic and invigorated. The person will feel more him- or herself and more capable of doing the right thing as he/she sees it.

Chapter 5: How Real Is Reality?

When something can be proven to exist it is said to be *real*. The ultimate proof of *reality* is what science concerns itself with. The natural sciences examine nature and the universe. It's not an easy process to arrive at scientific facts. The natural sciences use stringent scientific methods to establish *what is* and *what isn't*. The scientific methods used may vary from science to science, but according to "Encyclopedia of Science & Technology" they must have this in common:

Every scientific hypothesis or rule must be supported by evidence obtained by observations. Those observations must be repeatable by other scientists and must be observable by a large number of persons. Any scientific hypothesis can be changed if new observations, using different methods, give different results."

A common concern of any science is to eliminate any subjectivity introduced by a single observer. Many qualified observers have to agree on what they observe before anything can be considered for upgrading to scientific fact. Such discoveries and observations have to pass a peer review where qualified scientists discus the pro and cons of its validity. Much scientific philosophy has been written on the subject of the observer and how to eliminate any risk of errors and subjectivity. Observing things via instruments and translating observations into numbers and formulas have been used with great success.

Any discovery in science has to pass a peer review where qualified scientists discuss the pros and cons of its validity. Only after a consensus is reached and additional tests have confirmed the findings can a new discovery get upgraded to scientific fact.

The impulse that moves science forward, however, comes always from single individuals. No science would be performed unless we have somebody with an inquiring mind, one individual with a tremendous curiosity and an insatiable appetite for looking at things anew and firsthand. Such a person is usually at first considered a "mad scientist" until a time when he can get a sufficient number of colleagues to look at his discovery and have them confirm, or agree to, that they can make the same observation. They have to be able to duplicate the experiment and the observation in order to consider that there could be any reality to it.

In Clearing we are of course not primarily interested in doing physical universe research. Our prime interest, it could be said, is the scientist himself, the observer of things. *We see our mission as being "observing the observer"*. We want to look into how the individual *experiences* the world and the realities of the environment out there. How does a normal lay person come to the conclusion that something is real? It is less sophisticated than one may suspect. Yet, at its core it is contained in the scientific principles quoted above. At the core it's based on agreement and/or duplication. Let's look at some daily life examples.

When a traffic accident happens the police will find witnesses and essentially ask: what happened? Officers will usually get as many different accounts of the accident as the number of witnesses interviewed. One witness saw a green Ford hitting a yellow Audi car. Another saw a blue Toyota hitting a white Mercedes car. The witnesses will have different accounts regarding speed, maneuvers, the second by second timing of the accident, etc. The bystanders, of course, saw the accident from different vantage points, different points of view. Maybe they only saw part of it. The police will add up all these testimonies and find out where these agree and disagree. The officer in charge establishes a few points that all the witnesses agree on as facts. He then compares the rest of the testimonies until he comes to a point where he will conclude what probably happened, moment by moment, and finally state in his report: "This is what happened..." But it is clearly a process of thought and "negotiation" before the police gets to that point. This tells us, in terms of human experience, that arriving at what is real includes a process of thought and interpretation leading to some level of agreement.

Let's examine the two drivers for a moment. The driver that caused the accident momentarily didn't "agree to" the fact that there was a stop sign. Nor to the fact that another motorist was approaching. The accident and the collision "convinced him" of the reality of the other car. The judge in court convinced him about the reality of the stop sign. The guilty party had to pay a $500 fine plus damages to the injured party. The judge enforced a number of agreements the guilty party had overlooked or set aside in the accident. Apparently, these realities have a lot to do with agreement as well. If we don't agree, the physical universe and the courts will see to that these agreements are enforced!

When you buy or sell a house there is a lot of paperwork to fill in to make the deal official after the parties have settled the price. Experts will inspect the house for structural soundness and write reports. A broker will inspect the official records at the courthouse. A banker will inspect existing loans in the property and the credit worthiness of the buyer. Finally, a lawyer will draw up the title deed for the property and call a meeting. He will have the parties sign the papers and have several witnesses on hand attesting that they saw the signing take place. Finally, all official papers are filed at the court house; lots of paperwork, lots of signing. But all required by the law and the many parties involved. Without the paperwork and all the agreements it represents, the "deal didn't take place" in the eyes of the law. The law, in other words, here defines reality as agreement.

If you bump your head against the frame of a low door in an old house it will probably hurt. You will take a step back, rub your forehead and look at the door frame you ran into. In the future you will be more careful and more aware of that door and others like it. The door frame has become painfully real to you because you experienced the solid impact. The physical universe "punished you" for disagreeing with its laws. Two objects cannot occupy the same space according to physics. Once you agree to that law you will fare better in the future.

The examples above illustrate that our experience of reality is based on different types of agreements. In human affairs we negotiate, share or join agreements. Sometimes they are enforced upon us. In relation to the physical universe we accept things as they are. "Agree or else..." seems to be the message. Physical universe realities are realized through perception, observation and duplication. If we repeatedly observe the same thing it is real. If many scientists repeatedly observe the same phenomena under controlled conditions we have a scientific fact.

These types of agreements are routinely enforced when we momentarily seem careless or ignorant about them. They are enforced through disciplinary action when we talk about a social reality. In human affairs we still feel we could change things around if we worked real hard at it. We could appeal to the authority and have him show leniency towards us. He would ease the rules so we didn't get punished. On a bigger scale we could get the rules changed. We could become a leader or politician ourselves and change the rules and laws.

When we talk physical universe realities, we are up against tougher laws. The natural laws of physics are enforced through physical pain and unpleasant sensations when we bluntly disagree on their reality and break them. "Agree or perish" is the sinister message. There is no room for negotiation.

Subjective Reality

Something can be factual or exist for one person alone without having been agreed to. It can exist for you but not for others. We call this a subjective reality. Our private thoughts are subjective realities. A scientist making a new discovery will at first be alone with this knowledge. That's a subjective reality. His next task, as described above, is to convince his colleagues about the truth of this discovery. He invites them to look for themselves and responds to any criticism with scientific arguments. Once he has won a few over to agree with him he has a beginning new reality. The history of science and discovery is full of examples of how slow and difficult a process it can be to establish a new "objective" reality. The Earth was considered flat and the center of the universe for centuries, going back into prehistoric times.

When Galeo Galileo (1564-1642) claimed the Sun was at the center of the universe he was summoned by the Pope and nearly banned by the inquisition. He got off with a milder sentence of lifelong house arrest. The Italian monk Giordano Bruno (1548-1600) was, however, burnt as a heretic in year 1600 for saying the sun was at the center (although the sentence included other disagreements with Rome).

When the British doctor, William Harvey (1578-1657), discovered the function of the heart as the pump in the circulatory system, he waited 13 years to publish his findings. His findings challenged the prevailing teachings of Claudius Galen (129-200), the Greek-Roman medical authority from the 2nd century. Harvey was afraid his discovery would discredit him professionally. Dr. Harvey was the King's physician and feared to lose this high position. The findings when finally published caused decades of academic uproar and weren't accepted as facts until after Harvey's death. There are countless other examples of how slow a process it can be to have new scientific facts accepted as realities.

William Harvey

Even today, when you look at scientific literature, you will understand that new discoveries are delicate matters. When scientists write about their discoveries, they usually take great care in quoting works of their peers and the accepted authorities of their field. They know they have to do a very thorough job in showing how their work fits into the accepted tenets of their science for it to be well received. They know their findings have to pass a peer review in order to be considered valid and factual. This approval is unlikely to happen unless they are willing to give credit to the authorities in their field and submit to any pecking order that may exist. We here see an intersection between objective and social realities. That's the politics of science. The elements in play are discovery, acceptance, scientific reputation, promotions and fame.

Some people can "perceive things" while no one else is aware of them. These things can be factual and based on psychic ability and extrasensory perceptions. But if the rest of the world is convinced what a person insists "is real" is not there, it is labeled as obsessive thought, "ideas" or insanity. A person can claim she hears voices, that the Martians are chasing her, etc. This is so unreal with the rest of us so we say the person is insane. It is said that genius is a type of insanity. What the genius and the insane have in common, for sure, is an "attitude" towards the agreed upon reality of society and the universe. They can see things that no one else can.

Realities

We like to talk about a *person's or group's* reality. A person's reality is how that individual sees the world. This is based on his/her upbringing, education, values, own observations, etc. Sometimes we find it is based on traumatic incidents – physical trauma or emotional trauma. Whatever factors formed it, each person has a unique view on the world and some very personal values that color it.

Each organization or group, large or small, has a certain reality unique to that group. They have written and unwritten laws and rules. Besides the written rules there are agreements expressed as: "That's how things are around here" or "the new order of things", "the politically correct attitude", "the 'in', 'hip' or 'cool' behavior" in a sub-culture or youth group. You will often find that any social reality can be traced back to the founder or to opinion leaders of the group and their personal likes and dislikes. Likewise you will find values based on traumas that threatened the group. This is what is behind irrational aversions and attitudes of hate between groups. In 1942, during World War Two, Japanese-Americans mainly in Western USA were rounded up and kept under guard in camps till the end of the war. These were American citizens for a large part. But since USA was at war with Japan, starting with the bombardment of Pearl Harbor, no person of Japanese descent could be trusted.

History is full of examples of wars based on deeply held conflicting realities by the combatants. The victor succeeds because he can inflict more pain on the enemy and thus "prove" that his values are more "real" than the opposing ones. He is, in other words, enforcing the agreement he wants.

Mores, moral values, customs, rules, policies, and laws are all examples of group realities. They are values held by members of a certain group. If a member breaks them, the first action of the group is to discipline the member. This can be done by inflicting physical pain or symbolic pain. A thief that is being whipped would, of course, be an example of receiving physical punishment. A child that is being scolded for bad behavior and told next time he will get a spanking is threatened with pain. A group member that continuously breaks the laws and customs of a certain group will eventually become so "unreal" to the rest of its members that the perpetrator will become a non-member. The group will shun the member that now loses all privileges and contacts. In society, law breakers are eventually put in jail; in business, employees are simply fired.

Physical Universe and Agreement

When you are tired and see a chair you will probably welcome the sight and sit down. You won't give it a second thought. A theoretical physicist can, however, tell you that things aren't exactly what they look like. The solid surface of the chair is formed by molecules and atoms. Each atom is viewed as a microscopic "solar system". We have a nucleus ('the sun' in the atom) and the electrons ('planets') that are orbiting around it. There is mainly open space in this system comparable to the vast emptiness of our own solar system. When the electrons are being closely researched in a laboratory, it is still discussed if they are solid or simply energy; if they have a known single position or just a probable position. The Danish physicist, Niels Bohr (Nobel Prize 1922), and other leading theoretical physicists of the 20th century, furthermore discovered that the observer could change the outcome of an experiment simply by his presence and by the act of observing. The German physicist, Max Planck (Nobel Prize1918), raised the question in his Nobel Prize thank-you speech if there in fact was "anything there" when you looked at matter on an atomic level. The *implication* was that maybe the observer had an active role in putting it there. The *observation* was that matter, energy, space and time are not what we are so sure they are. Cutting edge physics of the last 40 years or so has even more intriguing theories. In the so-called String Theory 10-26 dimensions are used. The number of dimensions varies in different versions of the theory. There are the 3 known dimensions of space plus time. The extra dimensions (usually 7) are used mathematically to describe the composition and behavior of the electrons, protons and neutrons, the tiny sub-particles that make up the atom. The actuality of the physical universe seems to be shaky and fluctuating when studied by the brightest of minds in science. The reality of the same universe is however so agreed upon by the rest of us so we don't give it a second thought when we sit down on a chair but utterly rely upon its predictability and natural laws.

The English biologist and philosopher, Rupert Sheldrake, explains in his book "The Presence of the Past" that the physical laws, including gravity, the laws of chemistry, etc. can be explained as "habits of nature". He claims they are subject to change over the millennia. He offers evidence, especially from the field of chemistry and the forming of crystals. When a new compound is invented in a laboratory it may not crystallize for moths, although it should according to theoretical calculations. Then suddenly it may happen when a new badge of the new compound is produced. After that the compound now crystallizes every time. The compound has "learned" how to crystallize and adopts this new "habit."

The physical universe and all its natural phenomena can well be understood and explained as a set of agreements that are so broadly held that we totally take them for granted. If we disagree in any radical manner we will very soon be injured or killed as a result of transgressing its laws. Try to fly off a cliff by waving your arms, walk on water, eat fire, drive through a brick wall, etc., and you will end up in the hospital or graveyard very quickly. You have, it could be speculated, been excommunicated from the physical universe due to lack of agreement and duplication.

Through history philosophers like Plato, Spinoza, Leibniz, Emmanuel Kant, and many others have discussed if the physical universe simply was an illusion. Maybe it is. In a practical sense it's very real and very agreed upon. The laws of the country we live in could be argued to be an illusion. They have, after all, no physical presence except as written text which is only symbols and meanings. If you decide the laws do not apply to you you will however soon discover their reality. You will end up in court and possibly in jail.

Nothing can be viewed or understood unless we take a point of view to consider it from. Modern science, although it is the best thing the human race has going for it, clearly has its limited point of view. Nothing "outside the box" is considered to exist. Routinely, things and phenomena that don't fit into scientific thinking are bluntly disregarded. This is true in medicine where medical doctors usually reject any treatments, cures or therapies not originated, researched and endorsed by other medical doctors. It is true in many other fields as well.

The Zero Point

The above said, a point of view is a necessity when trying to understand and control things. Here is a simple illustration of how it helps take a confusion of particles apart: Tear up a piece of paper until you have dozens of small pieces. Throw this confetti up in the air and watch it fall like snow. Rather confusing as far as motion is concerned. Now, take one piece of the confetti and color it red. Throw all the bits and pieces up in the air once more, only this time follow the red piece of paper. Suddenly the confetti snow seems less confusing and easier to view. When you choose one particle in a confusion as the zero point and view the rest from there, you can suddenly face the whole mess and start to get some order and control. The confusion seems to fall apart. When it comes to data and problems, the same principle can be applied. Pick one likely datum as true and evaluate the rest from that point of view. You can even pick a wrong datum and it will still help you some of the way. You can find a greater truth from there and adopt that as your new zero point. In this fashion almost any confusion will fall apart.

A point of view is assumed in any subject or science. "We will only consider what can be physically sensed, measured and experienced" is expressing the most basic view of natural sciences. This view has cut through an endless morass of superstition and confusion. Yet, many phenomena of nature and living organisms are not registered or are bluntly overlooked by science. Maybe the state of our senses and scientific instruments don't catch it all. Also, down the road a little sentence was added to the scientific viewpoint: "Nothing else exists!" This is a lot less than science should teach or limit itself to. With this little sentence added, it has become a religion of sorts, sometimes called Scientism. It's a solid agreement among peers rather than a quest for knowledge. There is comfort in this, however, as the world seems orderly and predictable. No unaccounted motion or confusion at the fringes is taken seriously. It is simply ignored and sometimes even attacked.

Observer and observed

That leaves plenty of room for the inquiring minds of philosophy and religion. The very nature of man has been overlooked or ignored! In Clearing we have chosen the Being, the person's consciousness, as our fundamental zero point. We didn't start out with this. It simply showed up as the greater truth after years of research. It has worked very well as the zero point to use when sorting out existence with its problems and riddles. The reason it seems so hidden, is because it's from where we view things. Natural science looks *from* it—not at it. The obvious question natural science hasn't answered is: "**Who** does the perceiving, measuring and experiencing?" Since our goal is to "observe the observer" this omission becomes glaringly clear.

The reality of the Being has borne out in clearing work as the zero point for therapy, self-improvement and advanced abilities to the highest levels. There is no scientific reason to deny the true nature of man and his consciousness. We love science, the method; but not Scientism, the religion.

Clearing Work and Reality

We talked about, that there exists many realities around us. Basically each person or group has his, her or its own reality. Part of what clearing work is about is to enable the client to open up to new realities and gain the ability to view other realities. When you gain the ability to view other people's points of view, social interaction and communication become very positive and rewarding. Life becomes, once again, interesting and a continued discovery

As described earlier in this chapter, experiencing physical realities is closely related to perception and duplication. We explained in chapter 3 that the elements of communication are Cause-Distance-Effect leading to duplication and understanding at the receiving end of what sent from the originator. Reality could be defined as this element of duplication in communication. Reality is typically duplication in the observer of what exists 'out there'. This duplication is the dominating activity in natural science and naturalistic art.

'Duplication' can, however, also be the act of producing an exact copy of another person's opinions and ideas. Having such a duplicate in our own mind makes a degree of agreement with a new point of view possible. It doesn't necessarily mean agreement to a point where we now only can see it from that viewpoint. It simply means to get all the facts pertinent to the situation. It enables us to *also* see it from that point of view. We are building a higher reality, step by step, by adding points of view in addition to our own original viewpoint. This is how we increase our reality. We can suddenly see a situation or scene from all kinds of added "camera angles". It becomes multiple realit*es* and understanding*s*.

In some clearing work duplication of the physical reality of the environment is the first thing taken up. At a later stage the practitioner works more directly with points of view and the client's ability to perceive and understand other viewpoints. In DEEP Incident Clearing, for instance, viewing a traumatic incident through several points of view is a very important part. You would view the incident through the victims' as well as the transgressors' eyes. Even through bystanders' eyes sometimes.

But when we talk about duplication as an entry point, we talk about perception and contact with the physical universe. It can be very therapeutic simply to touch and perceive things as they exist around us.

There is a whole class of techniques, called basic objective techniques, devoted to improved awareness and perception of the objective world. They are easy to learn and are used both by professionals and amateur practitioners as they can be learned in evening courses. They have proven very effective with children. Our school systems have had their battles with kids suffering from 'hyper-activity' and 'attention deficit disorder'. Both these conditions respond very well to basic objective techniques. Children who have gone through such a program, either with a professional or a parent, tend to calm down and relax and get their attention and activity under their own control. They can concentrate better on the task at hand and simply have enough composure to sit still when the situation requires it. The can now direct their attention onto an assignment in class. The same techniques have, oddly enough, proven so powerful that some people, children as well as adults, suddenly become aware of their true spiritual nature. The techniques have routinely given clients "out of body" experiences. They could clearly perceive the physical universe directly without the use of the body's perception channels.

Footnote on "The Big Bang" – a Sour Comment

To the author and others it seems that modern physics and cosmology are on a wrong track. This is most evident in astrophysics where astronomers operate with black holes and dark energy, which supposedly make up about 95% of the known universe. Yet, these phenomena have never been sampled or directly observed – but it makes the math formulas work "beautifully"! The astronomers operate with "The Big Bang", the creation of the whole universe from nothing in an instant. Modern cosmology seems entirely to depend on mathematics and computer simulations – rather than observations and experiments. About modern cosmology and "The Big Bang" Rupert Sheldrake says, "Give us (the astrophysicists) one miracle and we will explain the rest." To him it seems a materialistic rewrite of the Bible's Book of Genesis and similar religious creation accounts – and I agree.

To the author modern cosmology and physics illustrate how peer-review and solid agreements can "Make up reality" and in the process hold back promising new research – in a similar fashion that the Catholic Church banned Galilei and Giordano Bruno. The new apostles seem to be Albert Einstein and Stephen Hawking.

They were brilliant mathematicians but not experimentalists. Much of modern science seems a desperate attempt to get rid of God and spirituality. Physics as it exists today is an excellent illustration of what is meant by Scientism. It is based on a solid agreement on materialism – and "follow the money" in the form of research grants and university positions, which both require peer approval. It also seems to be based on strong egos – scientists who want to demonstrate their own "genius" and outsmart the others with sophisticated theories and complex mathematical formulas. They are more concerned about being "interesting" to colleagues than in showing interest in the real world through experiments and observations.

To me a physics that is right also feels right. Somehow and down deep we have an intuitive understanding and agreement on how the physical universe and physics work. This then needs to be confirmed through further observations and experiments, of course. But when you replace intuition, experiments, and observations with mathematical formulas you replace the outside world with intellectual constructs. And in my opinion that is what we see today.

There exists an alternative cosmology and physics based on observations and experiments. It is known as **The Electric Universe** or The Plasma Universe. It is scorned by mainstream academia. Maybe it is just "too easy and obvious". It sees electricity and electro-magnetism as the major forces that hold the greater universe together. The weak force of gravity plays of course a role, if only minor, such as in our "local" solar system (sorry, Isaac Newton). Gravity in this theory is explained as a byproduct of electric and electro-magnetic forces. When electric forces are considered, black holes, dark energy and Big Bang become unnecessary mathematical constructs. The fantastic images captured by the Hubble space telescope can be explained as electrical phenomena and these phenomena can be recreated in the laboratory in small scale, using plasma physics and electromagnetic physics experiments.

Stephen Hawking, physicist and mathematician, symbolizes to me modern physics. He had a brilliant mind but due to his disabilities, cut off from interacting with the Universe.
It was "all in the head".

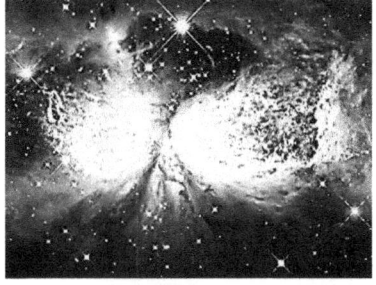

NASA photo: S106, star-forming region.
Similar spectacular phenomena can in small scale be reproduced in a laboratory, performing high voltage electrical experiments in a vacuum chamber.

The Norwegian scientist, Kristian Birkeland, around 1906. He examined the Northern Lights and reproduced the phenomena electrically in a vacuum chamber.
He was what we call "a mad scientist."

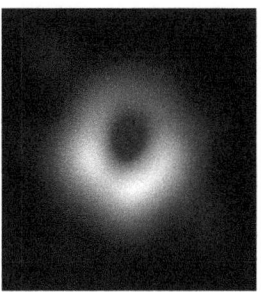

This image (April 2019) was obtained by radio telescopes and is presented as the first photo made of a black hole. Does such a faint image account for 95% of the energy and matter of the known universe? I doubt it. To me it seems very weak evidence compared to the abundant electrical phenomena observed in the sky.

Chapter 6: The Triad of Relationships and Understanding

In the previous chapters we have covered communication (chapter 3), the affinity scale (chapter 4), and reality (chapter 5). These three important attributes of life and living interact closely with each other. We say they form a triad. They form what we call the Triad of Relationships and Understanding. What this triad represents is at the core of human relationships. This triad uncovers the anatomy of understanding itself.

We have explained in detail each of the three elements. In this chapter, then, we are putting them together to show how closely they interact and how they are different sides of the same thing. Let us quickly review what affinity, reality and communication are:

Affinity: is most commonly seen as emotional response. It is affection or the lack thereof. It covers the whole emotional scale. It is defined as: willingness to occupy the same space as the object of one's affection. And as: consideration of distance.

Reality: there is a definite relationship between reality and agreement. Things are real to the degree we agree they are real. On those things upon which we disagree, we have very little reality. In personal relationships 'agreement' and reaching an agreement is prevalent. In experiencing objective reality 'agreement' is reached through perception and duplication. Any person of sound mind agrees on the reality of physical things because the person can perceive them and the person perceives the same as the person next to him or her.

Communication: is the interchange of messages and ideas between two persons. The basic elements of communication are: Sender - Distance - Receiver. The originator (Sender) sends a message over a distance to a listener (Receiver) with the purpose of having Receiver duplicate and understand the message. Human communication is usually two-ways. The parties take turns, exchanging messages and ideas back and forth.

Communication is Key

Communication is, by far, the most important aspect of the triad. This is because we can directly control our own communication. We can control what communications we send and, usually, we have pretty good control over what communications we receive. Also, the two other aspects (Affinity and Reality) can be understood as being qualities of the communication – although they can also be understood by themselves. But if we look at 'reality' in terms of communication, we showed how it could be explained and defined in terms of duplication and duplication is part of the communication formula. Any communication can be said to have the purpose to relay a reality.

We had a definition of 'affinity' saying "Affinity is a consideration of distance". Again, distance is part of the communication formula. Any communication also clearly expresses an emotion and is the usual way to relay emotions. In other words, live communication will contain all the three elements of: communication, reality, and affinity.

Human Relationships

A good study and a practical understanding of this triad go a long way in building and repairing relationships. Why? Because human relations, however complicated they may at times seem, can all be explained and understood as manifestations of this triad. People we have a good relationship with we want to be close to (affinity). We have much in common with them and find it easy to exchange viewpoints (reality). We can talk to them for hours without getting tired of it (communication). A good relationship, in other words, consists of a strong triad.

A bad relationship, on the other hand, is quite different. We can't really stand to be in the same room (poor affinity). We seem to disagree on just about anything of importance (poor reality). The communication breaks down all the time (poor communication). A bad relationship, in our terminology, consists of a weak triad.

A person whom you had never met would be neutral in terms of the triad of relationships. You wouldn't have a level of relationship and understanding, high or low. There would simply be a void that, at some point, could be filled with a good or bad relationship, with high or low understanding.

Building Relationships: How to build relationships has long been an art known to "people persons", including professional salesmen, diplomats and public relations personnel. Knowing and using the triad now removes it from being merely an intuitive art. Using the triad adds the missing knowledge to make it a method that can be taught and further expanded into a broad subject. Here are some examples of the basic principles.

Example: Let's say you want to make initial contact with a stranger. You start talking (communication). You compliment him (that expresses affinity). You pick a subject you can agree upon (reality). Some mutual respect and affinity will develop rather easily.

Talking about the weather is the classical neutral subject people easily can agree on. To build a good relationship, it is however a good idea to find something soon after you can compliment the person for. It can be anything from appearance, remarks, and possessions, to accomplishments. If you know the person a little bit, this step will have some obvious subjects.

The above small talk just ensures a positive first impression. But a positive contact is established and you can go on to discuss the things you wanted to discuss in the first place.

Your ability to build a positive relationship to any specific person would have a lot to do with your emotional response to that person. It is clear it would be very difficult to talk to the person if you didn't care about a person (low affinity). The way to talk to somebody, then, is to find something you like about him or her and to discuss something you can agree on. Things you agree on are more real. Reality and agreement, in terms of this triad, are closely connected as we have discussed.

In a group of, say, five persons, the one who didn't agree with the other four, would soon become unreal to the four and the disagreeing person's affinity would be seen to drop. This is an example of the relationship and understanding going the other way. If the agreement element drops (reality down), the two other elements will also drop (affinity and communication).

By disagreeing with the group, a member will usually see his status lowered. The other members will suddenly have difficulties understanding "what he is talking about". They will be less inclined to be seen with him as he is "strange" as that in turn would lower their status. This sequence describes a falling out of mutual understanding.

You will often find that the "born salesman" instinctively knows how to use the triad. A good salesman who *also* knows the workings of the triad will make an excellent sales trainer. He knows how and why to build a relationship to the customer and how to make the product real (reality) and wanted (affinity) by the potential buyer. He can rationally explain this to other sales persons. He can explain why skilled salesmen will talk about themselves. They do this just enough to appear more real, likable and trustworthy to the buyer. He will know why and how to get the customer excited and interested, even before trying to make a sale. He can do that, for instance, by sharing good news not related to the sales situation. This is to get the customer up the affinity scale and more receptive. He will know to explain how to make the product more real and attractive to the customer. He does this through information and hands-on experience and demonstrations. The "born salesman" does not necessarily know why his approach works and is therefore not a good teacher as he can't explain the theory. The person who is unable to sell anything can learn how to do that by studying the triad.

A public relations person will know how to formulate her message so it is real to the audience. Also, the affinity level she uses should match the affinity level of the audience. She would use the "Raising Somebody's Affinity" drill explained in the chapter on the affinity scale. She also knows she has to establish a mutual understanding even before she delivers the real message. She will have a feeling of how strong the communication line is and work on making it stronger. At some point she will assess if it is strong enough to carry the real message she wants to deliver. She will do any needed adjustments of how to deliver the message according to the situation. She knows very well she is not speaking in a vacuum but has to use live communication. If the mutual understanding should break down at any point she can quickly assess what has gone wrong and repair the affinity, reality or communication according to what she finds.

Repairing Relationships: The ability to quickly repair relationships is another obvious benefit from knowing the theory. As a rule it begins with repairing the communication. In a one-on-one situation, upsets usually happen due to out communication cycle. If you experience someone becoming upset with you, chances are you didn't pay attention to what she said, ignored it, didn't acknowledge, or misunderstood it or bluntly told her she was wrong. Maybe you were trying to push your own agenda one-sidedly. To clear up the situation you can simply ask: "What didn't I get?" "Was there something you said I didn't acknowledge?" "Was there something I misunderstood?" and the like. You then listen carefully and acknowledge without being argumentative, giving excuses, nor invalidating her points of view, etc. You simply listen, understand and acknowledge with nothing added. This can clear up even serious upsets in short order. There are more sophisticated methods that can be used in session. They are briefly outlined later in the chapter.

Learning

Besides being the principle behind building good relationships, the triad is at work when we want to learn things and acquire new skills. The student has to read books, listen to lectures, and observe the elements in action of a new subject he wants to learn. These are all ways of communication. The student has to be willing to be around the subject and be interested enough to spend considerable time in that environment. This is affinity-related. Finally, the student has to come to some state of agreement and duplication of the data taught. This is reality.

Faster rates of learning, practical ability to apply the subject, and ability to help students that are in trouble, are all made possible with a full understanding of how to use the triad of understanding in study.

To increase reality and ability to apply, the student should get in physical contact with the elements and do practical exercises in the new subject he is trying to learn. This is hands-on education, sometimes called practical. The hands-on is the best way to build up the necessary reality to become competent.

Any time the triad breaks down in education, one should back-step and see how it broke down. There are three principal reasons:

    1. The student didn't understand the words used, resulting in a breakdown of communication between teacher/textbook and student. This is remedied by the correct and frequent use of an English dictionary and specialized dictionaries. One should seek out and clear *all* misunderstood words in a subject that is hard to understand. Sometimes a brush-up course in basic grammar is what's needed.

    2. The subject appeared all theoretical with no practical use or understanding. This falls under low reality. This is repaired by hands-on exercises and by having the student demonstrate things physically.

    3. The student was rushed forward beyond his practical skill level. This has to do with too fast a pace. In application, skills related to a more basic area weren't mastered before going on to the next and more complex area. This causes the student to become confused and disoriented. We compare it here with affinity, although that is not the usual description. The fact is, however, once affinity is established one can have and tolerate the activity in one's personal space. Also, having affinity for a skill area is necessary in order to control it. To remedy this, one has to go back and work through earlier skill levels, step by step, and then carefully go forward.

Let us explain in another way how affinity fits into study: A student that progresses through a study should gain more and more certainty about what he learns and therefore become more relaxed and cheerful about it. We here assume the subject studied is free of falsehoods, is useful, and worthwhile. As the student advances through a longer study, the student should be able to learn related data faster and faster and often grasp new concepts even without having to read or hear it all. This indicates a heightened affinity and an increased ability to occupy the teacher's or textbook writer's point of view. No drawn-out or tedious communication is needed. No need to look at it this way and that way until finally the whole thing can be partially understood. No! At one glance at the data the student has got it. Let's illustrate the subject with some examples:

Example 1: A young man is trying to learn to become a mechanic. When he is first thrown into it the teacher uses a lot of new words. The communication is completely cut. The elements of communication are: Cause, distance, effect, with intention, attention, duplication and understanding. The student has no duplication nor understanding as he doesn't know what the teacher is talking about. He hasn't been around motors and cars and cannot agree or disagree with anything shown. He is completely incapable of "thinking like a motor", meaning mentally occupying the same space as the motor, and thus having a feel for what is being taught. His triad of understanding in the area is at the bottom. If the teacher knows his business, he will let the student look at different motor parts and name them for him. Then have him touch them and lift them. This gives the student some reality. The teacher will tell him the function of each part. That makes duplication and understanding possible. Actual communication is being established. By holding onto, lifting, and fitting together these parts, the student will little by little lose his back-off and fear of these motor parts and feel relaxed and quite cheerful about the whole thing. His affinity will come up.

Example 2: A master mechanic, who has repaired motors for years, can just by listening to a motor tell exactly what is wrong or exactly what three things to look for. Through reading about it (communication) and repairing a lot of cars he has gotten experience (reality) and is completely capable of "being the motor" (affinity). He can feel any bad performance of the motor as a physical sensation as if it were happening to his own body. When he hears the motor going 'clank, clank' it is painful to him. When it purrs like a cat it is a great pleasure to him. Obviously, he has high affinity for motors and a strong triad of understanding for motors.

The above gives the reader an idea of how the triad fits into education. The subject far exceeds what we can fully explain here.

Culture, Civilization and the Triad

Any culture or sub-culture can be described in terms of their special triad of relationships and understanding. This could be called customs and values. It is, however, the whole social fabric of a group we are talking about. This can be separated into its components of affinity, reality and communication. The spoken and written words are the communication components. This includes special terminology of a profession, lingo, slang, etc. of a group. It includes its media and other ways of community communication.

A sub-culture, like bikers, has: its own technology (bikes) and its group codes (reality); its special expressions, lingo, and magazines (communication); its own art, fashion and entertainment the members find 'cool' (affinity).

Reality of a culture has two separate parts: these are: 1. Technology and science; and 2. Social mores. Technology and science, obviously, impact our ways of thinking and living. They are the more progressive factors. The social mores is the conservative element but closer to how a culture defines itself. Social values of a country or culture are solidified through the moral values and laws of the land. Any progress in science and technology could change the reality of the culture to a marked extent. Yet, changing the culture and ways of thinking is a slow process as discussed in chapter 5, "Reality".

The affinity part of the culture is the likes and dislikes. There may not be any rational reason for not liking people with brown hair or to see blond people as beautiful—yet, it may be engrained in a certain culture. The same goes for fashion. The art world and entertainment industry of a culture will in many ways be the best expression of the affinity aspect of that culture or civilization. Art, fashion and entertainment are not seen as hard realities. The reason they attract us is, for a large part, due to the emotional content.

Understanding a culture as the collective triad of relationships and understanding of its people or members, gives us a new theoretical basis from where to describe it and explain changes and developments; determine relative the importance of phenomena – and it even gives us an inroad to change undesirable traits and values. Any group, company or sub-group will be characterized by a certain set of values that defines their special triad: their culture, or esprit de corps, etc. They have accomplishments and capabilities they take pride in – and acts they as a group find horrible. Corporations, professions, interest groups, government organizations, etc. will all have their own special brand of understanding; their own special language or terminology (communication); their own science and technology (reality); their own special values and moral codes (also reality); their own favorite aesthetics and entertainment (mainly affinity but also communication).

The ability of Beings to emit and share affinity, reality and communication is thus a very strong factor in all dealings of life. These elements are on our minds in all we are, do and strive after. They are always present, although it can take as many forms as human behavior can. It can be a progressive and uplifting factor as well as a confinement, even a jail, where we are held, due to affiliations. The way the group defines and understands itself can be a heavy burden as it can hold a group and its members on a destructive course in order to at least keep the group together. The desire for community and mutual understanding can be so strong it will overpower rational behavior and progress.

The above has a strong effect on any single individual. As a member of a group—as a person with a certain professional background, with certain interests and community background—the person will have his or her own personal brand of triad. What's new in this is not that all these different phenomena exist—they have been described since the beginning of history and existed since the beginning of time—the new thing is how they inter-relate. It gives us an opening in controlling the development of these phenomena, at least to a degree. Since they are "a force of nature", the degree of control is comparable to controlling a river or a natural event. We have some level of control if we keep at it without giving up too easily. One basic rule in making a positive difference is to take small steps, one step at the time. The person or group we seek to change can conceive of things being a little different and better if we promise not to upset their world. To bring about a major change, then, consists of taking many small steps in the same direction and allow each step to be experienced before taking the next. This step-by-step approach is important in all applications of the principles, be it in relationships, in education, or in clearing. In clearing work we call it going forward at the right pace.

The Triads in Clearing Work

When we talk triads and clearing the task is easier and more straight-forward. Our objective is usually not to change the person's "brand of relationships". It is to repair and increase the type of  relationships and understanding as they exist. This is also a broad way of expressing what we generally are doing in clearing and why the client came to us in the first place. The client wants to improve existing relationships, have more energy in doing what he/she loves to do, be able to better understand the viewpoints that surround him/her. The person typically wants more of what he/she already has going for him/her. But also to overcome some serious downfalls that work against the client. The downfalls are 'inabilities' that disturb or even ruin the client's life. It is unwanted reactions in certain situations and entire areas of the person's life that seem hard to deal with for the client. Inabilities to cope with certain situations and people can be worked on and repaired and cleared. The client's general level of affinity, reality and communication can be improved. That is what the practitioner and client have as their common objective for clearing work.

To the knowledgeable clearer this is a straight forward task. The clearer sees the Being in the chair, the client, as potentially pure understanding, as pure capability. At this highest level the Being is in perfect communication with people and things around him/her, having a great ability to simply be there and occupy the same space as. At some stage the Being can simply be the space and anything in it by pervading the area. The Being, potentially, has as well the ability to see all points of view while still maintaining his or her own point of view. The Being has the capability of total understanding.

In clearing work we seek to advance the client towards this high state of understanding, one part of the client's life at a time. In all clearing work the step-by-step approach is inherent. We always consider going forward in the right pace.

Handling Upsets

An upset can be seen as a sudden fall in affinity, reality or communication. When a person suddenly becomes upset, angry, offended, disgusted, very reserved, tearful, etc., etc. we see this sudden drop.

A woman, let's say, was talking to a girlfriend. The girlfriend suddenly came with what was perceived as a hurtful remark: "what do you call that color of the sweater you are wearing?" Our woman is somehow offended by the remark, turns around and leaves. The woman goes to the ladies room to compose herself. She doesn't like that girlfriend much after that. The triad between them has been damaged. It isn't really the point if the girlfriend intended it as a hurtful remark or not. Maybe she did and maybe she didn't. The point is how it was received by the woman. She was deeply offended. The remark triggered something in her mind. The triggering, rather than the girlfriend's action, was the break in their relationship.

The practitioner, running into this upset, can take it apart and restore the natural understanding that existed before the incident. First, the practitioner will establish if it was a break in affinity, reality, communication or understanding. Usually one of these stands out as the dominant aspect of the upset. By establishing the dominant one, the client gets a handle on the situation and some small relief. By further investigation the practitioner can establish, very quickly, exactly what was triggered. Usually it will lead to an earlier similar upset that to a stranger can look completely unrelated. This is, however, not for the practitioner to really be concerned about. The practitioner uses technical indicators to determine if he/she is on the right track and in hot pursuit of the original upset on this string of events. In minutes the practitioner can find the earliest upset and exactly how things went wrong. Use of this technique will result in that the whole upset clears up. By finding many such upsets, small and large, the client's whole outlook on life will change and she will be in possession of more of her natural potential for good relationships and understanding.

Chapter 7: Be – Do – Have
Modes of Existence

There are three modes of existence of considerable interest to us; those are Being, Doing, and Having. Together they form a cycle of action of any job or task. It is necessary to assume a certain role or way of being in order to perform a task. It is necessary to do the task right in order to get the result or product desired. The outcome or product of one's efforts is the having. These three modes form, in other words, a closely knit trio and together they make up the operating modes of existence as we see it in action in one individual or in larger entities, such as groups and whole cultures.

Be-Do-Have of a Baker

| Be: assuming an identity. **Being a baker** | Do: action, production. **Baking a cake** | Have: ownership, product. **Having a cake** |

By 'Being' we basically mean the assumption of an identity or role one plays in a certain game of life.

'Identity' can include physical appearance, one's character and personal values. 'Role' includes the position one holds. It can be one's professional job or the function one holds in a group or family unit.

By 'Doing' we mean action, performance, production. Other descriptions of Doing include: striving to reach a goal through action. 'Doing' is using energy and effort in order to bring about a certain end result.

By 'Having' we mean: owning, possessing, controlling, having a product. Having goes further than legal ownership. Any object one is able to control and freely use, one can take ownership of and is Having in our sense of the word. The ultimate ownership, in our sense of Having, is obtained when the Being is capable of pervading something. If a person is totally capable of permeating an automobile and all its mechanical parts that person will be in total control and mastery of that car. You see such ability in race car drivers and mechanics at the top of their professions. 'Having' includes legal ownership, of course, but is not limited to that. More important to living, and to clearing work, is the ability to permeate, master and control an object.

The bottom line of fully Having an object can be described this way: the object is perceived as being "out there", separate from self but easy to reach. You are comfortable with it. You know how to control it. You control *it*. It does not control you.

As mentioned, these three modes of existence form a closely knit trio, a cycle of action. We start with Being: taking on a role or title with its attributes. Having assumed a role or identity, we can now go into action and attack the physical environment by doing. By means of activity, we get more familiar with the environment and what it offers. We can also choose to create something new: a physical product. Thus, the game of life demands that we assume a way of being, an identity or role; the role enables us to Do, perform an activity or function; we perform it in the direction of Having, producing a product or end result. By doing one function over and over we gain experience and improve our Being, Doing and Having in that area. That is the cycle of existence. Here are some examples of Be-Do-Have:

Be	Do	Have
Provider/father	Work/earn money	A well provided for family
Housewife/mother	Care of kids, husband, house	A well-managed household
Programmer	Writes programs	Good software. Paycheck
Writer	Writes books	Published books. Readers
Cabinet maker	Makes kitchens	Installed kitchens. Paycheck
Police man, traffic	Enforces the traffic law	Motorists corrected. Paycheck
Tourist	Travels, sees new things	New experiences. Photos
Student	Studies, practices	Knowledge, skills, certificates

This be-do-have is also in the sequence of their importance to living. Ability to BE is more important than the ability to do. Ability to DO is more important than the ability to have. These three conditions, however, get easily confused and their real importance is turned upside down. In our culture it seems so much more important to have than to be. We are systematically being indoctrinated through advertising and peer pressure that all we need in order to feel well and happy is one extra thing: get a bigger house, a newer and faster car, a new gadget or pill, etc. If we have a newer and better car than the neighbor we feel superior. In society it is typically considered more important to have than to do.

These statements can be illustrated by looking at multi-generation companies. The founder of such a company usually had it right. He started with nothing but a big dream and a great understanding of who he had to be in order to succeed. This is the BE. He also had boundless energy and was working on his dream day and night. This is the DO. He ended up with a very successful company and a great fortune. This is the HAVE. Then second generation comes along—this is when it becomes interesting in our context. You will have heirs that are totally consumed by being rich and idle. They define their being, their identity, as being Mr. and Mrs. Rich, Junior. Their whole existences are lived in the HAVE of the founder. Usually, their lives are not any better due to all that money. They do not contribute with any renewal of the vision, the BE, of the founder. They see no good reason to DO anything except living the HAVE of the founder.

In successful second generation companies you will typically see the founder instill healthy values in his heir and successor. He makes sure Junior has great respect and interest in the company and gets the proper education to become a responsible leader. Most important is the practical education obtained by working directly under the founder. The heir adopts the necessary personal and moral values. This is in the realm of BE. The founder teaches Junior to work hard and tirelessly and how to work it all in order to be successful. He sees to that the heir actually does it and the father uses harsh discipline to make it happen; this is DO. Finally he will teach Junior "the value of the dollar", that it takes hard work and continued stewardship to maintain and improve the company and its net value. This is HAVE. The very successful heir will see the whole company and all its parts as a transparent organism. Junior permeates the company. Although this was an important definition of Having it here becomes a new level of Being as well. The heir can BE the company and all its parts. To that degree Junior has conquered a part of the physical universe and is in a position to conquer more. Indeed, this is the game of conquest in life—so important and basic so you see it in all successful endeavors of living in one shape or another.

When we look at BEING, we will find some people have a great ability to allow others their way of being. They nurture, teach and support others rather than try to take center stage. This ability to grant others the right to be the best they can be is one of the noblest traits and highest abilities of the human character. You see it in mothers, teachers and, we may add, in Clearing practitioners. Mothers, teachers, and practitioners, you could say, are in the business of growing Beingness. This is best done by giving their children, students, or clients a great sense of freedom within certain borders.

When you are around people capable of truly allowing others to grow, you will see their associates be happy, active and flourishing. This can be found in all walks of life. Often these people don't get the credit they deserve. Yet, they are so important to the health of families, institutions and companies that their absence would cause a collapse.

In the opposite end of the spectrum, we have people that completely refuse to let others be and express themselves. It can apply to selected persons or allowing any and all of humankind to be. In other words, they seem obsessed with the idea of erasing the other person from the surface of the earth. This can be done by overt or covert means. They will protest, object to, make nothing of, and criticize, etc. anything the person is, does or has. Such a destructive or antagonistic personality, if it is part of the person's character rather than a temporary reaction, is obsessed with the idea that anyone that is strong around him or her, is a direct threat to the destructive person's well-being and survival. Such people can indeed be very hard to be around and they account for a lot of human failure and misery. Usually we can shrug them off or avoid them. But if our daily life or livelihood depends on them the situation is different. They will, so to speak, get under our skin and poison our lives. Dealing effectively with such situations and individuals is important. Dealing correctly with such toxic and antagonistic characters has repeatedly been seen as the difference between success and failure; between happiness and misery; between health and illness in the affected individuals.

Be-Do-Have in Organizing

The principle of Be-do-have, in all its simplicity, can be used in making any group or organization more vibrant, effective and prosperous. The first thing to realize is that for anything to thrive, it has to have certain products that can be exchanged for other needed products. In a commercial organization this is self-evident. The employee has to produce what he/she is being paid to produce or the employee gets fired. The company has to have services or products it exchanges with its customers or it will soon go out of business.

The same is however true for any group, be it a government organization, an interest group, or a family. The exchange factor may be less obvious, the "products" less tangible or sellable in the open market place – yet, they are there. The traditional mom has to cook dinner, give birth to children, and take care of the household in general for the marriage to work. The traditional husband, on the other hand, has to provide for his family, provide a house to live in, fix up things, etc. to keep his end of the bargain. They have to be capable of offering each other company, affection, and sexual pleasure to consider the marriage in the first place. Any children have to grow and develop in order to eventually be able to take care of themselves and, directly or indirectly, take care of their parents in their old age. As toddlers they at least deliver joy, hope and activity and a lot of children's drawings that keep the family united and happy. Also, children are an important "product" in their own right of any marriage.

Production, of one kind or the other, is the basis for the morale of a group, the basis for its well-being and viability. When this production helps and promotes the main purpose of the group we have a vibrant, effective, and prosperous group.

The basic Be-do-have in a company is the production cycle. The Be defines the role, the job description. The Do defines performing one's duties with an end-product in mind. The Have is the actual completion of such a product. By first realizing what product one is supposed to deliver, one can go backwards and determine what one has to do in order to make that possible. Then one can make a job-description to determine what one's exact role or function is in the company. When each member goes through this re-organizing cycle the result will be higher morale and viability of the whole group.

The leader of the company can, of course, do this on the behalf of its members and clearly state what is expected. In doing this the leader will first take the puzzle apart and determine what products are being produced. This can be a wide variety of tangible and intangible products. Then the leader has to determine how these products dovetail into each other and add up to strengthening the basic purpose, production and prosperity of the company. The leader can then re-enforce the vital products and weed out those that don't add up to anything or to very little.

BEING in Clearing Work

In Shakespeare's play, Hamlet, the young Danish prince exclaims, "To be or not to be, that is the question!" and indeed, that is where everything begins in life. At birth we start with *being* a baby and take it from there. At every turn, early in life, our role and being is changed as we grow, learn, and get familiar with life and how to deal with people and things. We incorporate experiences; learn how to deal with all types of people and situations and it all gets reflected in our character and way of being.

Different identities are routinely adapted "because they work better". We dress to the occasion, so to speak, whether this is to appear and act tough, always meet adversity with a smile, always make a scene when things don't go our way, or prefer to "stay invisible". These traits can both be rational and irrational mechanisms of life. But at some point this whole evolution of assumed roles and identities can become so complex so we get lost or "lose our true Self". We experience an "identity crisis", have a "need to find ourselves" or we are simply awfully confused and clumsy in certain situations. This can be sorted out in Clearing.

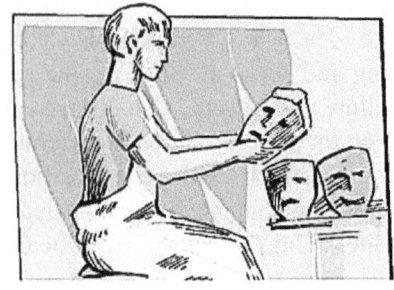

An important aspect of Identity is to be capable of attracting attention. An identity that attracts more positive attention than another is to be preferred. A valuable quality of Identity is its capability to attract respect and being reckoned with.

There is a phenomenon known as artificial identities. An artificial identity is a somewhat false way of being; something the person has become that is against the true self. The person has become "somebody else" to a degree. You see children 'being a parent' in manners and ways of thinking. This is not simply a genetic phenomenon. They copy the parents knowingly and unknowingly. It usually begins with a knowing copying. After all, the parents are their primary teachers and role models in life. The child builds up this way of behaving as a role it can choose. At some point it can, however, 'click' and the child has become that artificial identity, temporarily or permanently. It can be found that a girl is in her mother's identity in order to attract more attention from the father. She has seen her mother get all this attention and her solution to get some as well is to copy the mother. If it at some point 'clicks' it is not a matter of choice anymore. The girl has become her mother's identity. Artificial identities may 'click' as a result of stress. Once the stressful situation is over, the person will usually again be herself.

Another mechanism of artificial identities is choosing the winning identity in a conflict. You see defeated nations adopt the habits and manners of the victor. A person can be so overwhelmed by another person so the person becomes the other. This phenomenon, again, can start as a knowing copying but at some point it may click and become permanent and automatic. A person, as a matter of fact, can also have a large collection of these artificial identities and click from one to another depending of the situation and the danger one faces. When this happens, obviously, the person feels less than him- or herself. In criminology and pathology this helps us understand certain criminal and psychotic behaviors. The person is "someone else" for a period of time; then can become another "someone else" for another period of time. While the criminal commits the crime, he may act out an identity that at some point in the past overwhelmed him with violent intentions. It may even be the explanation behind bipolar disorder. The person clicks from one identity to another and thus has multiple personalities. The destructive personality, described earlier in this chapter, is seen to be so far removed from being his/her own good self that he/she can only experience other people as their enemies.

Clearing work requires a high level of client participation, and addressing artificial identities may not be possible in severe cases, such as in violent criminals, bipolar patients and truly destructive characters. There are other techniques that can be applied with success; but it requires a clinical setting. Since Clearing is practiced mainly by individual professionals, only a very few of them are equipped to handle this level of severity.

In DEEP Clearing we call these artificial identities **Characters.** The word Character originally means imprint as on the surface of a coin. We see these artificial identities as having been imprinted on the Being. They are different from the Being herself. Finding such imprinted Characters and getting the client to fully inspect and permeate them enables the client to recover any and all life energy caught up inside them. The client is capable of using the good parts of such an identity rationally. Nothing is lost, except the obsessive way of being associated with these subconscious and repressed Characters. We have found the DEEP techniques to be the most effective way to deal with artificial identities. Sometimes the client cannot run this with benefit right away.

Artificial identities can, however, be addressed in various other ways in Clearing. For completeness we outline them here. They all prepare the way for the running of DEEP. We can use techniques that address communication and help factors. Let us explain how a communication technique typically can help resolve the issue. The basic elements of communication, once again, are Sender-Distance-Receiver. Adopting an artificial identity can be seen as the Sender (the person the identity is modeled after) imposed itself so forcefully on Receiver (the one that adopted the identity) so that Sender and Receiver now exist with no distance between them. Receiver has obsessively become a carbon copy of Sender. By having the client establish a fictitious communication to Sender, he/she will be capable of again to impose a distance between Sender and Receiver. In other words, the client will be able to peel that identity off as if it were a carnival mask. The client can take it off and inspect it closely. This may not lead to a stable result with just one technique. But there exists dozens of actions that bit by bit will chip off this phenomenon of "being another" unknowingly. The benefits and gains from this are numerous. Usually, the identity the person adopted was, in the first place, a caricature of Sender. It is not the Sender-person on good and bad the Receiver-person took on but typically only the bad characteristics from an overwhelm situation.

This, by the way, is an example that the definition of Affinity as "consideration of distance" is a little more complex than closer is better (see chapter 4 on affinity). Grown children moving away from their parents will often experience that a troubled relationship transforms once this distance is established. They can now be "themselves" and establish a more self-determined and honest communication to their parents and improve the relationship. Once the artificial identity phenomenon is handled, the person will regain his/her own viewpoint and be capable of freely choosing own Be-do-have to overcome future challenges. Routinely, as explained, it leads to a better relationship with the Sender person.

Help actions and techniques are designed to straighten out a person's ability to more freely give and accept help. Since help is such an important factor in well-being and success as well as in relationships, this is an important point to address. The reason it often affects or blows artificial identities apart is due to the nature of help. When you help another person you routinely align your efforts completely according to the other person's intentions and needs. In other words, while working on the task you give up, in a sense, your own interests and 'become' the other person and add your power to his or hers. Thus there is an element of identification, of taking on the other person's identity if you will. In close relationships this can become so much of a routine so the giving person eventually goes into the identity of the person receiving the help. By clearing the help factor this subconscious mis-identification can, again, be straightened out and things will be seen in the right perspective.

Ability to DO and Clearing

The way 'Doing' is rehabilitated in clearing is best understood when we define Doing as 'striving to accomplish a purpose or goal through action'. 'Doing' is that middle section of the cycle, where energy is applied to getting the job done. If this forward motion and effort is interrupted for some reason the person will feel unfulfilled. The energy and the intention propelling it will still be at work to some extent. But now it bottles up as "charge", similar to static electricity. It has no clear objective to flow towards and has become a form of static disturbance. It is in the limbo of No-creation, the step 4 of the actual cycle of action (see chapter 1). The person's Attention Units are tied up in a distractive way.

A client may come in with a complaint that he cannot perform satisfactorily in a certain part of his life. His performance was fine at some point but now he is failing. The causes for this can be found and eradicated through clearing work unless they are purely physical. Even when they are found to have a physical or medical explanation, the performance can usually be improved considerably through clearing.

General techniques: There are many techniques that can rehabilitate ability to do. What they have in common is locating and cleaning up previous incomplete cycles of action. The practitioner, of course, will concentrate on the field of the complaint. By 'cleaning up' we mean to get the negative energy and charge removed from each instance of failure and in this way, piece by piece, from the whole area. Each instance of an incomplete or failed action will present a certain set of indicators or symptoms. The reason for the abandonment could be an upset, or two or more purposes or interests in conflict with each other. The halted action could be sitting on top of the client's earlier failures in the area. Depending of what the practitioner finds there is an appropriate technique.

We described above how *persons antagonistic to the client* can mean the difference between success and failure. Locating such persons in the client's past and present, cleaning off the charge this relationship has built up, and working out a practical plan on how to deal with such attacks in the future, can have a magical effect. In extreme cases it can appear as the practitioner pulls off a veil from the client's vision and perceptions and ability to act. The client will first timidly look around as if he waited for a new attack at any instance. When the client realizes he/she is "free at last" all parts of the client's life and activities are likely to improve. For this action to be effective it will have to be followed by a consultation where client and practitioner work out a plan of action to reduce the frequency of such incidents in the future and how to deal with them should they occur. Often it comes down to how to deal with one or two persons in the client's life.

Understanding the Words: There is another technique that boosts action level. This is more in the realm of education. Let's say the client studied engineering but chose never to practice. This may be a mystery to himself – as well as his parents and teachers. Obviously, the engineer never felt confident or competent in his field. Any of the above mentioned actions can play a role in rehabilitating this failed education. There is, however, a technique that directly takes aim at this particular case. The action consists of finding misunderstood words and symbols in the subject of engineering and clear these words and symbols to full understanding. This may lead back to earlier subjects in grammar school that were never fully understood due to misunderstood words. The practitioner's expertise consists in finding the right misunderstood words and quickly and precisely clears them up to full understanding using the appropriate dictionaries and material.

Simply describing the technique does not give it justice. Maybe that is why it is not broadly considered an answer to failed learning and education. But the fact is that misunderstood words can cause a student to give up a study or cease completely to be interested in a subject. Once a student understands the words, he can for the first time study the subject with full understanding. The understanding has to be to a level where he can transform it into action. Clearing up all the misunderstood words opens the door. It will release a river of dammed up understanding and enthusiasm for the engineering, provided he had such enthusiasm in the first place. He may have to re-study large sections of the subject to get fully up to speed. This is usually quickly done once the enthusiasm is back. It consists of putting blocks and pieces of knowledge and data together the right way. What the practitioner is capable of accomplishing is only to open the door and restore the original enthusiasm and get the engineer to realize how and why he lost his zeal.

Finding and defining words from subjects and textbooks, done as a precision activity, has broad applications in study. With school children suffering from 'attention deficit disorder' and 'hyper-activity' it is an important tool that sometimes magically resolves the situation. Usually it should be combined with other techniques to resolve these conditions completely. An array of other techniques is available to get the job fully done.

The DEEP Approach: In DEEP we can run out the counter-efforts present in the client. We find efforts to get a certain thing done, and we find counter-efforts right next to that but working in the opposite direction. These counter-efforts can usually be traced back to opponents. In DEEP clearing work we include seeing a conflict from both sides in a very literal way. We simply ask the client to assume the point of view of the opposition and view the whole issue from their viewpoint. This is done after first seeing the issue from own viewpoint, of course. By addressing the efforts and counter-efforts directly in this manner, the client will gain new ability to DO in the area. Running out the efforts and counter-efforts in many emotionally charged areas will result in the fact that the client in general will be more capable of doing work, both physical work and desk work.

Ability to HAVE

Ability to Have will increase as a general benefit from most clearing work. The Basic Objective Techniques we described in the chapter on Reality is an entry level action for bringing about an increase. Usually ability to have is not the direct subject of clearing. But freeing up ability to have is sometimes used as a remedy after running incidents and other actions that tend to take a lot of energy out of the client. If the client after an action or near the end of a session seems to be 'out of present time', a little bit groggy, etc. the practitioner will usually run a brief technique that orients the client back to the present environment. The clearer will typically point out different objects in the room for the client to look at or touch. This gets the person back into present time and to being fully alert in the environment.

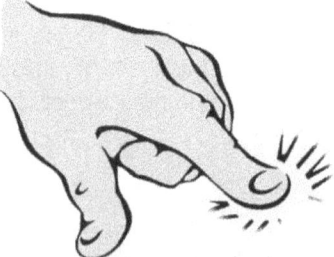

Chapter 8: Spirit – Mind – Body

There are three main components that make up a human being: 1) there is **the spirit** or Consciousness; 2) there is **the mind**, which is different from the spirit and the body; and finally, 3) there is the best known and best understood component: **the body.**

The Spirit

The human spirit is a distinct entity of consciousness. It is the part of us that is 'being aware of being aware'. It is separate from the body; separate from the individual's memories and training; separate from the person's experiences and hidden memories in the subconscious and unconscious part of the mind. It is not what is called the astral body or the aura. These are energy phenomena mainly produced by the human spirit but they are much more complex entities. At the very core, the human spirit is a very simple and happy Being, capable of perception and considerations.

The Spirit is the most important and permanent part of a human being. What we mean by 'Spirit' is the person or personality as it persists through this life and many lifetimes for each individual. You refer to the same "I" or "me" at any stage of your life. It is the core personality of an individual. The spirit is your basic self, a very powerful and capable fellow who over time has been trapped and burdened with all kinds of painful experiences, losses, false ideas, confusions, and relationships gone bad. It is not in as good a condition as it could be, by far. It can, however, be rehabilitated.

The idea that you *have* a soul is incorrect. The correct concept is that you *are* a soul. The soul, spirit, or consciousness is the very core of your being. It's *who* you are, the real you.

The mission of clearing work is to restore this core individual to his or her 'own good self'. It is to free the person of all the chains and burdens that hold him/her down. The power and abilities native to a Being are very impressive. In the course of clearing the core personality is who we want to contact and work with. We are not trying to teach or relay new information to a client through clearing. Once the client has understood a few basic definitions and concepts of the method and technology, the person has to find her own answers. What then happens is that clearing enables the client to strip off layers of *added* false ideas, confusions, traumas, and other burdens of life.

A spirit or consciousness, in its purest form, is non-physical. It does not have mass, wavelength, nor a fixed location. It has however abilities. It has the abilities to make decisions and set goals, to make and hold considerations. It also has the ability to perceive. "The purest form", you could say, is a theoretical state since it is impossible to measure. It can only be recognized through intuition. In practice you will find the consciousness decides to have a location in space and does have a recognizable wavelength, does surround itself with a tiny but measurable mass. The consciousness of a human being is usually located nearby or in the head. Some of the first considerations this Being operates under as a human being are to communicate, feel affinity and experience the reality of the environment. At its highest recognizable level the consciousness *is* universal understanding.

The Being normally occupies a position in or near a body throughout life. At death, the spirit leaves the body. The origin of the word spirit is 'breath', meaning 'breath of life'. When the spirit leaves the body at death, the eyes of the body become glassy and dull; the body collapses; the 'breath of life' apparently stops. The spirit, however, lives on as a consciousness capable of animating a newborn body at a later time.

The Mind

The mind is a communication and control system between the Being and the environment. The first object of control is the Being's most intimate possession, the body and its brain. The mind is not the brain. The brain is 'hardware'. In a modern analogy the mind, with its recordings and data, can be understood as the needed software while the brain is the hardware normally needed to run it. The Being itself is the 'computer operator' as well as the 'programmer'. It 'writes programs' knowingly, such as in learning; and unknowingly, such as during overwhelming and traumatic incidents. Later on the Being depends on these 'programs' when it has to respond to situations and emergencies.

Hardware: Brain

Software: Mind

Operator: Spirit

A computer system consists of hardware and software. You can't see the software except as a disc or CD; yet, without it nothing much happens. The operator is the uncontested boss. He is exterior to the system, responsible for the input and for reading and understanding the output.

In Clearing, we see the mind as a network of communications and pictures, energies and masses; and of stored thoughts, emotions and efforts. These phenomena are brought into existence by the spirit when operating in the physical universe and interacting with other Beings. The consciousness establishes various systems of control so it can continue to operate a body. It operates the body in order to control and conquer the physical universe. Life seems to have as its motivation to manifest itself, to survive and thrive—each individual as its own organism. Once raw survival is accomplished by a person or organism it strives for higher levels of thriving and success. The individual seeks gradually to "improve his lot in life". The individual seeks to extend its influence and control to additional and ideally all parts of life. At any given moment the mind helps the Being compute all the factors involved in this quest. From minute details of how to find lunch to major goals and ambitious plans with all the many factors involved in their planning and execution. The mind is thus a service mechanism that is owned, operated and maintained by the Being. It takes care of the practical planning, calculations, and executions of actions and initiatives related to the organism's survival and success.

The Being, in other words, is the boss possessing free will. The mind is the trusted but "hired help" whose job description is to assist the boss in succeeding in whatever the boss decides to do.

The consciousness is an intimate part of any mental activity as nothing happens in the absence of a boss or an operator. Mental activity is not just a mechanical or preprogrammed process as some schools of psychology want us to believe. There obviously are such things as predetermined mechanical responses in our mental activity. There are, however, also the x-factors of human behavior, free will, human error, pure idiocy as well as brilliance and genius.

The Mind and its Parts

We use various models to get a better practical understanding of important functions of the mind. In the first model the *functional principles* rather than structure are examined. This model outlines principles important to clearing work.

Some will ask: "Where is the mind located?" We give our bid on that question later in this chapter using another model. When it comes to function it is enough to say: It is a function, a 'black box', between the spirit and body. As mentioned, we see the mind as software and the brain as hardware, while the Being, the consciousness, the spirit is the owner and operator of this mind/brain system.

In this present model, we see the mind as having two main parts. The first of these is called *the Conscious or Rational Mind*. The second is *the Subconscious Mind*. There is a third system, a type of mind that controls body function. This is covered later.

The Conscious or Rational Mind

The conscious or rational mind is the portion of mind that deals with *rational thought*. This part works like a well-functioning computer program. This part is used when we solve problems and come up with accurate predictions and estimations. The capabilities of this part of the mind are impressive. This mind is hard at work when we resolve a multitude of very different problems of any imaginable kind: in daily life, in education, in science and research, in unfamiliar situations.

When a motorist drives a car without problems, she uses her rational mind all the time when she observes traffic and responds. She has to estimate the condition of the road, speeds, directions, other cars' condition and capabilities—even other drivers' condition. She does this almost automatically. Examples of the rational mind's functionality can be given from all parts of a person's life where things go well.

The way this mind operates is through combining and forecasting scenarios. It combines perceptions of the immediate environment; with data about the past (mental images); and estimations of the future (in picture form) and draws conclusions from this.

Intelligence can be defined as the ability to recognize differences, similarities and identical things. In other words, when we clearly can discern when things are different from each other; when and how some things are similar to each other; and when two or more things are identical to each other, we demonstrate intelligence. A well-functioning rational mind includes a data system where all data and facts are filed in a way that makes it easy and accurate to find them again. Yet, it's the Being who possesses intelligence just as it is the programmer and operator that possess the intelligence when using a computer system – not the system itself. It is important to realize that all the data and programs of the rational mind are monitored and controlled by the consciousness. Without the Being's awareness and being in charge we just have a sophisticated system that is ready for use but idle.

The Subconscious Mind and Bypass Reactions

The Subconscious Mind is that part of the mind that operates under a person's level of awareness and consciousness. It can be considered a huge storage area filled with treasures but also as the home of primitive survival patterns and instant defensive and aggressive reactions. The subconscious mind in general contains our forgotten experiences that we still use as basis for our thinking, feeling and acting. It influences us in countless ways. In Clearing we are mainly interested in this part of the mind. And we are mainly interested in the primitive survival patterns "learned" during traumatic and overwhelming incidents. These hidden experiences are the basis for what we call *Bypass Reactions*— responses of irrational thoughts, emotions, actions and habits that are happening outside our control and having a negative effect on us. They seem to happen automatically and bypass or overpower our rational mind to a greater or lesser degree. Since these thoughts, emotions and reactions are in conflict with what our rational mind tells us the two sides, the rational side contra the automatic subconscious side, generate charge between them. We have two conflicting or opposite poles. This generates what is known as emotional charge. Finding, releasing or dissolving emotional charge is what we essentially want to accomplish in clearing—and it is the essence of what any therapy seeks to accomplish.

Bypass reactions can be anything from irrational fears, to losing one's temper, to violent or criminal behavior, to odd habits and compulsions, to fixed ideas and obsessive thoughts. Accumulation of bypass reactions goes even further to be the main non-medical cause of neurosis, depression and psychosis.

The Repressed Mind

The part of the subconscious mind that contains the primitive and often irrational survival patterns, the collection of bypass reactions, is in DEEP called *the Repressed Mind*. It has, of course, been isolated and labeled by other researchers and writers in our field. Often it is simply called the subconscious or unconscious mind. Eckhart Tolle calls it for the Pain Body and defines it this way: "This accumulated pain is a negative energy field that occupies your body and mind. If you look on it as an invisible entity in its own right, you are getting quite close to the truth. It's the emotional pain body. It has two modes of being: dormant and active."

Samuel Sagan, MD, of Clairvision describes the same phenomena using old Sanskrit terminology. He uses the word Samskara to name emotional imprints or scars, the same that in DEEP and elsewhere is called stressful or traumatic incidents—or rather the mental imprints after such experiences. He goes on to discuss the complete collection of samscaras which he calls by the Sanskrit word, Manas. He translates this into English as the Reacting Mind. Here is an interesting quote:

"Since animals can become neurotic, we can assume they also have samskaras (i.e. emotional scars). The reflexes observed by Pavlov in his work with dogs present clear analogies with the conditioning of the samskaras.

"An important Sanskrit word, as said, related to samskaras is Manas. Manas refers to the layer in which we think and experience emotions. More precisely, manas has to do with the thoughts and emotions which are reactions directly related to samskaras. The concept of 'reacting mind' (manas) will be developed at length later in the book."

Frank A. Gerbode of Traumatic Incident Reduction (TIR) describes it this way (slightly paraphrased): 'The average person usually has a fairly large number of traumatic and stressful incidents, with different themes in common. These sequences of incidents overlap each other to form a network of traumatic incidents which we call the *traumatic incident network* or *"Net"*. The object of TIR is to reduce the amount of emotional charge the Net contains' (end quotes).

Since each author uses his own terminology in context with other technical elements, we prefer not to use their words. We use the term "Repressed Mind". We could have used the Unconscious Mind as Sigmund Freud did (and also Carl Jung in Collective Unconscious) or the Subconscious Mind as Pierre Janet, Carl Jung and others did. But both terms also have a positive meaning as a storage place for useful memories and experiences that just are out of reach.

Our term, *the Repressed Mind* underscores that it is material that is *held* out of consciousness. The Repressed Mind contains traumatic incidents that never arrived at full consciousness due to circumstances or the disturbing content. But it also contains things the person actively pushed out of consciousness and repressed. This includes own bad actions and misdeeds and much other stuff we actively try to forget, deny we had any part of, or alter to a degree so our recollection is a complete falsehood.

Our formal definition of the Repressed Mind is:

1. The Repressed Mind is the repressed or never viewed part of the subconscious mind. It seems to have a will of its own.

2. That part of the subconscious mind that contains emotionally charged material and bypass reactions. It tends to bypass the rational mind and react directly to factors in the environment that are perceived as dangers. It is a collection of conditioned reflexes, of primitive survival patterns, that were "learned" during stressful and life threatening situations. It can be triggered by the same or similar elements in the environment. It seems to have a will of its own in the form of out of control thoughts (dictates), emotions and impulses that are in conflict with the rational mind. Part of this mind is also own misdeeds and failures that we repress, deny, alter or "try to forget".

Traumas: A major contributor to the repressed mind and its bypass reactions is traumatic incidents. The subconscious mind has a huge collection of *recordings* of such incidents. These recordings contain the thoughts, emotions, feelings, efforts and body-sensations experienced during the actual incident. The incident is a moment where the person was confused and overwhelmed. There are physical traumas as well as emotional traumas. These recordings are very detailed but hidden. The process of recording such incidents goes on even when the person is unconscious. The accuracy of these recordings has been proven time and again where client's detailed recall of operations and severe accidents were compared to objective accounts from personnel at the scene.

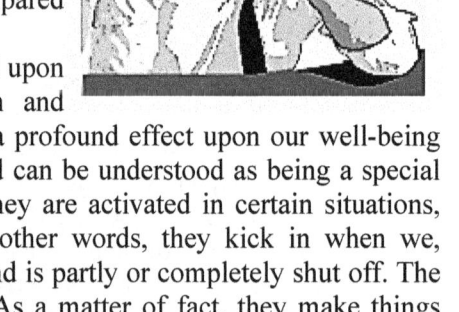

Due to the physical and mental pain these traumas inflicted upon the person, the experiences remain areas of heavy occlusion and confusion. They remain hidden to the individual. Yet, they have a profound effect upon our well-being and behavior – even health. This hidden compartment of our mind can be understood as being a special 'black box' that contains pre-programmed emergency routines. They are activated in certain situations, especially when we are in danger, exhausted or distressed. In other words, they kick in when we, apparently, are in poor control of our situation and our rational mind is partly or completely shut off. The problem is that these emergency routines don't work very well. As a matter of fact, they make things worse and usually cause disasters of their own!

Under normal circumstances the incident-recordings remain in place unknown to the individual. A man may remember falling off a ladder five years ago, but he has 'forgotten' all the details of the incident. Yet, the accident exists as a detailed recording in the person's mind and it has a profound effect upon him each time he sees a ladder.

Logic and Bypass Reactions

The reason the bypass mechanism of the repressed mind is such a negative force is due to the "logic" it operates on. Above we defined 'Intelligence' as the ability to discern differences, similarities and identical items. This ability does not extend to the repressed mind. This part of the subconscious mind is "stupid!" It works in a robotic way and leaves no room for intelligent thought. The "think" it operates on is to identify things with each other indiscriminately. Each little reminder of the content of an incident can become a trigger for the whole traumatic incident with its content of heavy emotion, pain and irrational thought and behavior. It is a conditioned reflex of sorts where new triggers are added and become 'live' as time goes on. The person sees a police car and short circuits and runs his own car into a tree. The police car was the trigger. It was associated with a speeding ticket, that was associated with an earlier car accident, that was associated with loss of control, that was associated with... just about anything else, including health conditions caused by a number of earlier accidents. The irrational associations, the conditioned reflexes, or 'software routines' kicked in and caused the panic, the loss of control, the accident, and new health problems on top of the existing ones.

The repressed mind is an accumulation of trauma, loss, own misdeeds, and our "worst nightmares."

Here is another example, again, with a car accident: a woman is in an accident and hurts her back. It happened driving near City Hall. A green car, an old man walking a dog, loud music from a band were all present at the time of the accident. After her back has healed the woman passes the spot; a band is playing. She feels the stinging pain in the back once more and the fear that was a natural reaction when the accident occurred. Later she feels a similar pain and fear whenever she hears a band or sees an old man walking a dog. The repressed mind has short circuited the various elements present in the accident with each other, including the back ache and fear. This irrational association can develop so she feels pain and fear each time she sees City Hall on TV! All the elements and perceptions in the hidden recordings have become short circuited until we have a completely irrational conditioned reflex mechanism that repeatedly is going off for no good reason.

The bypass mechanisms can lie dormant and never become activated. It takes a number of trigger elements that match up with the recording of the original incident for it to be "woken up". Once that has happened, it is very likely that any such mechanism remains in existence and gets triggered from time to time. A radical change of situation or environment may put it to sleep again.

While a person is on a high emotional level (see chapter 4) he/she is less likely to experience the "wakening up" of the repressed mind. He or she can remain rational throughout adversities. The most typical circumstances for reactivation are when the person is physically and mentally worn down; is tired, overworked, and not taking care of health issues. It all adds up to less resiliency. These conditions also approach the general content of stressful and traumatic incidents, moments where the person was more or less knocked out or overwhelmed by circumstances.

Activities that simply raise the emotional level of a person are therefore a workable approach to rise above many of the negative effects of this mechanism. This includes taking care of one's health, getting plenty of sleep, doing things one loves, getting exercise and having fun. From a Clearing perspective it includes actions that raise the emotional level of the client without addressing the actual incidents and traumas. But contacting the actual recordings and reviewing them carefully will completely overcome their potential threat. We do this in what is called DEEP Incident Clearing. We review the original recordings with all their irrational thoughts, negative emotions, and traumatic body memories. Once that is done, we transform traumatic incidents to life experience.

Network of Incidents

We have explained how one element gets associated with all other elements in the incident unselectively. In the example with the car accident near City Hall, any reminder, such as seeing City Hall on TV, eventually got powered up and could trigger the recording of the accident. The incident's content of pain, fear and discomfort inflicted itself on the woman.

Above we quoted Frank Gerbode's definition of the Network of Traumatic Incidents or the Net. That definition of what we call the repressed mind is very relevant here. Because such network of incidents also exists. The illogical association is at work connecting similar incidents. Mainly we are looking earlier in time. Lighter incidents connect up with much heavier ones that happened earlier, even in earlier lives. The earlier traumas are the hidden culprits despite they happened many years ago. The later incidents trigger the earlier, and even more hidden and unsuspected incidents.

Often a complaint the client presents to the clearer apparently is rooted in a recent incident. If close and repeated reviewing of that incident doesn't resolve the situation completely, the practitioner will ask for an earlier starting point to the event as that could have been missed. If that is dealt with without complete resolution, the practitioner will ask for an earlier similar incident. The clearer can in this way often backtrack a whole string of incidents.

Example: Let's say, a man is having troubles with operating machinery. He brings up a feeling of panic when he is operating his lawnmower tractor. This is a typical bypass reaction. A recent accident with the tractor is contacted, the details reviewed. The earlier incident it is sitting on is a break-down the client had with his car 5 years ago. The incident is contacted and reviewed. An incident from childhood is contacted and reviewed next. It is an accident he had with his bicycle at the age of 12. Earlier than that, there was an accident involving a tricycle at the age of 4. Finally, in our example, an incident at the age of 3 is found where the client as a little boy stepped on a toy car and fell and got hurt badly. The toy got ruined and the father blamed his son heavily on top of that. We have an irrational association of: Lawnmowers-Cars -Bicycles-Tricycles-Toy cars, plus hundreds of other elements and details. These incidents were all rolled up in a ball and working in unison in making it painful and confusing to deal with machinery and vehicles of any kind.

Sometimes the action will take the client earlier than his birth and into what appears to be earlier lives of the Being. This is not a new discovery, even in more officially recognized therapies. C. G. Jung, a personal student of Sigmund Freud and world renowned psychotherapist, talks about it as well – just to mention a famous name. This observation is, however, a well-guarded secret in official psychology. The datum just doesn't fit the model of the brain being the mind and personality.

Another type of incidents that leads to bypass reactions and short circuits in the repressed mind is incidents leading to guilt. These incidents consist of bad deeds the client has committed and of secrets that the client seeks to keep hidden or forget. Thus they get repressed and distorted and fall out of sight, only to react on the client from "the hidden deep". They can be cleared in a similar fashion and traced to earlier similar bad deeds. To use these techniques successfully, the client's responsibility level has to be sufficiently high so he/she can recognize his/her own causation rather than feeling accused and being defensive about the bad deeds. Therefore, these techniques are reserved for more experienced clients. The types of earlier similar incidents this clearing work reveals can go way back as well.

As a note on going earlier; it should be pointed out that once the client is reviewing an old incident a more recent one can be triggered as well. This should be taken up and reviewed. What gets triggered is not always earlier in a linear fashion. It may just be more hidden and forgotten. So we are dealing with a network of incidents as Dr. Gerbode points out, and we review what is offered.

Formation of the Bypass Mechanism

There are two elements that explain why bypass mechanisms are formed and stay in place. They both work in the same direction:

1. As a warning: the recordings of the dangerous incidents seem to be held in place as a warning system. The pain and emotional content is activated when the person approaches a situation similar to the original dangerous incident. The slight pain and emotional content is a red light that tells the person to steer clear of danger and of repeating the bad experience. It's a conditioned reflex mechanism that is triggered and it bypasses the rational mind and works instantly.

2. Emotional pain: Another reason is that the recordings contain pain and heavy emotional content. It spans from unpleasant to horrifying. When triggered by similarities in the environment, the recordings tend to force pain and disturbing emotion upon the client. The client consequently *shies away from viewing* the recordings themselves. They remain occluded and hidden. This is a "fear of the dark" phenomenon. It's safer not to look.

If the bypass mechanism came about as a design by nature, the lesson seems to be that it teaches us about dangers through physical punishment. This may work in animal training. Small conditioned reflexes, or 'warning programs', are installed that make a red lamp light up before any accident or breach of rules happens. In a very limited sense it works in child rearing as well. A mother slaps the fingers of her 3 year old son when he reaches out to touch a hot stove. Next time the boy sees the hot stove, his fingers hurt a little bit before he touches and he stops the motion.

The problem, however, is the indiscriminate identifications of elements with each other that happen in bypass reactions. As the repressed mind builds up more and more, warning signals will go off for no rational reason. Finally, the only way the person can avoid the pain and heavy emotional content is to remain locked up and inactive; and that doesn't work either! When you add to that, that verbal content in traumatic incidents is part of what the person reacts to, you are headed for chaos. Certain words and phrases can trigger irrational behavior. Especially this language factor makes the repressed mind totally unworkable as an emergency system. Sentences and irrational decisions embedded in painful incidents can become imperative commands. "The stove!" yelled as a warning can later lead to an obsession with stoves. What may work for animals does not work for human beings, mainly because of the language factor. A person can be seen to unknowingly replay incidents. If a man was brutally beaten and yelled at as a child, he will carry that pattern of behavior in his repressed mind. Say, his father repeatedly beat him and yelled in anger at the same time, "This will teach you!" Later on, the son will feel sore in his behind and angry when he tries to learn things in school. Teaching got associated with pain and anger. That is what the beatings taught him. When he in turn becomes a father, he is prone to act out or repeat the same pattern on his own son. The young father is convinced of the value of a "good beating". He yells "This will teach you!" while punishing *his* son. He is passing on the curse of the family. This goes a long way in explaining how brutality and certain irrational behaviors seem to run in families. It explains, for a large part, why the world at large seems to be a violent and chaotic place regardless of the fact that all mankind seems to wish for peace.

Let us return to the individual and give some examples of the bypass mechanism at work: somebody is hearing bad news meant for a stranger but the person has a violent and inexplicable reaction to it. Somebody is having a little accident or mishap but becomes *very* upset. Losing one's temper; panic; phobia; having repeated accidents in a certain area; shyness and irrational fears can all be traced back to the repressed mind. You can see these phenomena every day if you look for them. Besides causing occasional over-reaction, the mechanism can also take permanent control of a smaller or larger part of a person's life. An example of this could be sadness and depression, including regular thoughts of suicide, or avoiding all crowds or certain places. Some clients have strong fears and dislikes for certain types of people, animals, or sites. Be it the opposite sex, salesmen, dentists, doctors, snakes, spiders, heights, speaking in public, etc., etc. If the dislikes and reactions have no rational explanation it's a sure sign of the repressed mind at work. There is a rational way to respond in trigger situations. A person should be able to stay in control of self and face dangers and surprises in the environment. Caution and fear can be rational reactions or irrational ones. To get to a rational state of mind in critical situations, the person may need to do clearing work. The charged and traumatic incidents have to be reviewed and inspected closely.

The Body-Function Systems

The third "mind" or control system is the part that monitors and controls body functions. This is an even heavier type of "mind" since it does not contain what we usually call thought activity. It operates primarily on the body's physiology and partly on what we call body-memories that seem to reside in the nervous systems and the body itself. It contains subconscious and unconscious programs that control the body and allow and prepare for conscious control as well. These systems operate in the Effort band.

Eastern practices talk about what is called the Etheric Body, an energy field that surrounds and permeates the physical body. That seems to play a role in what we here call the body-function systems. The American cell biologist, Professor Bruce Lipton, also acknowledges this energy field.

The body-function systems regulate and operate the physiology: nerves, glands, muscles, and so on. The systems regulate the involuntary systems (heartbeat, digestion, etc.) and carry out the person's orders via the voluntary systems (movements, use of senses). We can at occasions bypass the physical control systems of nerves and biochemistry and cause an effect on the body directly. According to Bruce Lipton, medical researcher Canace Pert, and others, our cells are loaded with special receptors on their membranes – and this system of receptors responds to three types of signals: to biochemistry, to nerve signals and to the subtle energies of emotions. There are these three channels of influence of the body, its organs and cells.

The Body

The human body is probably the best researched subject in all of science. Anatomy, physiology, and all the branches of medicine are studied every day in countless hospitals, universities and laboratories. The body has been examined and studied since the beginning of time. You should think we knew all there was to know about the subject a long time ago

Yet within the last 30 years, a new branch within biology, called Epigenetics, has added a whole new dimension to our understanding of organisms and the body and the body-mind connection. The human body is estimated to consist of 37 trillion cells. Each cell can, in its own right, be seen as an independent organism that is working in symbiosis and harmony with all the other cells. Each cell is sentient and has a degree of perception, intelligence and consciousness. The cells respond to their environment—first and foremost to their biological environment, such as the blood stream and its content of nutrients, toxins, hormones, etc. But there is a chain of cause and effect, starting at our minds and our perception of the environment. The mind, with its thoughts and emotions, activates the brain that in turn activates the glandular systems and the nervous systems throughout the body. Hormones, etc. affect the cells on a chemical level. So the cells get messages from the mind and the brain through these channels; and as explained above, emotions can affect the body's cells directly.

Stress: Essentially there are two types of signals and modes. There is stress mode or defensive-aggressive mode on the one side. It is a state of fear or anger and contraction. Then there is a relaxed but active mode on the other side. This is a happy mode of growth and expansion.

The above is according to Bruce Lipton and others. Lipton explains this in detail in his book, "The Biology of Belief". He explains the chain of events and the science behind it all in an easy to understand language.

It has long been known that the stress and fear mode will shut down the body's immune system, the system that fights disease. The body does this in order to allocate all its resources to defend itself. It goes into 'fight, flee, or freeze' mode. If this stress mode lasts for an extended period of time, the body and the cells are prone to contract a number of diseases. In the happy mode, on the other hand, the body allocates its resources to maintain a fully functioning immune system and to maintain health and growth. This is the mechanism of stress being a major cause behind disease. The body simply lets down its internal defenses to man its external defenses.

Placebo and Nocebo Effect

When a patient gets well from taking a simple sugar pill instead of real medicine, we talk about the Placebo effect. The patient got well from *believing* it was strong medicine. In other words, it wasn't the pill that cured the patient but *the belief and conviction that it would help* that cured him. This phenomenon is well known to all medical doctors and the pharmaceutical industry. They are usually in a state of despair and ridicule over it.

One medical doctor and author, among others, has a different take on this. Dr. Lissa Rankin in her book "Mind over Medicine" explains that, according to her research (including many studies done by other scientists) the patient receiving the placebo medicine will go from a state of constant stress throughout the body to the happy and relaxed state. In other words, the placebo effect gives the natural internal defenses a chance to work. In the absence of stress the body simply cures itself. Many of these stress factors come from the environment and the patient's inability to deal appropriately with them.

Dealing with all these stress-factors is different and far removed from simply using positive suggestions like, "take this pill and you will get well". The stress factors are usually real and should be dealt with. It can be self-limiting, self-invalidating and debilitating thoughts and beliefs.

Both Dr. Rankin and many medical researchers talk about what they call the Nocebo effect. It is the opposite of Placebo. It means that negative beliefs and convictions, including "death sentence diagnoses" (such as 'you may have cancer – we need to do further tests.') expressed by a trusted doctor, can be taken as a death sentence and cause a rapid decline in health.

Clearing and Health

What clearing work can contribute with is to shed light on stress-related conditions. We can find the negative beliefs that lead to negative emotions and body sensations that are locked into the body. These encapsulated energies affect the heath in a downward direction. They put the body in a state of nervous alertness and lock down the workings of the immune system as described above. Also, traumatic incidents can impede the blood circulation and flow of life energy to a specific part of the body and simply place an area or organ under stress, leading to illness—call it psychosomatic if you will. It may still need medical treatment. But for a more permanent recovery the mental and emotional sides need to be taken care of as well.

The health and physical wellbeing can also take a hit from stress factors in the environment. Having too much to do, being under attack from bosses, colleagues or family members can all lead to stress and illness. The clearer will in such cases help the client organize her life so she has a plan for dealing with these sources of stress. This alone lightens the burden and can lead to recovery from minor illnesses, such as a cold or a flu-like condition.

By handling factors in the patient's environment and the traumatic and stressful content stemming from the repressed mind, swifter and more stable recovery is possible. This should be done as a follow-up after normal medical treatment. Most medical doctors are very aware of the importance of the stress factor in treating the ill. But unfortunately medical schools seem to be focused on the use of drugs and surgery only. Mainstream medicine only accepts physical causes for illness. There has in the last several decades, however, been a strong demand by the public for alternative treatment of many origins; from acupuncture to chiropractic; from homeopathy to nutrition—and countless other methods. All this activity reflects that the body and our health are some of the most pressing issues of life. It also reflects that all the answers haven't been found yet. Many patients start with traditional medical treatment. If that doesn't help they go to alternative practices. The rising popularity of these alternative treatments shows that many patients find that Western medicine is not working fully in their case.

The stress factor in illness is routinely estimated to be a factor for as many as 75-85% of patients. In Clearing we offer a well-researched approach to the problem of relieving stress and psychosomatic conditions. What we can do for the body, then, is to clear it from subconscious stress factors including traumatic factors. This is usually done while a medical doctor is the primary caregiver. If a client has an occasional ailment that is less serious and doesn't need medical attention, the complaint can be taken up and checked for thought components. It is important to point out that clearing is not designed to diagnose or treat illness, be it medical or psychiatric. The subject is primarily intended for personal and spiritual development. We do, however, encourage medical professionals to look into the subject and, where appropriate, work together with a practitioner in getting the 'stress element' fully inspected and eliminated.

Another Model

Any model of the mind is an abstraction, of course. A model is a useful tool in understanding important mechanisms and aspects. In the above model we got to understand some mechanisms important to clearing. But we didn't really address the question of *where* the mind is located. We did touch upon that the body seems to be controlled by more than one system (some schools say that the body IS our subconscious mind). Our work with Clearing has however shown us that there is an age-old model that seems to give some interesting answers.

The Aura or Energy Body

The aura or energy body has been recognized for millennia in Eastern spiritual and medical practices. Also Christian saints are always depicted with a halo or aura. In Clearing we call this energy field *the Energy Body*. It is a product of the spirit and body rather than being the spirit itself. In the West it has in recent decades been subject to intense studies. Barbara Ann Brennan, originally a NASA scientist, has for instance given detailed descriptions of its anatomy. The energy body consists of different

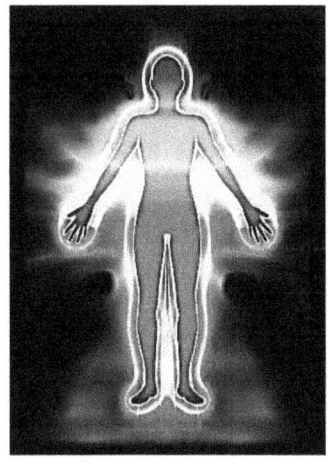

layers. Brennan talks about 7 layers visible to her and 3 invisible ones. But she points out that it is a continuous spectrum of finer and finer wavelengths—the concentration of the shortest and most coarse wavelengths being closest to the body. The outer layers permeate the body and all the inner layers. If you go to fairs covering Spirit-Mind-Body, you will undoubtedly be able to find stands where they offer to photograph your aura and give you an interpretation of the photo afterwards. They use special cameras based on what is called Kirlian photography. We do not use aura interpretations but find it relevant and of great interest that the energy body actually shows up on the film.

In DEEP Clearing our interest is focused on three bands, three aspect of our psyche that apparently reside in the energy body. The phenomena are Thought, Emotion and Body-control (Effort). In Eastern inspired systems the first layer closest to the body and permeating it, is called the etheric body. It is the seat for regulating the body and its functions. Outside that we find the second layer, the emotional body. Outside that again is the third, the mental body, the layer holding thoughts and mental processes.

Thought, Emotion and Effort are covered in great detail in part two of this book. But let us just say here, that the energy body seems to be the storage place for thoughts, emotions and efforts and that these phenomena determine our faith in life. They define who we are as identities as they contain what we think, what we feel and what we do. They contain all the thoughts, emotions, feelings and efforts (habits) that we use in everyday life. By thoughts we mean concepts, ideas, decisions, etc. It is content that usually can be expressed in words. By emotion we mean a band of mental activity that is more intuitive and spontaneous. It is our unreflected mental reactions to the environment and people. You could say 'Instinctive' except much of our emotional responses are actually acquired from all kinds of experiences, including trauma. Finally the effort band contains the actual blueprint for our actions and behaviors. It contains physical habits and routines as well as irrational body reactions and body sensations. In DEEP clearing we call this type of memory Body Memories. So the layers of thoughts, emotions and efforts of a person could be said to be the mental house the Being lives in. The body, of course, is the physical home of the Being. *All the phenomena of these three or more energy forms are as a set called a DEEP Package in this book. Our subjective experiences in life are recorded as sets – in DEEP Packages.*

We find the model of the energy body with its layers useful in DEEP clearing; thoughts, emotions, and body memories obviously have a physical location in or around the body. We sometimes ask clients *where* a certain thought, emotion or body memory is located and most clients have no difficulty in simply pointing to the spot. It helps the client to gain control over the phenomena. Gaining control is a first step in cleaning out one's mental house of irrational or unwanted thoughts, emotions and body memories.

We do not take our model further than that. We do not theorize over the remaining 7 layers or so. We are interested in improving the actual 'house' our client lives in. Clearing the three layers of thought, emotion and effort takes care of that and it will some fine day allow the client to ascend to new heights, starting this new journey from a 'house' in very good order.

Head, Heart and Hand

We need not resort to Eastern philosophies and energy bodies to understand thought, emotion and effort. Both Christian and Judean traditions talk about head, heart and hand. This includes the American youth movement 4H (here the 4 H's stand for head, heart, hand and health.) The three elements of thought, emotion and effort correspond closely to these classic faculties or elements of a human being. It is about what we think, what we feel and what we do. They go under different labels. Besides head, heart and hand we meet it as mind, heart and body; and as mental, emotional and physical.

Note that effort and hand correspond to body and action. This is important here, because what we classify under the effort and body level are things like body posture, body language as well as impulse and action. So we have a wider category under the heading of Effort that covers the physical band: the physical doing of something as well as the mental precursor to physical action which is impulse. (See also illustration at the end of the chapter.)

Three Parts of the Brain

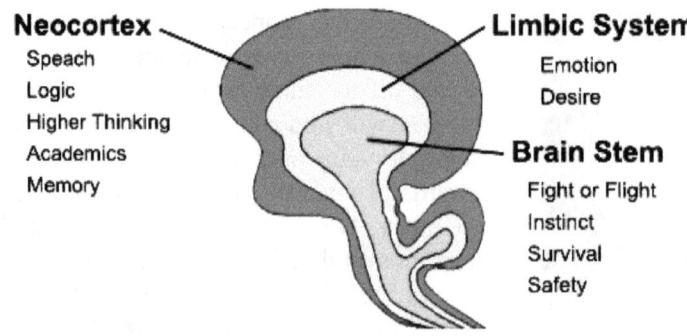

While we are at different models of the mind, etc., we also need to take a look at the brain. The American doctor and neuroscientist Paul D. McLean formulated the theory of the triune brain. It was mainly researched in the 1960s. In 1990 he finally published the book "The Triune Brain in Evolution." According to Dr. McLean the brain evolved in three main stages. First the primitive reptilian brain developed. It is located in the brain stem. It controls basic body functions, body motion and instinctive raw survival behavior, such as aggression, dominance, defense of territory, procreation, and ritual behavior. Here we have the seat for action without much emotion or thought.

On top of this developed the emotional brain (the limbic system or paleo-mammalian complex). It is seen as responsible for the motivation and emotion involved in feeding, sex, and raising of the young.

Finally there is the neocortex (neo-mammalian complex or cerebral neocortex.) This brain is only developed in higher mammals and especially in humans. McLean regarded this as the most recent step in the evolution of the brain. It deals with language, rational thinking and planning. The three parts of the brain, as formulated by Dr. Paul McLean, correspond very well to the model of thought, emotion and effort. We have reptilian brain = effort; limbic system = emotion; neocortex = thought. There is an excellent description of the triune brain in the book, "The Body Keeps the Score" by Bessel Van Der Kolk.

Several Systems: In summary, there seems to be back-up systems when it comes to the mind. They are not necessarily exclusive of each other. It is not all-in-the-brain nor all-in-the-energy-body nor all in the-heart-and-body. Some schools, like Focusing and HeartMath, actually say the body IS our subconscious mind. We don't hold the client to a specific model. We simply ask where and how it is experienced subjectively. The client sometimes points to the head, sometimes to the body or to the immediate vicinity, the field. Whatever the client says is taken as his experience and that is what matters.

Belief and Results

Models are models and they can be difficult to coordinate sometimes. The above models will change as research and science progresses. As Alfred Korzybski said, "the map is not the territory." This applies to these models. We are still using the best maps we have.

You may ask: "Do I have to believe in these models and other data in this book to benefit from Clearing?" The answer is "NO!" You don't have to understand electricity to benefit from electric light. You don't have to understand the inside of a computer to use one and benefit from its capabilities either. You may, like the author, be totally ignorant about the inner workings of computers, programs, etc. They will still work for you. The same could be said about clearing. We are telling you the theory that led to DEEP Clearing. You may have an issue about man as a spirit, earlier existences, the models used to explain the mind; talking about auras and energy bodies, etc. All a practitioner will need from you is that you work honestly with him/her, follow the instructions given in session and answer the questions.

Regarding earlier existences, should it come up: any incident can be run as a fictitious incident with benefits. The practitioner simply asks, "Can you imagine an earlier similar incident?" If 'yes', the client can tell what could have happened.

Our mission is not to convince people about the ideas. It is to make people well. That happens in present time, here and now! What happened in the distant past or in past lives will be all forgotten and gone once it has been fully reviewed in Clearing.

The DEEP Package

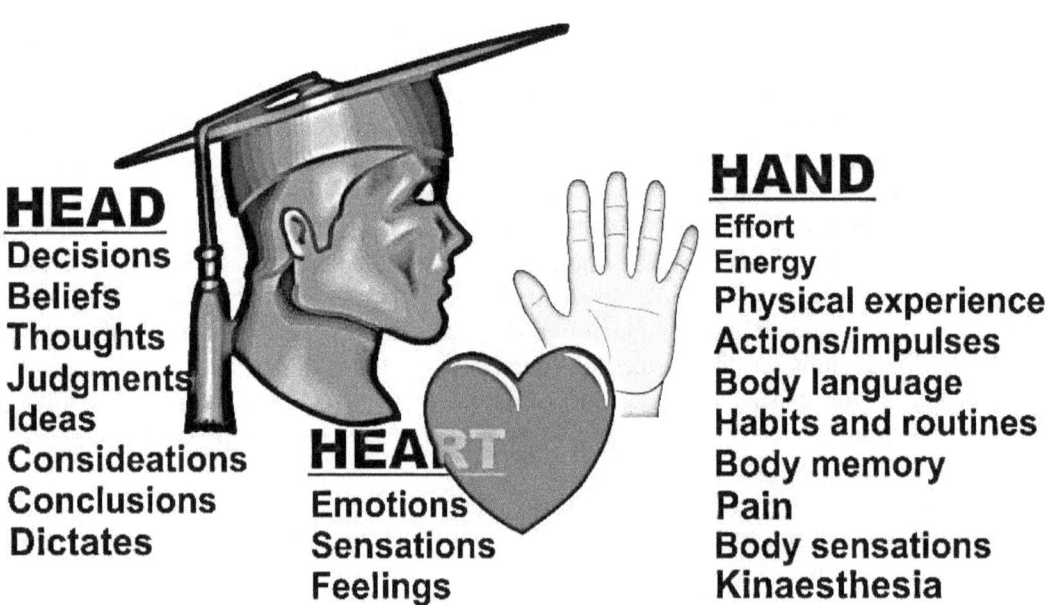

An important concept in this book is **the *DEEP package.*** It is the set of personal recordings the person keeps of a subjective experience. All the elements in the illustration are in play and can be part of such a recoded package. In the text such packages are sometimes called Thought–Emotion–Effort and sometimes simply a DEEP Package. D.E.E.P. stands for Decisions, Emotions, Efforts, and Polarities. Polarities refer to conflicts between two parties.

Chapter 9: Life as a Game

Living life can be compared to playing a game. There are different types of games. The four most important types are: 1) opposition Games; 2) competitive games; 3) Man against the environment games; 4) Complementary games.

Opposition Games

When we look at a ball game, such as soccer, we see players expending a lot of physical energy in an attempt to conquer and control the ball. The players demonstrate great skill in holding on to the ball as a team and forwarding it towards the opposing team's goal. They execute all kinds of skills and tactics in order to get an edge and to score. Once they have succeeded in scoring they have to prevent the opponent from scoring a goal on them. On a professional level no efforts are spared in getting one's team to the top. It includes tough practice sessions with grueling physical training, ball handling and tactics. Also, team routines, consisting of practicing designed plays to get around the opponent players and then score.

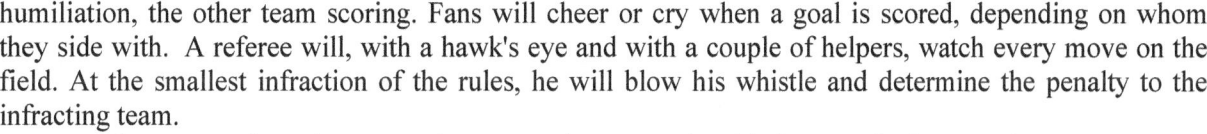

On game day the goal keeper is the last line of defense in preventing the unthinkable, the ultimate humiliation, the other team scoring. Fans will cheer or cry when a goal is scored, depending on whom they side with. A referee will, with a hawk's eye and with a couple of helpers, watch every move on the field. At the smallest infraction of the rules, he will blow his whistle and determine the penalty to the infracting team.

When we analyze the game of soccer and compare it with dozens of other popular games, be it a game of chess, horse racing, card games, even figure skating and mountain climbing, we find they have certain things in common. We can isolate eight key elements: 1) We have *players*; 2) a *playing field*; 3) a *clear objective*; 4) there are *rules*; 5) there are *obstacles or opposition*; 6) there are *challenges, variety*; 7) There is an *outcome*, a winner and a loser; 8) there is a *payoff*, such as excitement, status and honor, or material things, including money. A main reason for engaging in games is however to experience the payoff as excitement. The joy of winning, the chill of losing and the whole spectrum of emotions and sensations connected to playing or watching the game. Let's take a closer look at soccer in this perspective.

1. Players: In soccer there are 11 players on each team, each player with his role and skills. **2. Playing field:** We have a 100x50 meters field covered with grass and a goal in each end. **3. Objective:** The overall objective of each team is to score goals, and to score more goals than the opponent. **4. Rules:** The detailed rules are enforced by the referee. **5. Opposition and obstacles:** Soccer is an opposition game, where the teams are permitted to attack the other team. The opposition, of course, is delivered by the other team that defends and counter-attacks. There are obstacles imposed by the rules and by the role or position each player is given. For instance, only the keeper is allowed to touch the ball with the hands. **6. Challenges and Variety:** All the unpredictable factors of a ball game make up for the interest and fascination it attracts. The bouncing of the ball; the ball slipping through the hands of the keeper; the superb pass; the fantastic kick resulting in a goal; the sudden determination of a defender, etc., etc. If we knew it all beforehand it would be uninteresting, it wouldn't really be a game. It for sure wouldn't have the fascination and excitement that draws the crowd. **7. Outcome:** There is winning or losing, the outcome of the game. The game is of a finite length such as 90 minutes of playing time in soccer. It's a well-defined cycle of action. **8. Payoff:** A soccer game is mainly played for the excitement of winning and losing. That is what the players, the fans and anybody else around the game have in common. In professional sports there is of course big money at stake as well and professional careers. In soccer there are heroes that are hailed and losers that are booed, etc., etc.

Other Opposition Games, Chess

Opposition games are characterized by the two sides are allowed to attack each other within the rules. In chess we have the players attacking each other on an intellectual level with carefully thought out moves on a chess board. Even though the game is radically different from a ballgame, as there is no physical action involved, we can still find the eight key elements.

1. Players: We have the two players of respectively white pieces and black pieces. You can of course also see the pieces as "players" and the two chess combatants as generals engaging in battle between black and white armies. *2. Playing Field:* is the checkered board consisting of 64 small squares. *3. Objective:* to corner the opponent's king in a chess mate situation. *4. Rules:* the allowed moves of the pieces. *5. Opposition and obstacles:* Each player confronts the opposing "army" of pieces on the chess board. Obstacles are enforced through the rules and the allowed moves of each piece. *6. Challenges, Variety:* What will the opponent do? What are the consequences of a certain move as we go five moves forward? *7. Outcome:* The game is over when one side is chess mate. There is a winner and a loser. *8. Payoff:* The game offers intellectual stimulation and entertainment. Even though it is not seen as a game of emotion, it provokes strong feelings in the lovers of the game. Also, successful players certainly build a reputation.

More Games

In most board- and card games there are more than two sides. Often the rules state, "Played by 3-5 players". You may have the option to attack any opponent you meet. In Ludo you can send an opponent back to start. In Monopoly, you can charge an opponent play money if he checks in on one of your expensive hotels. In most card games each player plays for himself, trying to outsmart and win over the other players. Often there has to be more than 2 players to provide enough challenge and variety. In Solitaire card games the outcome depends on wits and also a lot on luck. 'Luck' here accounts for delivering the variety and emotion. The same could be said about many computer games. Here the player's luck, quick reaction and wits are tested against the computer game environment.

In such single man's games, you still have the eight key elements. In a computer shooting game it would be something like this: *1. Players:* You have the person who plays the game, yourself, and maybe fictive opponents, such as hostile soldiers and gunmen. *2. The playing field* is your computer screen. *3. The objective:* is to win in battle over the armed enemy. *4. Rules:* The program dictates the rules by what you can and cannot do. *5. Opposition and obstacles*: are provided by the game designers. In a sense you are up against the designers as the opposing force. *6. Challenges, Variety:* You don't know what will happen next. Where is the next threat going to come from? If you after many plays know the exact moves and threats of the opponent you will probably get so bored with it that you look for another game. It is only fun when there is a challenge of your skills, your alertness, and ability to act. If you win every time there is no longer any variety and challenge, essential parts of any game. *7. Outcome:* Part of what makes games attractive is that they will soon end; you are not stuck in that environment. They play out after a well-defined period of time and then you can go home and forget all about it. You were entertained in the moment. In contrast, our major undertakings in life drag out for years and years and we are stuck with them. Bad outcomes can result in hardships such as loneliness, poverty, starvation and even death. Therefore we say, "This is not a game!" *8. Payoff:* In a single man's game the payoff is excitement and entertainment; also improving skills, alertness and ability to act in that environment.

Competitive Games

In the above we mainly described Opposition Games, games where you are allowed to attack the opponent. There is another type of games we call Competitive Games. Here, each player performs on his/her own and the performance is then compared with the other competitors. The best performer is the winner. This is true in running and most other races. Take downhill skiing. Each skier is the single runner on the course. The next runner is started when the course is clear. Each skier competes directly against the clock and only indirectly against the other skiers. At the end of the day the winner is, of course, the fastest. We have sports, such as figure skating and gymnastics, where a panel of judges rates each performance in order to find the overall winner. Let's see how that plays out using our eight key elements. Let's take Olympic figure skating for pairs:

1. Players: There are the competitors, such as one pair of figure skaters from each nation. *2. Objective:* To deliver the perfect performance according to standards set by the sport and judged by the judges. *3. Playing field* is the ice in a sports arena. *4. Rules:* There are rules regarding equipment, no doping, and standards of how to judge a performance. *5. Opposition and obstacles:* The opposition is the other contestants and their performance. The obstacles are the physical environment, such as equipment, ice and arena, the limitations of the human body. *6. Challenge, Variety:* Slick ice, condition of equipment, physical and mental fitness on the day, the judges, the reactions of the crowd, are all elements in play and they provide plenty of variety for all involved. *7. Outcome:* the pair that is judged to deliver the best performance (high in difficulty, done with least errors, artistic impression) is the winner. *8. Payoff:* Olympic gold medal with all the media attention and opportunities that follow.

Man against the Environment

An activity such as Mountain Climbing done for leisure is the sport of choice for some. Here we have the mountain climber taking up the challenge that some steep mountain seems to impose. If we compare this activity to our eight key points, we again find a good fit. *1. Players:* Our mountain climber with the fellow climbers. *2. Objective:* Is simply to reach the top and plant a flag. *3. Playing field:* The mountain and nature. *4. Rules:* There are many skills to learn and master, many rules of the trade to understand before a person can call himself an accomplished mountain climber. The rules here are imposed by nature and laws of physics, such as gravity and how to use the equipment. Break them, and you may be in severe danger. *5. Obstacles and opposition:* The mountain, gravity, the weather conditions are all obstacles. There is no man-made opposition but nature offers plenty. *6. Challenges, Variety:* Many unforeseen obstacles will be encountered. Many things can go wrong and that account for challenges and variety. There are dangers to overcome and many small victories to have while climbing the mountain. *7. Outcome:* Once the top is reached and the flag is planted the main objective is accomplished. To get down safely and live to tell about it is a less glamourous part of the mission. *8. Payoff:* Overcoming the challenge and live to tell about it. In terms of emotions and sensations they are many during the climb as well. There is a reason why the most emotionally tense moments in movies are called "cliff hangers."

Elements of Life

When we consider that what we usually call 'games' are regarded as entertainment and amusement, it can sometimes be baffling to see what hardships, including utter exhaustion, injury and even death, players and participants are willing to subject themselves to in order to play and possibly win. Some sports, such as car racing, mountain climbing, boxing and downhill skiing, are extremely dangerous sports. Apparently, games and their eight key elements have such a profound appeal to us humans that we will do just about anything to experience the sensations and excitement they generate.

Games are usually considered something we do after work. We get home, we change our clothes and now we can have some fun. The playing of a game is a short cycle of action. It clearly has a clear start, an action phase and an end. Once the game is over it's over. We can walk away from it and forget all about it without consequence. Due to the short time span games last, it is easy to become unattached afterwards and analyze what went on. To analyze games is a favorite pastime for coaches, players, spectators, and sports commentators alike.

Some people have "no time for games". They see life as too serious and the stakes of living are too high. They go out there in the real world every day and do what has to be done. They regard 'mere games' as only suited for children and irresponsible adults. Yet, we see their children imitating these adults in their games, even war games.

When we analyze the activities of this 'the real world', something strange will soon become clear. The elements of games are not reserved for or confined to leisure time games. We find that the same eight elements of players, objective, playing field, rules, obstacles and barriers, challenges and variety, outcome, payoff, are what we live and breathe every day at work, in relationships, in politics and war, when we travel, etc. They even have to be part of any story and entertainment or we don't find it interesting.

The Games of Mr. Jones

If we take a responsible provider and family man, Mr. Jones, who goes to work every day to provide for his family, does a good job and works on his promotion, he is subject to rules and regulations imposed on him from family, work place and society. Mr. Jones may have a dream of putting his kids through university,  being able to afford a bigger home, taking the family on vacation every year and excel at his job so he ends up in a senior executive position. To achieve all of that are his objectives and goals in life. These goals are pretty much what we call "the American Dream", a perfectly legitimate and socially acceptable set of goals for a man and his family. Our society depends on dreams like that. The obstacles and opposition in this setting may simply be to compete and deal with other career people with the same or similar goals.

Mr. Jones, in terms of rules, has to follow several sets. At work he has to follow company policy and produce what he is supposed to. He has to impress his bosses sufficiently to keep his job. If he is diligent in following and enforcing the rules, it may give him an edge when it becomes time to consider his promotion. He also has to follow the rules and laws of society to stay out of trouble. At home he may be the King of the Castle. Yet, he has to play by certain rules to keep everybody happy. He may be wise in suppressing outbursts of frustration and bachelor behavior and instead do what is expected of him. He may be, to a large extent, the one who sets and enforces the rules in the first place. To keep the 'game' of happy family-life going, he now has to abide by these rules. When he married Mrs. Jones, they came to some sort of agreement on what 'game of life' they wanted to play together (depending on the character of their marriage, Mrs. Jones, of course, could be the real Queen and Mr. Jones her Prince Charming).

In terms of creating some enjoyable variety, Mr. Jones has many choices he can make in each sphere of his life. At work he can come up with brilliant solutions to problems beyond what is expected of him. He is setting new standards, expanding the game rather than breaking the rules. His superiors realize Jones can play a bigger game closer to the executive rule book of the company and may promote him to the next level. This results in a bigger pay check and new payoffs in the form of new freedoms. He can do more of what he wants to without breaking the rules of the games he is playing in life. The opposition and obstacles Mr. Jones encounters at work may simply be the work load and the many different tasks that are thrown at him. He may also compete with  colleagues about favors and promotions. In society Mr. Jones has the freedom to engage and participate in more games in order to experience opportunities and variety. He can volunteer for projects with his expertise. He can go into organizational work or into politics if he is so inclined and capable. Each time his spheres of interest change the rules and challenges change with them—as do the payoff. Hopefully, at home is where Mr. Jones feels most relaxed. With the family, Mr. Jones can of course do things out of the ordinary, recharge the batteries and have a good time. Mr. Jones will probably take his wife and kids to ball games. The game generates all sorts of excitements and sensations; emotional outbursts and release. It releases tensions in Mr. Jones that built up during the week in the more serious games of work and as head of the family.

Work and Games

What exactly is the difference between sports- and leisure-games on the one side and work on the other? In work the outcome is a practical result, a product. The payoff is the product that helps us to survive and thrive better. Work, per definition, should result in such a product that is of use to someone after the job is done.

A game, on the other hand, has as its main function the enjoyment of the moment. There is the voluntary engagement in the short time span of a leisure game. Also, any good leisure game must have a strong element of competition, challenges or opposition as this is key in providing the emotional engagement and excitement. In work this is not necessarily the case. Work is more oriented towards the future, manufacturing of products and services for further use and helpful to practical survival.

Complementary Games

In work and life we find what we call Complementary Games. These are games where there is no clear opposition or competition. A complementary game is a constructive game where there is teamwork going on. The objective is to bring about a desired condition or product.

In sports this can be found as teamwork within a team. A ball game without teamwork within your team is a lost game. So a complementary game is a game of teamwork and cooperation towards a clear goal, condition or product.

Let's say Mr. Jones wants to build a new and bigger house for the family. We have a complementary game with the desired objective of a new and better house. Let's see how that fares against our eight key elements:

1. *Players:* There is Mr. and Mrs. Jones who start and finance the project. There is an architect, an engineer, masons, carpenters, plumbers, electricians, etc. who have the necessary skills to carry out the family's objective. These are all players – each player bringing his or her special skills and  expertise, energy and time to the project. *2. The objective* that pulls them all together is the vision of the completed house according to the Jones family and the architect's plans and blueprints. *3. Playing field:* Is the framework for the project. The town they live in, the lot they bought, the available methods, resources and technology for building the house. *4. Rules:* There are many rules to follow in order to succeed. There are building regulations and the many rules within each profession of the involved professionals. *5. Obstacles and opposition:* The obvious obstacles are money, time, what is technically possible. Oppositions can also happen in the form of hostile building inspectors, fraudulent suppliers and contractors. Maybe dissatisfied neighbors who complain about the fences and other details of the project. *6. Challenges and Variety*: There are plenty of challenges and unforeseen factors in such a project for the Jones family: The money; "Will the house be ready in time?" "We need a different furnace;" can Mrs. Jones get her dream bathroom? Etc., etc. Maybe Mr. Jones and the architect have to fight the building inspectors to get things done the way they want them. *7. Outcome:* There is, of course, a clear cut outcome of the project. The finished house, ready to be moved into. *8. Payoff:* Such a project will provide a lot of activity and emotional engagement for the Jones family. In the end the payoff is of course a better house to live in. For all the assisting participants there are payoffs too: employment, demonstrating professional skills, money, pride, etc.

There Must Be a Game!

Life is a battle, a contest, a struggle—sometimes a rat-race. At times we have clear opponents. Very often it is rather a contest against the environment or against economic pressures and hardships.

By simply being alive we have entered the field of contest. The overall game on Planet Earth for all life forms seems to be to survive and succeed. For each human, animal and plant it seems to be to persist as an organism through time, to grow and prosper until the time span is up. Then the next generation, our children or progeny will take over. Every life form, every man, woman and child; every animal, of whatever species, be it on land, in the air, or in the sea; every plant and tree; even every insect and microscopic organism such as bacteria – they all have this in common: to survive and thrive on two levels: 1. To survive and thrive as their own organism; 2. To survive and thrive as a species.

This apparent course "Survive and thrive!" that we follow can take many forms and unexpected turns. By itself it is very broad. It could be compared to telling a large group of children to "Play ball!" without defining what kind of ball game it refers to. Only a series of practical circumstances, agreements and choices will narrow it down to an actual playable game. When we talk human lives and look at all the games we engage in, it's also clear there is great latitude and freedom of choice. All the choices possible account for the opportunities and variety we see in careers, luck in life, personal fortune, etc. We see this clearly among siblings or a particular class of graduates from a high school. High school reunions 5, 10 and 20 years after graduation are always revelations of how different "the game of life" turns out for graduates starting at a relatively level playing field.

In leisure games opponents are matched equally, in strength and competing under the same rules. In life this is rarely the case. Rules and opponents are not clearly defined. Sometimes an apparent enemy is really an ally. More often an apparent ally turns out to play against us. Yet, any single human being will soon find his or her niche and define the game (or games) to play. Games in life are defined by goals and purposes and the roles and identities attached to them. "Becoming a rocket scientist", "being a farmer", "being a nurse", "pursue a career as a classical violinist", "being a mother and house wife", "being a good father and husband", etc. – each defines a whole package of the eight key elements of a game. That is the game of life the person will experience and play with all its ups and downs; with all the challenges and the emotional engagements that follow.

To have a game, any game, seems to be a basic human craving. It seems we need a game at all costs. If we can't have the game of being the pampered celebrity living in luxury, we can at least have the game of doing a regular job or perhaps being a patient or a victim of a disaster. Even a bank robber plays a fairly well-defined game. We are all writers of at least one great novel: our life's story! And we want it to be as interesting, exciting and as unique as possible. You will find any human Being has a number of games going on at any moment. Mr. Jones is engaged in being a father, a husband, being a corporate man, a driver – not to speak of his ambitions to become the mayor of his city. Each of these games has its own set of rules and possibilities. We play these games because they generate interest, contest, activity, joy of possession and emotional engagement.

No-Games-Conditions

There are scenarios we describe as no-games-conditions. Such scenarios only have very short endurance. Often such a scenario is set up as the goal we strive after oddly enough. They are seen as the ultimate prize of victory for the game we are engaged in. Getting there, or getting there first, means we have won! Once it is obtained for real, however, it soon becomes clear it is unbearable in the long run. A busy executive may dream about the day he retires. He wants to sit at the beach with his wife and just relax; a drink in his hand while the family dog chases the seagulls and ducks. Much of what he does is to make this dream come true. When he finally gets there it may kill him. If he had no thought of what he wanted to do at the beach, besides relaxing, or with his retirement in general, it is certainly a complete vacuum, a complete no-games-condition where life becomes utterly uninteresting and boring to a point that it ruins the person's health and happiness. There is no variety or challenges, nothing to focus on or be interested in. Freedom is all around him, but freedom alone is a no-games-condition. You see time and again that persons retiring from all-consuming jobs die shortly after they retire and apparently for no good reason. It's not because they retired due to bad health. It is more likely that this dream, this glorious image with no action in it, was so an utterly no-games-condition when realized so the person died from boredom, lack of variety, and lack of interest in life in his new environment.

We strive after a life in luxury and in peace and quiet.
Once we attain it, we realize we miss the game.

The lesson to learn is: *there must be a game!* Achievement of goals can only briefly be celebrated; the joy they generate is short-lived. If our retiree in time had prepared a second career, or at least an activity that could interest him seriously, chances are that he could enjoy a long and interesting retirement. He would have had a new game to keep him active and interested in life. He would experience a long retirement in good health and happiness.

Freedom and Games

Freedom can only exist for an extended period of time when it is defined within rules and obstacles. When we have clear-cut rules that are enforced we have a game. There are things you mustn't do. Those are obstacles. There are things you are free to do. This is 'freedom' or maybe 'freedoms' as we know it. If there are no rules there is no game, no contest is possible. The freedoms are not clear either. If the rules aren't made known but enforced, we have a strange cut-throat environment similar to the one described in George Orwell's novel "1984". On the surface it may look like "the best of all worlds". It soon becomes clear, that this is just the sugar coating of a police state where citizens mysteriously disappear never to be seen again.

Obstacles in general consist of inhibiting ideas, as expressed in rules – or simply in the mores of a group and traditional thinking. Obstacles can also be space, energy, masses and time one has to avoid or overcome in order to succeed. Freedom as an abstract idea is the total absence of these barriers. Unfortunately, this is also a condition without thought or action, an unhappy condition of total emptiness. Surrounded by too many obstacles and barriers, we humans long for freedom. But once we arrive into the Utopia of total freedom, we find ourselves purposeless and miserable. There is only tolerable freedom when contained by obstacles and defined within rules. If the obstacles are known and the freedoms are known there can be life, living, happiness and a worthwhile a game!

If you have access to a group of pre-school children, you can easily set up an experiment to see these principles in action.

The first scenario would be where you allow the kids to do whatever they want to do; they can go to bed as late as they want; you never wake them up early; they have all the toys and indoors and outdoors space and facilities they would ever want; each kid has its own TV, video player, computer tablet, library of children's books, etc. They are free to fight with each other and they know you will never scold or punish any of them. You see your only role as satisfying their smallest needs and providing the things they seem to want. In other words, they have total freedom, or as close to it as possible in the real world. Soon you will see a group of kids that are constantly fighting, constantly misbehaving and unhappy most of the time. They will suffer from 'attention deficit disorder', 'hyper activity', be bored and constantly be misbehaving, including fighting each other, destroying property, giving you the hardest time they can dream up.

The second scenario is with a similar group of pre-school children. You may use the same facilities, only this time there is a clear set of rules and numerous do's and don'ts that are enforced fairly. The children have a clear schedule, including bed time, mealtimes and periods set aside for different activities. They have clearly defined indoors and outdoors activities and schedules. The resources given to each kid are sufficient but limited. Children that do well in the group are rewarded. Children that misbehave or attack the other kids are punished fairly. The rules are transparent, quite simple and evenly enforced. You expect the children to behave and perform. If they don't, they get punished in the form of reduced privileges, less treats, lowered status. You will see these kids become much better behaved, much happier, better capable of sharing and showing other social behaviors. They may protest bedtime, but once they know it is fairly enforced it will give them a sense of security and predictability. The evening when they for some unusual reason are allowed to stay up late will stand out as a very special evening in their memories.

Choosing of Games

To have a game you need the eight elements in one form or another. You should have team mates, allies and opponents or opposition. You need a purpose and a prize. In the game of life you see the formation of all kinds of games with strange alliances, rules and playing fields. When you look over the multitude of life forms, the abundance of possible playing fields on this planet and in this universe, you get the overall scope and possibilities of the games of life. All these venues and potential players offer the possibilities of organizing all kinds of teams and contests. Two groups can engage in a contest. This is a given opposition game in many sports. In commercial life we see competitive games within an industry. The relative success is here expressed in expansion rate and the market share one company gains compared to the others. In the military you see friendly competition among regiments and, of course, the hostile opposition game of war against an enemy army. In politics you see a competition among individuals and parties to gain voters. And you see opposition games among parties as they attack each other's political positions.

An individual can team up with animals and plants against, let's say, the physical universe and here we have a game. We can have a man and his horse conquering the vast space of the Wild West.

Any single individual is at any given time engaged in a number of games. By examining the potential playing fields and players of this person, one can map and clarify the various teams he is part of and those he is playing against. If an individual is only playing for him/herself, and not belonging to any other team, it is certain that this individual will lose. He/she has too much potential opposition from the remaining of life. This condition is known as self-centered egoism. The individual may look like the lone hero and live in that delusion. We will, however, find an individual who is overwhelmed by the rest of life and incapable of getting much done. The person is selfish to a degree that he/she can't form any needed alliances or is made the target of countless opponents across the boards. To enjoy life and succeed, one must be willing to be part of life across much broader spheres.

Levels of Engagement

We talk about three levels of engagement. The initial level is called **Self-determinism.** The person is in control of self and his or her side of the game. This is what we see in sports. There is a healthy level of competitive spirit, good energy, good control in tactics and execution. This is the state of mind of players of any game who enjoys the game and continues to do so. Clearly, we have the "them and us" situation of an opposition game, but none of the parties has declared victory or defeat. A person who is generally self-determined is in a healthy state of mind. The person can be combative or easy going as the case may be. The determining factor is if the person is in control of his/her side of life and is capable of overcoming obstacles in good spirits. The person can freely move around and 'play offense or defense' according to what is required.

Below self-determinism is the level of **Other-determinism.** The other-determined person is beaten down or losing; something else than self has taken control. The opponent can be another person or team. It can even be the person's own subconscious or repressed mind that has taken over. An Other-determined person has to a degree become a slave of something else. We see slave masters in the form of drug pushers, oppressive regimes, despotic organizations or victorious armies. But Other-determinism happens on many levels. Even mental illnesses, where the person has lost him- or herself to forces outside the individual's control, is said to be other-determined. Other-determinism comes about when the person has lost the game, or completely lost interest in it—yet, continues to be the unwilling or unknowing participant. It's a state of No-creation, a limbo where the person is dragged around. The person simply hasn't disengaged from the game.

Multi-determinism is a state where a person is in control of both sides of a game. It is above self-determinism. A referee is multi-determined in relation to the two competing teams. An executive is in the role of being multi-determined in relation to any conflict taking place among employees under his supervision. A chairman of the board of a large corporation is in the role of being multi-determined in relation to any conflicts between departments and even between different companies owned by that corporation. You could say a multi-determined person has graduated from a smaller game. The executive rose to the higher role through promotion. The chairman of the board rose to an even higher 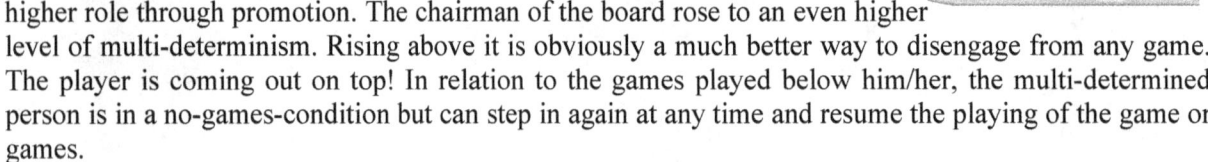 level of multi-determinism. Rising above it is obviously a much better way to disengage from any game. The player is coming out on top! In relation to the games played below him/her, the multi-determined person is in a no-games-condition but can step in again at any time and resume the playing of the game or games.

In summary: At any given time, any human being is engaged in a large number of games, knowingly and unknowingly, in the overall game of life. In many matters decisions are made elsewhere that may affect our lives radically. Yet, often there is nothing we can do about it. In some games we are moved like pawns in a chess game. We are other-determined in relation to such games. There are the games we engage in knowingly and openly and those are the games we are self-determined participants in. These games engage us by generating interest, contest, activity, emotional engagement and joy of possession. Finally, there are a considerable number of games we are multi-determined about. Teachers are, or should be, multi-determined to any games among their students. The executive is multi-determined to the skirmishes taking place on lower organizational levels. He is called upon to sort out conflicts and make decisions over the heads of the conflicting parties. These games are considered "old hat" or "kids' games" to the multi-determined individual. He/she can play them in his/her sleep. The multi-determined person knows them so well so they no more offer the contest, challenges and variety he/she wants from a good game.

Games and Happiness

Throughout this chapter we have pointed out that a major reason for the playing of games is the payoff in the form of all the emotions and sensations they generate. Emotions and sensations are the paymasters. They make us feel alive and engaged. They make it worthwhile to play. In chapter 4 we explained the affinity scale; a scale that plots all the major emotions in a succession of aliveness. The connection between games and emotion enables us to see the emotional scale in a new light. The scale can be seen as a scale of success: Ultimate survival and success at the top, failure, agony and death at the bottom. When things are going real well we move up on this scale, feeling happier and more alive. When we are having heavy opposition and barely are hanging on, we move down the scale. When we get pushed down into an overwhelmed and other-determined state of mind we are near the bottom of the scale. Our luck and happiness is at a real low.

Analyzing the connection between games and the affinity scale gives us a new insight about happiness. If we define happiness as being high on the affinity scale, we now have a way to *manufacture* happiness. If we engage in games in life that have a clear and constructive objective; games where the obstacles are possible to overcome; if we work at it hard and overcome those barriers – we are winning. When we finally achieve our objective we will experience a high level of satisfaction and happiness. If we keep engaging in winnable games and make sure to win most of them, we will have a successful life, full of emotion and sensation. We will work towards real satisfaction and happiness; we will enjoy life and sometimes be fully happy. The happiness is the ultimate reward for winning our most important games in life.

Such a moment of happiness is, however, an end-point of sorts. It's a no-games-condition. It won't last forever. It is quite transient. So enjoy the moment and the rewards but keep in mind that you have to dream up new worthwhile and obtainable goals. Engage in fulfilling them and simply keep on going and you will feel alive and sometimes real happy. So we need to have dreams (objectives), work hard at them, and realize the most important ones to experience the joys of life and the big moments of happiness. There are games we lose if we play for real. This is inevitable. Winning all the time after all isn't fun. So remember to learn from the losses. End the cycle of action on these games so they don't linger on as "burdens of limbo". Concentrate your energies and efforts on winnable games and work at it and your future is bright.

Much of what we do in Clearing can be understood as ending cycle on the lost games so they no longer are burdens of shame, blame and regret. They are no longer burdens you feel compelled to drag along. Having shed all this "luggage of limbo" we can concentrate our efforts and spirits on realizing our dreams and create a bright future.

Games and problems

Another way to look at this games theory is to look at it from the perspective of problems. A problem could be defined as 'an intention versus a counter-intention'; 'a purpose versus a counter-purpose'. You want to go somewhere but the car won't start. That is a problem. Or you want to go to point A but your spouse insists on going to point B. That is a problem too. Intention and counter-intention. Problems align very well with levels of engagement. A self-determined person will operate on a set of purposes which are often opposed by an opponent's counter-purposes. A person that is truly multi-determined in an area is above that as he/she controls both sides of the game. In the area the person is multi-determined in, he/she will have minimal problems of the type that makes up every day's annoyances. In feudal times, the tenant peasants may have struggled and starved. They may have been in fights with their lord of the manor; over payments and rights; over keeping their farmhouse and land; over keeping their own children at home, etc. The king, who was way above these conditions and fights, may not even have heard about their fights and plights. He could however interfere at any time to make things right. A sovereign king as an archetype is the clear expression of multi-determinism.

Other-determined persons (including the tenant peasants) will have undesirable problems all over the place. The counter-intentions they are up against in various areas seem so formidable so these persons are in a complete overwhelm.

There is however also another lesson to learn from this relationship between games and problems. The fact is, a person *without* problems seems to be unhappy. It has been proven repeatedly that if you come in and *solve* all the problems for a person, he/she will waste no time in engaging in other very similar situations with their problems. The person wants the objectives, obstacles, challenges and games of which these problems are an intimate part. As it works out in clearing, it has been established that problems are a commodity the person wants. The problems are attributes of the games the person is engaged in. Instead of solving the problems *for* the person, the clearer can work with a person's ability to *create* problems at will. When the client can create problems, bigger and bigger, he/she is capable of creating more desirable problems. The person becomes more self-determined and better suited to play a bigger game.

Games and Roles

In Clearing we see the individual as a very powerful Being – a Being who potentially is capable of playing any game successfully. This is not what we see in our fellow man and society today. The reason is that we have played so many games over the eons. Each life-time of our long journey of millions of years offered a new set of obstacles and conditions, a new environment with its rules and challenges. Each major game required that we took on the appropriate role in order to play the game at hand successfully. We had to "dress up for the game", so to speak.

This action of "dressing up", of taking on the appropriate role, can be illustrated this way, using the game of ice hockey. Here the players have to put on all types of clothes and equipment before entering the field. There is offensive equipment as the skates and hockey stick, allowing the player to play with speed and power. There is defensive equipment, such as the helmet, clothes and cushions that protect against blows and collisions – not to speak of insulation against the cold. What we have is a player optimized for the game of hockey but not much else. He wouldn't be able to drive a car, sit around and talk in the living room, hold a job in an office, work in a store, make love to his wife, etc. if he was stuck in that outfit.

Obviously, such a situation is far from optimum. But in one form or another, we all have such fixed identities. In DEEP we can deal with such unwanted fixated identities directly. This is done in what we call DEEP Character Clearing.

The cycle of action of a major game in life is: it starts out with a desire, a goal, a mission the individual pursues. Let's say, a woman sees her mission in life as 'to heal people'. To do that effectively she has to enter a healing profession. Let's say she decides to become a medical doctor. She goes to

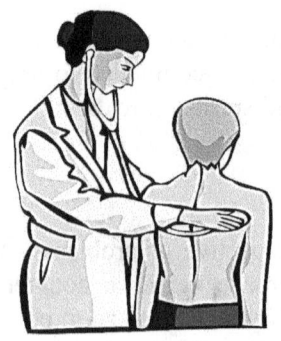

medical school to get fully educated in this role. This includes learning all the science, the medical procedures – all the skills of a doctor. It also includes joining the medical profession and acting professionally in the brother- and sisterhood of hospitals and clinics. The cycle of a career is: 1. We have a desire to do a certain line of work, make our contributions to society along these lines. 2. We become trained, educated and experienced in this profession. We assume the professional role and duties that is optimum for this line of work. 3. We do the role for years but finally get stuck in this role. 4. It becomes a fixed persona, identity or role that we carry with us. 5. We get into a new environment and game where this role is completely unsuitable. As a result, we have to overcome the confusion that this conflict generates. The confusion may reside on a subconscious or unconscious level. We restrain ourselves to be able to function somewhat in this new environment. As a result, the Being has to restrain self more and more. This goes on lifetime after lifetime. We manage to sort out some of these confusions but others stick to us.

In Clearing we can address these old confusions and identities and end cycle on the outdated and irrational ones. As a benefit from this work the client extracts the experience and wisdom contained in all this living. Clearing work resolves the subconscious and unconscious conflicts and releases the life force tied up in the past. Clearing converts old confusions and hang-ups to life experience.

Games and Clearing Work

Games and problems are intimately connected as we have seen. In doing Clearing, we work in the direction of higher levels of freedom and control—with multi-determinism as its ultimate goal. When we address the person's ability to have or not have problems, we are directly working on the person's ability to play a game. The practitioner will find games and problems across the client's spheres of engagement and the practitioner can help sort them out. Total multi-determinism across all parts of life is an ideal and theoretical level of having super-human awareness, control and understanding. It is worth striving for. We know, however, should we fully attain it, it would be a no-games condition. Since any client is engaged in almost an unlimited number of games, most of them outside awareness, we can safely take any game in sight and bring it up to a level where the client can be an active participant in it or rising above it and let it go. There will be plenty of other games now emerging over the horizon and coming into consciousness, games to engage in and play.

To be an active participant and enjoy the game the person needs to be self-determined about playing. To be able to leave the game behind, and still be in good shape, the person should rise above it and disengage through multi-determinism. During Clearing, many games long forgotten and now submerged, will surface. Most of these games can and should be disengaged from. Some games, closer to the client's immediate life, are better simply discharged and rehabilitated. Both disengagement and renewed engagement is accomplished by getting rid of the mental charge surrounding the problems of the game and by increasing the client's understanding of what he was, or is, engaged in.

Obsessive Games-Conditions: One particular condition is of interest beyond what's already discussed. There is a scenario often called an *obsessive games-condition*. The participants have engaged in an opposition game only partially known and understood. You have rivalries, in-fights and personality clashes where the objective is to defeat the other side although this is highly irrational in terms of practical value and survival. Such conflicts are routinely found to be dictated by the repressed mind. There may be a mis-identification of what or who the opponent is or what the opponent is seeking to do. One side may be living in a conflict of the past where the impressive opponent looked exactly like the colleague at work she is battling—or so she sees it. Maybe the colleague at work is fighting another fictive opponent in his behavior towards the woman. By sorting out the true nature of such an irrational games-condition and finding the true interests of the client, such obsessive games-conditions are usually resolved just by dealing with the one person doing clearing work. The client will be in a position to let it go and the other side will usually snap out of it as well if he is not pushed or provoked.

Unadvertised Games: Also, you will routinely see people engaged in "unadvertised games". They are supposed to perform a certain function but have long since constructed their own little game to replace that. They have other fish to fry. A person could, for example, be an investment adviser but now he overcharges costumers when he knowingly is giving bad advice. A woman could be in charge of hiring people for her company but she is really looking for a new husband rather than good workers. To really look at and understand the games around us, and the actual games we participate in, can be mind-blowing. In terms of games, it could be said that clearing work as its overall goal has to enable the client to arrive at a better understanding of the games he/she is part of and enable him/her to become a better player in the game of life.

Clearing work in general is designed along the lines of offering a game to the client, never a no-games-condition. Also, techniques address the games of life. In Eastern practices, such as many forms of meditation, the students are made to contemplate the highest virtues and the Divine Being for long periods of time. This may cleanse mind and spirit for many. It is, however, very different from the practice of clearing.

In Clearing, the client is guided into the bustling activities and confusions of his/her own life in order to sort out the games he/she is playing and the levels of engagement that exist. Obsessive games-conditions and "unadvertised games" will surface. Other-determined games the client has long forgotten about will as well. Severe losses in some important games-of-life will have impressed themselves deeply on the client as emotional scars. All this can be viewed through the Life-as-a-game theory and each game sorted out so the client can disengage from many unwanted games; become more self-determined about others; and multi-determined about most old games.

In DEEP we can address unwanted traits directly and trace them back to outdated roles and games. This takes some preparatory work where all the pressing issues of the present are being sorted out.

A clearing action cycle in general is a short and well defined cycle. The team locates an issue to work on. The client confronts it and looks at it from many angles and viewpoints. It's resolved and the client experiences joy and relief as a result. The goal is not for the client to disengage from all games in life but make the person more aware of the games he/she is engaged in and enable the person to overall "play a better game of life!"

Part 2: DEEP Theory

Chapter 10: Emotional Charge
Releasing the Power of Your Mind – from Within

Have you ever seen someone explode in anger or burst out in tears for apparently no good reason? Has it ever happened to you? Have you ever seen a driver erupt in road rage? Have you ever had irrational fears or felt hopelessness?

What we see or experience is emotional charge at work. It makes us say the wrong things at the wrong time. It makes us do irrational things that we regret afterwards; and it makes us feel unsafe, uncomfortable and even depressed although there is no obvious reason to feel that way. So what is this emotional charge? What do we know about it and how do we overcome it? That is what this chapter takes up and analyzes at some length.

Emotional charge can, for now, be described as a type of mental energy that somehow is stored in the repressed mind. Typical for emotional charge is that it is an emotional reaction that is disproportionate to the situation. The person is losing his/her temper; losing his/her "cool". The emotions have taken over, so to speak. The rational mind has been set aside. To better understand the nature of this emotional charge, also simply called charge, it is important to get a fuller understanding of emotion.

Emotions are Energy and Communication

We covered emotion and the affinity scale in chapter 4. We stated that emotion is a type of mental energy closely related to being alive. We stated that the higher the person is on the affinity scale, the more

energy and aliveness the person has available. We also learned that emotions act as signals to the body. Emotions generated by the Being affect the nervous system and the endocrine system and cells directly and enable the body and the person to respond physically to danger in one way and to positive things in another way. So emotions have some obvious physical effects on the body. Emotions can be understood as part of a communication system between the Being and the body, and between the person and the environment. The Being uses emotions to control the body to avoid danger and unpleasant things; and to approach and get needed and wanted things. Once these emotional responses are all settled in in the body-and-mind system they seem to work on their own. Situations and things get an emotional value assigned to them and the person "knows" what to think about them. Some little girl at the dinner table "knows" that fried chicken is "bad", and ice cream and pancakes are "good". She has assigned *emotional markers* to the different foods and they instantly tell her what to think and what to eat or not eat.

In a healthy state the emotions flow freely. We go up and down the emotional scale in response to the situations we deal with. We avoid or fight non-survival factors, dangers and all kinds of negative things. We seek and embrace survival factors, the positive things we need and want. So emotions energize us and help us respond well to the environment. A healthy emotional life, in fact, acts as a perfect guiding system; as a trustworthy compass. And it responds almost instantly to situations. We don't have to sit and think before we respond. This fact alone can be critical in the face of danger, physically or socially.

Another aspect of emotions is that they are an important part of our communication. If we want to relay any message effectively, we have to express ourselves with emotions. The emotions work as waves of energy. They travel on a different wavelength than thoughts and mere words. The printed word has a lot less impact than the spoken word expressed with emotion. The emotions energize the communication in their own way. Messages with emotional impact really communicate and can get others to act and react. Emotions in communication are so powerful that they can completely bypass rational thought. In politics, for example, some boring economist may know exactly how to fix the economy and country but nobody wants to listen to him; while some personable candidate knows exactly how to appeal emotionally to the voters and gets elected to office despite her lack of skills in economics. So emotions are important parts of our communication and interaction with others. The higher emotions on the emotional scale, such as strong interest and enthusiasm, are pure fuel. In the appendix you will find an expanded affinity scale. The expanded scale lists a number of levels above enthusiasm, such as elation, being in action, games, etc. They are levels that contain a lot of live energy. Such positive emotions are badly needed in order to succeed in any project, small or large. The lower emotions are just as important. They work as signals to the organism and to other people. They work as emotional markers. Antagonism and anger-signals express and fuel hostility towards someone or something that is seen as working against own survival and success. A signal is sent to the body to get in fighting mode. The person expresses antagonism/anger at the opponent or enemy. The anger is the fuel that provides the energy in an attack.

Pains are signals of acute danger on a body level. Fear expresses and signals danger and risk for overwhelm. "Get out of there before it is too late!" seems to be the message. The fear-signal is similar to pain but earlier and warns against looming pain and overwhelm. Grief can be a cry for help. Deep grief is a signal to pause, reflect and regroup. Apathy also has a clear function as a signal to the body to do nothing, or as a communication to an overpowering enemy of surrender. It may act as a white flag, if you will. There is an emotion of pretended death just below apathy where the person "plays dead" and maybe saves his life that way. The attacker simply walks away. So, even the "negative" emotions have clear functions. Also, the lower emotions, such as especially the anger band, are used to control others by stopping them from doing unwanted things. Other emotions, such as fear and grief, are used as an appeal to stop certain behaviors and are thus an attempt to control others by appeal. An emotion like enthusiasm is used to inspire and motivate others and control them by example and positive energy.

It is therefore important that the emotions flow freely and reflect the situation. It is important that we can express all the relevant emotions when communicating with others. If the person is stuck on one emotional level that doesn't reflect the situation, the person is less capable of handling the situation and getting others involved. An enthusiastic person, for instance, may act recklessly in critical situations where a bit of caution and fear would have saved the day. A too conservative or fearful person may never seize an opportunity offered to him/her. An entrepreneur may have a good project but lacks the emotional energy and charisma needed to get others involved.

What we do in DEEP clearing is to restore this natural state of freely flowing emotions. Our focus is therefore, for a large part, on emotions and feelings that are not flowing naturally but have been locked up in past incidents, situations, subjects and identities. These locked up emotions are the basis of emotional charge. If they "explode" out of context with the situation, we see these over-reactions and under-reactions described above in the chapter.

Also, during our history in life, we have installed a lot of arbitrary markers that the person needs to inspect and maybe revise. By unlocking these emotions we restore vital energy to the person. We restore a healthier and more balanced emotional life where the person acts and reacts on what *is*, rather than on what *was*.

Emotional Charge

Emotional charge appears to be an electrical phenomenon in the psyche. It can be understood as bottled up energy. It is mental energy that has been suppressed and repressed; its natural flow has been blocked. Release of this energy can be registered on a so-called bio-monitor or skin response meter (electro-dermo-meter). This instrument measures electrical resistance and changes in the resistance of the body and its energy field. When bottled up energy is released as a current of emotional charge, it shows up as a reaction on the bio-monitor. This coincides with the person feeling the emotional charge passing out of his/her system and a sense of relief. That one could register changes in the psyche this way has been known for over 100 years. Among others, The Swiss psychiatrist C. G. Jung experimented with such an instrument around 1906-07, and published an article about it in "Journal of Abnormal Psychology" in 1907.

The Biomonitor

The bio-monitor is an instrument that measures electrical resistance in the body and its energy field. When the introspector is asked questions that are emotionally charged, the instrument will give a reaction. The bigger the reaction the more charge is available to be discharged. Discharge of thoughts can be done by communication. The introspector is simply kept talking about the charged subject. Pains and heavy emotions will also cause the monitor to react. But here the discharge is best done using the pinch test method, described in the box below. (Photo: a Mindwalker 4)

The Pinch Test Method demonstrates how the bio-monitor registers charge. It is also a demonstration of a basic technique in DEEP, called *Repeating*. A volunteer holds the electrodes as shown in the photo. The person leading the experiment asks the volunteer to roll up his sleeve. With permission the volunteer is given a good pinch in the arm. This is painful and is only done with permission and as an experiment. The volunteer is now asked to let his attention wander and think of other things. The bio-monitor will show no particular reaction. The volunteer is then asked to recall the painful pinch. He will feel a shade of the pain and more importantly here, there will be a distinct reaction on the bio-monitor. Recalling the pinch several times, the pain as well as the reaction become less and less. Finally there is no meter reaction and this coincides with the moment where the volunteer feels no more pain from the pinch. The pain won't disappear by just talking about it. It will have to be accessed and re-experienced in its original form. The method is used in Repeating where a well-defined discomfort, a DEEP element, can be dissolved by repeated re-experiencing. There are many DEEP elements to be found in a traumatic incident.

When we follow up on this electrical aspect of emotions and emotional charge, we can learn something important about how to release this charge in clearing work. Also, a fuller understanding of this in DEEP clearing has enabled us to gain new insights in how to deal effectively with this phenomenon of charge that is so central to clearing and to any form of therapy and self-development.
We know from physics that electricity is a flow of charged particles between two poles. In a copper wire we have a flow of electrons between the positive and negative pole of a battery. So we have a plus pole and a minus pole and the electrical flow is generated between these two terminals. As long as the electrical circuit is intact, we have a normal flow between the two poles. We have useful energy we can

harness in all kinds of electrical appliances and devices. If the circuit is broken or if we have a short circuit the electricity won't flow. We have no result or an electrical disaster, such as a breakdown of equipment or a fire.

We have another electrical phenomenon known as static electricity. If we charge up an individual with static electricity, the hair of the person will stand on its ends as shown in the picture. This is a classic experiment in physics class. If the person then touches an electrical conductor, such as a water pipe, this overcharge of negative electrons will instantly flow and escape and the hair falls down to its normal position.

We can use what we know about electricity as an analogy to what happens in the mind regarding emotional charge. If we for now describe emotional charge as repressed emotional or mental energy in the mind, we get a situation similar to static electricity. We have electrical charge building up around one pole and with nowhere to go. The hair of the subject will literally stand on its end. If the person then flows this emotion and energy as a communication to someone else successfully, the bottled up energy is discharged and the hair will again flow naturally around the head of the person.

Just expressing or flowing this emotional charge can give some relief but the relief will not necessarily happen. It will have some therapeutic effect to "speak one's mind". It is well known that a "frank and heated discussion" can cleanse the air between two parties. But one big problem with most heated discussions is that none of the parties is really willing to listen. The one party tries to flow his/her charge to the other. But it is instantly cut off and met with an opposite flow of accusations. So an orderly line or connection that can carry the charge either way is never really established. Typically when the two sides part they experience a little relief as they have spoken their minds. The relief may be based on the fact that the party has clarified his/her own position to self. But since no orderly discharge took place the parties are likely to collide again in the near future and now with more intensity as their disagreements and positions are clearer. In the case of open hostility or war, there is absolutely no benefit or relief to find in "open exchanges or discussions". Instead, it is a spark-producing device, so to speak, where we don't have an orderly flow between the poles but an electrical discharge in the form of sparks and short circuit.

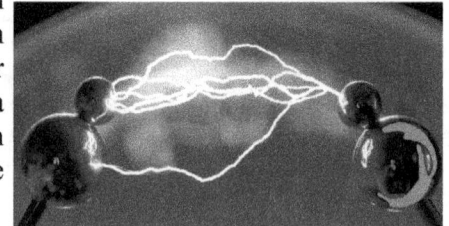

The most durable spark-producing constellation is where we have two enemies that are at war with each other. None of the parties has any intention to back down. Each party is "absolutely right" and the other party "completely wrong". Each party is completely unwilling to see the other party's point of view. In DEEP clearing we can address this kind of situation and mechanism by running viewpoints. This is covered in the next chapter and in the technical materials of DEEP Incident Clearing and DEEP Viewpoint Clearing. The introspector is made to view the incident or the long running conflict and war from both points of view, own viewpoint and the opponents viewpoint.

Inspecting the poles is what we do in DEEP clearing. The introspector is made to take a close look at the elements that built up the pole or poles in the person's own mind. These poles, also called mental ridges, have the characteristics of being "things". They have a tiny mass, they can generate energy, and they seem to have a location in or around the Being. They can be worked on as objects and physical phenomena. We do so to change their characteristics and eventually dissolve them. In DEEP we emphasize the introspection element. We have the client introspect the somewhat flimsy but still physical nature of what generates the charge. We are not that interested in rational explanations of "why the client and the client's spouse had an argument and reacted the way they did." Our objective is to have the introspector self-determinedly inspect the mental "machinery and electronic circuits" the person had installed at some point in time. We can help the introspector to change them to a more workable condition. We are entering a layer of the mind "where the lava is still hot" as one client put it.

Inspecting the Poles

It takes fixed positions or isolated poles in the mental landscape of the mind to generate emotional charge. Such fixed positions can be experiences and it can be identities the person has dealt with or identities and roles the person has taken on. It can also simply be emotional markers, emotional values the person has assigned to things. We assign these markers to friends and foes alike, to situations, entertainment, things, foods as mentioned, subjects, and so on. In some traumatic experiences the emotional markers are very strong. The person never wants to go there again! They seem to be bent in blinking neon as eternal warnings of horror! Yet, in DEEP clearing we can access them all and turn them off at the switch. The bothersome markers and responses from trauma and overwhelm are kept alive as subconscious warnings. They prompt a readiness and alertness, a fear if you will, to prevent the same thing from happening again. When they are activated they work as single poles that generate emotional charge and emotional responses. The emotions take over in a defensive routine that bypasses the rational mind. No orderly discharge is taking place.

So experiences, identities and things with their emotional markers make up the negative poles in the mind. Such a pole has, as mentioned, a tiny mental mass, typically contained in related mental holographic pictures. There are persons, animals and objects and phenomena in the pictures and each acts as a component within this pole. When a situation in the present warrants it, the pole becomes active. The charge gets regenerated. The emotion therein prompts a certain response that bypasses the rational mind. There is a generation of charge but no actual discharge as long as the negative pole remains hidden and completely out of awareness. Persons and clients in general often say "I want to get rid of the charge I have on such and such a subject." People have charge on anything from mother-in-law's, to cats, to the opposite sex, to authority figures, to spiders, to flying, etc., etc. They come in and want to get rid of this charge. That is why they go in therapy or want to do clearing in the first place.

Triggered charge can often be felt around the head. It can also lodge in body parts. It can be body parts that were injured in an accident; a bad shoulder, a stiff neck after a sports injury. Or an abdomen  filled with knots after an operation. It can also be charge that simply is stored in the body, not related to a physical injury. A body part is simply used as an available place where the charge can be deposited. We can for example address and handle the charge the person has on spiders and the person will experience that the neck feels less tense and stiff after the session. It is a futile endeavor to try to find out why this charge lodged in the neck. It seems that different clients have their own favorite part of their body where they store charge in general. It can be in solar plexus and stomach; it can be in neck and shoulders; it can be around the head or in the abdomen. It is usually within the torso and head. The so-called chakras also seem to be storage places for charge.

So if the person suffers from headaches of psychosomatic origin there is no reason to believe it stems from some head injury from past lives. The important thing to notice about triggered charge is that it is here now and can be perceived. Therefore it can also be addressed as a "physical manifestation" in present time by the introspector. No reason to chase endlessly in past lives to find out "the exact battle" where the person was injured or killed to cause this exact pain. When the clearer starts addressing the pain as a present time manifestation such an incident may turn up or not. If it does, it can be run as a traumatic incident. If it doesn't, the clearer can discharge the discomfort anyway. The most used method in DEEP is to have the introspector piece by piece experience the discomfort in session. This principle is described in the pinch test method above. (There are many other techniques found in the DEEP Toolbox that are used to discharge discomforts.) We have to search out the original discomfort. This technique can be used on emotions, efforts and other DEEP elements coming up. There is minimal pain connected to this. It is done very gradually and under professional supervision. The discomfort will soon disappear and a new related item is taken up. The clearer asks in turn for emotions, feelings, efforts and thoughts connected to the complaint and works on these aspects. When working on an item the discomfort will briefly be felt, then recede or completely disappear. When we say it has gone flat, it means: receded to a low level of discomfort but not totally gone. When we say it has blown, it means: it has completely dissipated or disappeared, sometimes in a spectacular way. Using the array of DEEP tools to work on a discomfort or emotional charge, and addressing it from different angles and viewpoints, including all thoughts, emotions, feelings and efforts surrounding it, it can be blown fully

DEEP—the Acronym

Scale of Physicality. At the top is non-material. At the bottom are physical body and physical matter.

In the above we talked about poles in the mind and the poles having mass, a degree of physicality. This discovery is very much at the center of DEEP. The acronym DEEP stands for Decision, Emotion, Effort (or Energy) and Polarity (or Point of view). 1. Decision is about what we think and decide. 2. Emotion is about what we feel; 3. Effort is about what we do. In common English we would say DEEP is about *subjective experience*. The poles that generate charge come about as a process that starts at Decision or thought. The decisions and thoughts evoke some Emotions. The emotions lead to Efforts and physical energy. Effort is about what we do. It is motion and concerns about motion. We are confronting the physical world with its forces and motions. So we have subjective experience of the Being meeting the real world and its forces. In the real world we are dealing with these physical forces and motions. In life the handling of motion and mass leads to more solidity and mass in the mind. Daily repeated efforts are also called habits.

> Efforts have a physical side and a mental side. A physical effort or force is a vector with a direction and a certain magnitude. The motorcyclist drives in a certain direction (e.g. north). The weight and the speed of the motorcycle determine the magnitude of the force. The dog's effort is the direction and amount of pull in the leash. If the biker ran into the tree, he would simply experience the tree's effort or force as a solidity and resistance. Efforts that work against a person or entity are called Counter-Efforts. Own efforts are simply called Efforts.
>
>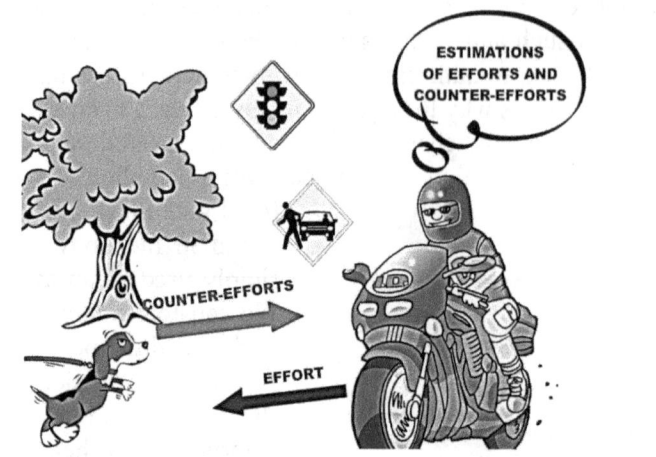
>
> Efforts also have a mental side. The driver must constantly estimate the counter-efforts he meets and his own efforts needed to overcome them. He keeps an eye on everything: pedestrians crossing the road, dogs on a leash or no leash; barriers like trees and traffic lights. Each counter-effort becomes a vector in the biker's mind. It has a direction (possible outcome and impact) and a certain speed or force assigned to it. Through experience the biker has made mental vectors of all kinds of counter-efforts and needed own efforts to overcome them. He uses these data and experiences to estimate situations with their dangers and his options
>
> Should the biker be so unfortunate to collide with the tree, the impact and injury would be recorded mentally as an effort colliding with a counter-effort. In this case it produces pain and injury. We can address the mental or psycho-somatic side of this by addressing the two colliding vectors or forces separately. By running the counter-effort and effort, one after the other, the solidity of the injury can be resolved and the pain be relieved.

An important factor in bringing about this solidity is that efforts are met with counter-efforts (see illustration). It can be in the form of opposition from other people or resistance from the physical universe. It takes work to overcome the physical universe. Also being hit by a physical object is a counter-effort in our use of the term.

Emotions are likewise met with counter-emotions, as in a heated discussion or a dramatic situation. Thoughts are met with counter-thoughts, as in a debate, a chess game, or in problem solving where all the options are considered. Through these natural processes solidities and poles form in the mind. We have the P in DEEP that stands for 'Polarity' or 'Point of View'. In a polarity we have two poles in conflict. P as 'Point of view' means we have one pole, not necessarily in conflict but simply holding some position, either physically or mentally. So the acronym DEEP stands for Decision, Emotion, Effort/energy, Polarity/point of view and those elements and their variations are what we address. We can address two poles in conflict that generate charge between them – or one pole that generates emotional charge around itself like static electricity. When we are dealing in one pole there is still plenty of counter-thoughts, counter-emotions and counter-efforts to be found inside, which led to the formation of this pole. There is no shortage of games and abandoned games in this universe – and remnants of all this is what makes up the DEEP elements of the mind.

Above the thought-emotion-effort bands we have 'non-material' in our illustration. This is the realm of knowingness; of pure data. Here we have understanding it its purest form (see chapter 6). When we understand something fully it becomes a non-material knowingness. We know something without the need to think about it, feel about it or have physical contact with it.

It is of course obvious that efforts or actions can lead to emotions that can lead to thoughts, so in practice it is not a one way street from thought to emotion to effort and habit. In dialectic materialism, as formulated by Karl Marx, thought is only seen as a reflection of the material universe: a person sees something and describes it in words and the words are the thoughts. According to this philosophy there is no thought prior to motion. (Motion is, we repeat, what we call effort/counter-effort in these materials). Thoughts, according to Marx, come about when we observe or experience the physical universe at work. New thoughts come about when two forces collide and the observer or experiencer mirrors the two forces and combines them into a new thought, a synthesis. In our opinion this strictly materialistic view is too narrow. The flow goes both ways and thought by itself is a powerful force, not just a mere reflection of the physical universe. Efforts and energies give birth to new thoughts but new thoughts also give birth to new efforts and energies.

Thoughts can lead to efforts
and efforts can lead to thoughts.
The physical world inspires us
but we also have new ideas
of our own we want to build.

DEEP Element > < DEEP Element

There are many small vectors inside a pole and between poles. The conflicting forces and the layers of thoughts, emotions and efforts make up a confusing structure which is perceived as a solidity.

We have:

Thought><Counter-Thought
Emotion><Counter-Emotion
Effort><Counter-Effort
Pole><Counter-Pole
There is also DEEP element against DEEP element:
Thoughts>< Emotions
Thoughts>< Efforts
Efforts>< Emotions

It may be perceived as a confusion as in the illustration. In practice it is not that complicated to work with. We see it as opposing vectors. We simply complete one element after the other, one vector and the opposing one, until it all is gone. Usually it falls apart long before all the formal steps are done.

In practical DEEP clearing work, we work with well-known issues, such as fears, upsets, problems, traumatic incidents, relationships, roles and identities, etc. First we get the story. Then we take up that DEEP element the introspector offers and work the layers of effort, emotion and decision in the most accessible order. Since emotion always seems to be available in working with DEEP items, that is where to start, unless there is a clear indication to the contrary. It is however a long standing clinical observation and fact that Decisions and Thoughts are the most important elements to arrive at in clearing up charge. 'Decision' is the General in an army. It is the top manager and CEO of a corporation. The thoughts surrounding a major decision could be said to be the staff officers surrounding the general in an army. In a corporation 'thought' compares to the top management level. So decision and thought are not mere reflections of what is happening in the physical universe: what is happening on the battlefield when we talk army. Or what is happening in the company and marketplace when we talk corporations. Decisions and thoughts are the controlling forces that hold the form: they keep the soldiers in line and the enemy at bay; they shape the corporation and its strategy in the marketplace.

The order of importance in clearing work is decision and thought at the top. Emotion and effort may compete for second place. In physical injury incidents the effort is ranked higher than emotion.

Physical pain, by the way, comes about when two efforts collide. In emotional incidents, emotion ranks higher than effort/physicality. Still, in any type of DEEP work the most important element to arrive at is the decision and thought level buried in the issue. And the central irrational decisions are the most important of all to find and discharge. They work as Dictates from the Repressed Mind. Only when they are cleared up is the issue fully dealt with, only then is permanent change possible.

What makes DEEP more effective than maybe all other self-improvement and therapy systems is however that we address any issue on all three levels. If only the thought level is addressed on an intellectual level, results are very poor as in early psycho-therapy. If we get the central thoughts and decisions that were made at the time the issue formed, the results are usually very good. If we unburden the area for its emotions and efforts and then get the thoughts and decisions that hold the whole issue in place and alive, the results are spectacular. The emotions and efforts don't necessarily just clear up by themselves. It is not enough that the top management of a company realizes what has been wrong with their strategy in the past. They have to make the whole organization understand and realize not to stick to old routines but bypass them and clear them out of the system so the staff can follow the new strategy with some enthusiasm. Otherwise the old emotional and behavioral habits and routines will still have a life of their own – and that needs to be addressed directly. So by clearing up the existing emotions and efforts we address the whole spectrum and we get better access to the decision level where we find the important decisions more readily. Also, the barriers to implementing a new strategy are removed. There is made room for a fresh start not burdened by bad habits and old routines and the lack of enthusiasm. If you only get the rational explanations of an issue, as in early 20th century psycho-therapy, it can be compared with some professor in a business school understanding what went wrong; an insight that only by chance will have some influence on the company in question and its performance. In early psycho-therapy there also was this wrong idea that it was only the psychiatrist that could understand the patient's case. The psychiatrist was a medical doctor who had specialized in psycho-therapy. From medical practice the psychiatrist was used to diagnose the patient and then *do* something to the patient. The psychiatrist would maybe conclude, "What is wrong with you is that your father was an alcoholic" and that was the end of the "treatment." In clearing practices, including DEEP, the approach is radically different. The practical session approach is covered in a later chapter. But in this context it should be said, that the most important element is that *the introspector* understands his/her case and sees his/her life in a new light due to the clearing – not that the clearer understands all the finer details. And quite frankly, *the introspector has to do the hard work.* The clearer merely guides the introspector with a light hand. Often the clearer can bring about positive radical changes in the client without knowing exactly what is going on and without the least need for "diagnosing and treating the patient".

Intention as Cause

We emphasized in the above the importance of reaching the thought level in clearing work. A definition that reflects that can be found in Frank A. Gerbode's book, "Beyond Psychology – an Introduction to Metapsychology" (2013). He defines Charge as repressed, unfulfilled intention and attention (See footnote 1 at end of chapter.)

Seeing it as a repression of intention and/or attention underscores several important aspects. It underscores that charge is a bottled up phenomenon and that the person can do something about it. 'Intention' is a thought-form that produces energy; and 'Repressed' means it is being stopped by the person herself or possibly by an outside force. Attention is a thought-form as well; and repressed attention means that the person simply gets overwhelmed and refuses or fails to experience what happened. If the person can overcome any resistance to either execute or perceive and freely let the intention or attention flow to its completion the cycle is ended. There is no energy-producing intention/attention left to repress. The Intention, of course, can also simply come to consciousness, be reviewed and be ended or canceled by the person.

Often the intention in question is very irrational or socially unacceptable and the person – or society around her – will actively repress it. This means that the person will repeat irrational behaviors over and over without knowing exactly why. It won't really complete as the intention itself is hidden and repressed. When brought to consciousness the person can therefore simply see it for what it is and decide to withdraw it – simply end cycle on it by canceling it.

When it comes to repressed attention it is usually the result of an overwhelm. What took place happened too fast; was too violent or hurtful; too embarrassing or humiliating; too painful or life-threatening and the person was unable or refused to take it in. The person simply couldn't process what was happening. The person will not only shut off what apparently happened; the person will also shut off experiencing own reactions (thoughts-emotions-efforts) to the event. Undoing these repressions and have it all flow to their completion or end cycle on them is what we do in any successful stress and trauma therapy.

Outside Repression

The repression of intention may apparently come from the outside in the form of disapproval or opposition. This can be hard for the client to detect as something he/she can do anything about. In DEEP we resolve this situation by running the repression from the viewpoint of the repressor. The person has internalized this opposition and it is this internal battle that is playing out. By apparently viewing the conflict from the opponent's point of view it resolves easily. That is how we handle repression or counter-vectors. This is covered at length in the next chapter about Points of view/Polarities – the "P" in D.E.E.P.

It can of course also be the person stopping herself in doing or saying something she will regret. This is what we call a Secondary Effort. It can be run as such.

"I Love My Story"

In classical 20th century psycho-therapy the therapist would trace the patient's difficulties back to childhood and consider the work done. "Your mother loved your sister more than you, and that's why..." "You were teased and bullied in school and that's why..." etc. Many patients loved this. They now had acceptable answers for their shortcomings and problems. But as the American psycho-therapist and life coach, Debbie Ford, points out: "We live inside our stories." "We love our story." She also says that unless we break out of this "our story", we shall not expect a radical change or improvement. We can only expect to feel a little better about ourselves and continue "our story" by adding new chapters. We can add happier chapters to being "an abused child", growing up with alcoholic parents, "being an emigrant", etc. But we still define ourselves in that role rather than starting a new game where we use all our abilities and power. To really move on, we have to leave the role of 'victim of abuse' and even 'survivor of abuse' behind us and redefine ourselves. If we release our power from within the road is open to be who we really are, leaving behind "our story" with its limited role as the butterfly leaves behind the caterpillar. In various regression therapies, including past lives recall therapies, "the story" is also emphasized, but in quite a different way. You take up stressful or traumatic incidents and go through them repeatedly. Then you ask for an earlier similar incident to run. And when that is run you ask for an even earlier one. In this fashion you can go hundreds, thousands, even millions of  years back in time. This is all very fascinating by itself and often very therapeutic. For one thing, it makes the client realize that his/her existence isn't limited to this one body. But still, running all these incidents is all about the story. "I fell out of a spaceship 10 million years ago and that is why I am afraid of heights." In the best of these modalities the irrational intention or decision at the bottom of this is looked for and found. They know the importance of finding the original decision or thought. The unfortunate astronaut may have said to himself, "oh, I am lost. I will never see my loved ones again!" And that in a sense explains his fear of heights. I am trained in a number of these modalities and have practiced the regression approach extensively. I had a great time as a practitioner and as a client, receiving clearing, with these modalities. I have been inspired by them. I was especially inspired by Robert Ducharme's R3X. Yet, I often saw regression therapy clients who were all excited and blown out at the time but when it all settled down were still afraid of heights.

And here we are at the point I want to make: unless you take great care in flattening the emotions, efforts and decisions as you go along running a series of incidents, these elements are not gone for good. They will stick up their ugly heads at a later time. On the other hand, if you take care of flattening these DEEP elements as you go along, the "fear of heights" may have permanently disappeared after running one or two incidents thoroughly.

The emotional charge is not the same as the story. The emotional charge and all the DEEP elements for that matter, have to be addressed directly to be flattened and blown. Experiments along the lines of the pinch test method strongly support that. One experiment, done in 2011, is available as video at our Youtube account for the Ability One Group. We ran a series of incidents with an older incident running technique and then reran the same incidents with DEEP Incident Clearing. There was plenty of charge left to handle and this got completely handled with DEEP tools. And this experiment shows the difference and validity of the DEEP approach. The heavy emotion and the other DEEP elements—each element needs to be fully experienced as itself, outside the context of any story it is part of to be permanently dealt with.

In DEEP Incident Clearing we do use the personal story, the story of the loss, the accident or stressful situation. But we use the story to find a string of DEEP elements we can work on. The real change in the case comes about when we have permanently dealt with all the DEEP elements related to an issue. It soon becomes clear to new DEEP practitioners that the client's favorite DEEP elements are not just stemming from one incident. They are used again and again in the client's life as a personal style of living, of emoting and thinking. They are used in a similar fashion as novelists have their favorite expressions and their favorite ways of describing persons and incidents in their novels and stories.

Releasing the Power of Your Mind—from Within

In conclusion of running "our stories" versus running DEEP elements, let me say this: We tend to consider and react to our story. After all, it is so interesting, so fascinating. It makes us unique. But we tend to overlook the tiny masses and poles, the DEEP elements our story or stories activate and string together and re-enforce in the mind. Telling one's story is a first important step in therapy but a limited one. After all, it is concentrating on the past and not the future nor one's future development. When we take great care in flattening the DEEP elements we encounter in clearing as we go along, the internal landscape of the person's mind changes to the better. The decisions, emotions and efforts used in one incident are part of the person's basic vocabulary and style, so to speak. They are elements the person uses again and again when dealing with all kinds of situations. By blowing the most irrational ones and helping the person to get the others under control as a personal vocabulary he/she can use or not use, we assist the person in becoming more open and flexible in mind and spirit. We help the person to be able to do new things and pursue higher and more ambitious goals. We help the caterpillar become a butterfly.

1. Footnote: Dr. Gerbode's definition of charge is actually: "Charge is repressed, unfulfilled intention". But he explains in the text that Attention is a form of intention. "You have to *intend* to pay attention to something." In other words, in his definition the word Intention covers what we call Intention and Attention – as explained in chapter 2.

We find his formulation can be confusing to some students. So to follow the terminology of this book we use this form: "Charge is unfulfilled intention and attention." Also, we have found, and explain throughout the book, that all the DEEP elements present have to be addressed in order to fully handle the charge in a stressful or traumatic incident.

Chapter 11: Viewpoints, Identities, Polarities

There is power in viewpoints. Strongly held viewpoints have been known to change history. An example would be Martin Luther, a simple German monk, who around 1517 stood up against Rome and the Catholic Church and made it tremble in its foundation. His views led to the creation of the Lutheran Church that now has spread throughout Northern Europe and throughout the world.

Also his name brother, Martin Luther King of the Civil Rights Movement in the 1960s USA, had very little resources but a strong belief and viewpoint. His steadfastness eventually made the white establishment surrender to the black Americans' demands for respect. Now there is a street in every American city named after him.

There are countless other examples like this from history. Negative examples would be dictators like Adolf Hitler, and Josef Stalin who held very strong and extreme political views. They got into power based on these views and caused the death of millions as a result.

Power, it could be said, is simply the ability to hold a position. In the case of for instance Hitler, he had of course the back-up of the Nazi party and the military enabling him to hold his position. But Nazi Germany started with an idea and a strong, if destructive, point of view. The Reformation by Martin Luther started from a strong and righteous idea, a clear point of view the monk wouldn't back down from. So did Martin Luther King and the civil rights movement.

The difference from simply a strong idea and what we here call a point of view is that a strong point of view develops into an identity with decisions, thoughts, emotions, actions and habits. It has goals, ideals and routines. So the strong point of view quickly develops into an identity. An identity may develop into a political movement or an organization. It seeks to have all the elements necessary to succeed. It develops and organizes itself over time to better succeed in forwarding its basic goal and mission.

Points of View and the Mind

The focus of this book is not politics or history. So let us turn to individual lives, to the human mind and psyche.

We talked about poles of the mind in the last chapter. The most powerful poles of the mind are points of view. It can be own points of view and other people's points of view. We hold some points of view of our own and we have a clear idea of the points of view that surround us and we sometimes are up against. These are other people's points of view we have a copy of. We don't necessarily agree or disagree with their behaviors or opinions; they are simply imprinted as small models or programs in our minds. We are holding these viewpoints in our own minds and you could say we have

set up a mental model of our outer world that tells us what to expect and not expect. Like kids play with dolls they name Mommy and Daddy, Brother and Sister, we have set up this internal world populated with characters important in our lives. In our own minds we find friends and opponents, helpers and people who wanted to take advantage of us. When we talk traumatic incidents there are notoriously perpetrators and wrong-doers who we may only know from the length of the incident; be it a robber in a robbery or a motorist in a car accident, etc. The point is that all these characters, all these points of view with their characteristics, are alive as imprints in our own minds. They exist as toy models and imprints in our psyche. They exist as small programs and routines, complete with expected behaviors, feelings and thoughts.

They exist internally in our minds independent of the external, the real person, who may, or may not, act in the same fashion as their counter-parts do in our mental world.

This state of affairs, having poles to love or hate, to fight or fear, to agree or disagree with, actually links up to chapter 9, "Life as a Game". Because these points of view we hold, these characters populate our games of life. We see other people and the external world through this filter of our internal mental characters. We tend to classify our experiences and the people populating them according to this gallery of characters that are imprinted in our own psyche; and we tend to act and react based on that. In the following we introduce the most important DEEP techniques and how viewpoints or identities are an intimate part of what we address. We use, 'points of view', 'identities' and 'characters' as synonyms in DEEP.

Points of View in DEEP Incident Clearing

DEEP Incident Clearing is the DEEP technique for clearing traumatic experiences. We have the 'P' in DEEP meaning 'Polarities' or 'Points of View.' In a physical trauma we can have two persons colliding, resulting in an injury. To deal with that in session we view the two sides, the two colliding vectors, separately. First we review the experience of the injured person. We have the introspector view what happened from his/her own viewpoint, the victim's point of view. Then we have the introspector take the point of view of the outside force (the wrong-doer, the repressor) hitting self, the to-be-injured person, and the introspector carefully reviews that. The surprising thing is that our victim has a detailed recording of the other person's subjective experience as well. Not only the other person's movements but also an amazing amount of details about the other person's state of mind, including his/her motivation at the moment of the collision.

For example, a soccer player is tackled by an opponent player and is injured. First we run the victim's own experience and body memory of the accident. This means we return the introspector to the incident and have him go through it as if it were happening right now. After doing that several times, the introspector will experience some relief. We also find his emotions, thoughts and decisions. But that is only half the work.

It was the opponent player who was the negative cause of the victim's injury. So the

normal human reaction is to blame it on the wrong-doer and leave it at that. It may be hard to see how the clearer or victim could do anything about that. However, the injured person has this detailed recording of the other player's actions from that player's point of view. And the amazing thing is that it is really the conflict between these two separate *recordings* both internally held by the victim, these two vectors, which cause the *permanent* damage! What we mean by 'permanent damage' is that once the injury is healed the victim may still have long term effects from the collision in the form of fears, aches and pains that now don't have an immediate physical explanation. It is often heard in football that old injuries keep plaguing players and that these old injuries make the players more fearful and less brave when playing ball. It is like the body and mind are presented with all kinds of warning signs that pop up when a similar situation comes about on the field. The aches and pains, stemming from the now fully healed injury, are ways the body warns the player against repeating the injury. What we seek in clearing is not to make players completely fearless and reckless. But we do want to free such a player from the 'inexplicable pains' so he can assess situations on the field without such luggage. Instead of responding based on repressed memories, the player can respond based on his experience. He can do a split second risk evaluation and attack the ball with optimum courage and aggressiveness. Sometimes, of course, he will conclude that the risk is greater than the potential gain. In other words, instead of becoming an injured player once again or one afraid of the game, he has become smarter and wiser about the game and of greater value to himself and the team.

He will no longer be plagued by the psycho-somatic aftereffects of old injuries. And due to his experience he will be subject to fewer injuries now and in the future.

The Other Viewpoint

The way we address and eliminate the outside force (the opponent player) is the following: *We have the introspector (victim) assume the viewpoint of the other player* and have our hurt person go through the incident from that point of view. We neither need to call in the opponent player nor contact him telepathically—or anything like that. We simply have the victim see the incident through the opponent's eyes. We are talking about the victim's internal copy of the opponent's point of view. This is the opposite vector, the repression that holds the incident suspended. This runs beautifully with a wealth of details that amazes the victim and everyone. Again, an amazing amount of details of the opponent's perceptions and the opponent's emotions, feelings, thoughts and decisions are available to us in session—to the introspector and the clearer.

By working both sides, the two colliding vectors, the mental mass (the ridge) in the mind will dissolve and the person can now come up to present time, so to speak. The frozen moment in time, battling a hostile force or opponent, has become liquid and can now resolve and it virtually evaporates. The same polarity can be explored when it comes to emotion and thought.

The difference from running an incident just from the victim's viewpoint and running the same incident from all charged viewpoints is quite significant. This is because any resistive charge in the mind is so resistive because it is a confusion of colliding vectors. If we were hurt in a car accident we may rightfully blame it all on the offender. It was her fault and the court agrees and has ruled it that way. It was after all her that ran a red light. But in session it is important that the introspector examines his/her part in holding the opposing viewpoint, the opposing vector, in place; because it is this colliding viewpoint that is the other side of the ridge. It contains the opposing forces. When the introspector is made to put on the wrong-doer's glasses, or for a short while is made to walk in in the perpetrator's shoes, or drive the colliding driver's car, the recordings are suddenly seen for what they are. *The two sides are held suspended against each other in the introspector's mind* – and realizing that the whole thing falls apart.

It has surprised many an introspector to be able to "read the opponent's mind" by reviewing the incident from the opponent's viewpoint in session. Apparently, this information was recorded at some subconscious level when the incident originally took place. It went however unnoticed at the time and every time the person looked back at the incident. Maybe the pain, horror, confusion, etc. of what happened made it hard to look at. The person just wanted to forget the whole thing. Consequently the recordings from these viewpoints persisted. In the safe situation of the session with a trusted person as guide the introspector can now recover all the details. It seems quite magical to be able to retrieve all these details years later. And often the introspector will realize that the motivation of the opponent was much more benign and caring than believed.

In DEEP Incident Clearing we will often view incidents from many points of view. Not only the victim's and the wrong-doer's. But also other participants, be it other drivers, the police, onlookers, etc. We can even ask the introspector to see it all in a bird's eye view. As long as there is emotional charge we can run a viewpoint with benefit. In a sense the session can be compared to using many cameras in film and TV to get all the angles and details. Since the original mental recordings of the incident are "holographic recordings", recordings we can see in 3 dimensions and with a lot of details and perceptions, this makes sense. Ideally the introspector will recreate the experience of being there, the full 3-D experience with sounds, smells, motions, emotions and thoughts. When that is brought about the introspector has permeated the recordings fully and the solidity of the scene will dissolve. It is as if the recordings stayed solid and in place and waiting as a reminder for that moment of full pervasion. A metaphysical interpretation of this could be that it stays in place until we have learned our lesson; until we have transformed the trauma or overwhelm situation into a life experience. The fact is that full pervasion and understanding of an overwhelm situation or trauma makes it cease as an overwhelm or trauma. We have mastered it and can move on a little wiser and more experienced. It is quite magical!

Is the Client Prepared?

The above session outcome is not happening every time and for everyone. Fortunately we can produce excellent results with less than the ideal situation. Some clients have poor memories and can only retrieve part of it. To other clients it is too overwhelming to dive into these trying times of the past. A lighter approach is called for. Therefore it has to be pointed out that the DEEP techniques are  advanced techniques and may appear too difficult for some to start out with. In our own practice we use many other clearing techniques with inexperienced clients. The most basic one is simply to be a good listener and help the client sort out his/her own thoughts. But our approach when we do DEEP is that clearing is a journey from being an ordinary human being towards higher states of being. Our potential as spiritual Beings is just about unlimited and impossible to imagine. In developing the DEEP techniques, our goal has been to push the frontier upwards. The DEEP techniques are not necessarily the fastest techniques around. During development we have had these two criteria in mind: to produce stable results and to help the person obtain higher states of being. We know practitioners who boast they can handle all the client's complaints in 5 hours. They cannot find anything to clear after that. We have checked out several of these techniques. We found them beneficial but we could see plenty of room for improvement in the client at the end of such a run – and so could the client we may add. Therefore we take such claims as being the way these services are being promoted rather than being something that can be substantiated. To obtain stable results and spiritual progress, not just spiritual high-points and occasional blowouts, does take some hard work and dedication. DEEP is devoted to those people who are willing to do this work and then reap the rewards. We hope and believe that you are one of them.

DEEP Character Clearing and Viewpoints

DEEP Character Clearing (DCC) is our most advanced technique. Oddly enough, it is also the first technique developed in DEEP. This was simply because our first motivation was to move the limit for personal development upwards. The action will be covered in detail in a later book. In this book we only cover the principles of the action. In this chapter we cover what is relevant to viewpoints, identities and characters.

In DEEP Incident Clearing we often dealt with wrong-doers who were strangers to the introspector. Still, the introspector could find an internal imprint of such a person's behavior and character for the length of the incident. In DEEP Character Clearing we address long term relationships, usually troubled ones, those that haunt us and keep us awake at night. We typically deal in archetypes and "karmic enemies." In other words, we deal with long term opposition games of life, with their goals and players. Even though these games are also taking place between real people, the players are being colored by the identities anchored in our own psyche. The games we play with them seem to follow old scripts that repeat themselves. The 'P' in DEEP here stands for Polarity, a counter-pole, rather than just diverging points of view.

"The battle of the sexes" is an example of a classic opposition game. The battles a typical human being has had with spouses, fiancées and "exes" have made their marks.

When you look at an average Being's karmic history there are countless such relationships and battles. Many different roles have been played by each spouse. The person carries all these patterns of behavior in the subconscious mind. The patterns and games are repeating themselves in new relationships. When we handle identities in DCC we have the introspector look at these roles, one at the time. Own role and the opponent's role are both carefully discharged. So are the ideas and goals they operate on. After completing DCC the person can rise above playing these strange and destructive games.

There are a number of modalities in existence that are dealing with these opposition games and polarities. We have examined a number of these techniques that already existed. A common denominator was that they emphasized running the goals rather than the identities. We found this to be a grave error. We found that it was crucial to spend up to 90% of the time on dealing with the identities. In dealing with the thoughts, emotions and efforts contained in the identities we are dealing directly with the mental masses and ridges. Of course, the goals also had to be inspected and diffused so the mechanism wouldn't simply charge up again in life. But unless we first took care of the tangled substances in the identities it wasn't really possible. It wasn't possible to get to the goals as they were surrounded with high voltage electrical fences, so to speak. We wanted to get past the fences and find the switch that could turn off the power that energized fences as well as the goals. Just going for the goals was like spotting lightning at a distance. There was no access and no switch in sight.

The research that led to DEEP Character Clearing was started in 2005 and it took several years and a lot of trial and error before it became clear that the way to go was to concentrate on the identities rather than the goals. In the present form of DCC we spend several hours concentrating on one identity, then we go on to look at the other side, the opposing identity and spend several hours concentrating on that. It may seem slow and tedious in terms of number of goals handled. But as we go forward we find that it was time well spent. Much of the basic charge on the case has been removed and therefore the clearing work goes faster as we go forward. It is the completing of the first pair or the first couple of pairs that really changes the outlook of the person. The person moves up the scale of determinism from other-determined through self-determined to multi-determined (see chapter 9, Life as a Game). The person expands his/her viewpoint from living in a little box – to viewing the world from a mountain top concerning a basic conflict in the person's life. The overall end result of the running of DEEP Character Clearing is a high level of multi-determinism; an ability to embrace friends and foes alike with compassion and savvy. You don't fall for a potential opponent's tricks to pick a fight. Your ability to network and gaining power through this form of expansion is evident. We don't claim that you will gain super-natural powers. You won't be capable of teleportation or materializing objects into existence by thought-power alone.

But you will shed many false identities, false characters as we call it. After shedding these false characters, the Being gets into its own character, the person becomes his/her true self. You will be capable of seeing yourself in others; seeing their basic good intentions and *their* struggles to survive and succeed. So the outcome is a higher level of wholeness, a higher level of integrity that comes naturally with shedding false characters that were obsessively engaging in conflicts, infights and obsessive games-conditions. Your increased ability to seeing yourself in others also extends to having a more flexible mind, a richer imagination as you can see their points of view. You can see new points of view; create new and more constructive games – complimentary games where everybody wins.

DEEP Subject Clearing

In DEEP Subject Clearing (DSC) viewpoints and identities play a smaller role. The technique addresses troublesome subjects. It can be anything from 'fear of spiders' to 'early school days' to 'my career' to 'doing my chores' to 'dealing with the boss', etc. We simply take up subjects the person has charge on and wants to handle. The action is more exploratory. We don't have all the details yet. It is well suited for less experienced introspectors as well as for entering a new area with a more experienced person. Using a number of questions, we get the introspector to look at all angles surrounding the issue. A question may uncover a DEEP package that is taken up once that question has been answered. Based on the data uncovered in DEEP Subject Clearing we can later address the issue with other techniques. Central identities and incidents to the subject are routinely found and can subsequently be addressed fully.

DEEP Body Clearing, Basic Version

In DEEP Body Clearing (DBC) we view the body as an organized collection of organs under the person's command. The body works like a human organization. There are local command posts that need to be in touch with levels of command above it and below it. But we also have body parts and organs that may have local problems. We address these trouble spots and view them from the body part's point of view as well as from the person's point of view. The introspector can actually have a conversation with an ailing kidney, find out what the kidney is complaining about and hopefully remedy the matter. DBC is mainly intended to get the person in better communication with his/her body. It is neither a medical procedure nor a body work procedure; just a light first aid based on communication that should be followed up by an examination and treatment by a health professional if something is found wrong.

A more comprehensive version exists in training materials. In Deep Body Clearing many aspects of a spiritual being dealing with the physical body are examined and cleared.

DEEP Viewpoint Clearing

DEEP Viewpoint Clearing (DVC) is an alternative DEEP technique for running incidents. It is alternative to DEEP Incident Clearing where the story and the mental picture recordings of the story are at the center of interest. In DVC we review an incident based on the characters taking part in it. We examine each charged player's or participant's state of mind, including the introspector's. The technique has proven valuable with experienced clients as running incidents after many sessions can become tedious. But the characters, their roles and the games they play with each other are still charged.

Introspectors, who for various reasons were reluctant to running incidents, are raving about DVC and the results they got from it. So finding an alternative technique for dealing with stressful experiences and traumatic incidents was a high priority. We have come up with DEEP Viewpoint Clearing that emphasizes the players and their dealings with each other rather than the story and the mental image recordings. And it seems to be a valid and far reaching approach.

Dialogue or "Hello-OK"

A number of simple DEEP techniques are contained in what is called the toolbox. Chapter 15 covers the techniques. A tool from this box assists the clearer in working a certain area to complete an overall technique. We will briefly cover one toolbox technique here as it is very relevant to this chapter on viewpoints. It is called 'Hello-OK'. It is typically run between the introspector and a character. In the example below the character is 'Jim'. It goes like this: "Say 'Hello' to Jim." "Have Jim say 'OK' to that hello." "Have Jim say 'Hello' to you." "Say 'OK' to that hello." This is run for one or two rounds in order to establish a communication line. Then we go into relaying messages. "Is there something you want to say to Jim?" "Have Jim receive that." "Is there something Jim wants to say to you?" "Receive and acknowledge that." This simple tool can lead to all kinds of conversations between the introspector and this character of his/her own mind. It serves to illustrate how we tend to compartmentalize our thought processes and minds.

Similar techniques to Hello-OK have been in use in psychotherapy for many years. At a conference we heard a speech of a former psychiatric nurse. She had been working at a psychiatric hospital and used a very similar technique when she was given a chance.

She was a nurse, not a psychiatrist, so she could only do it now and then when she got the doctor's permission. She found however that many of the patients had a major situation with a person important to them. It could be a spouse, a boss, a parent, etc. It could also be a loved one who had died. The patient would spend much of his/her time thinking about that. The nurse used the technique to get all the undelivered communications out in the open and acknowledged. Once that got cleaned out an amazing high percentage of these patients were cured to a point where they could get released from the facility.

Her story illustrates several important points in a very simple manner. It illustrates how important communication is to our well-being. It illustrates how we compartmentalize our minds into characters. Also, characters that represent hostile and dominating people in our lives can have a devastating effect on our well-being; likewise can the loss of a loved one. The ill effects can be dealt with using simple means. And let me add, it illustrates our understanding of emotional charge as unfulfilled or undelivered, repressed communications, where the communications can be intentions and thoughts, emotions and efforts – the key words being 'unfulfilled, undelivered and repressed'. We use the Hello-OK tool in context with the major techniques described in this chapter. When exactly to use it, is covered in the technical writings later in the book. But obviously it can be used as a stand-alone assist as well.

Attached Entities

Addressing viewpoints in clearing extends beyond our minds. In several religious practices and modalities there is much talk about bodiless spirits influencing us and sometimes haunting us. So in certain circles there is a lot of interest and importance attached to the phenomenon of these life-entities. These entities are spirits without bodies and possibly spiritual fragments, such as foreign attention units stuck to us. They can be attached to our own body or person without them doing much besides being asleep. In certain kinds of advanced procedures these entities can be contacted, awoken and released. Although this can be fascinating, we see it as a phenomenon that shouldn't be overrated in importance. In DEEP our focus is on handling the person's issues. When we do that the phenomenon of attached entities will usually sort itself out. Often it will be found to be a character in the introspector's own mind that, so to speak, manifests a mind of its own, a sub-personality. Our whole effort in DEEP is to integrate such viewpoints as this makes the person more whole and able. But should such attached entities come up and take center stage, they can be addressed as any other viewpoint. They will either integrate or blow. We have found that concentrating on these case phenomena as something foreign running our lives easily can be overdone at the expense of looking at the person's own case issues. In DEEP we concentrate on the person's case and issues; on the person's personal development and increased ability. Working in that direction the person grows and soon any attached entities are seen as small disturbances that will blow or sort themselves out. Should a stray attached entity turn up and take center stage it can still be addressed directly using the DEEP tools.

Other Beings and Viewpoints

Besides the above, we can contact bigger entities and identities in clearing work. A couple, a family or a group seems to have a group-mind consisting of all the guiding principles and collective memories of the group (a field of consciousness or morphic field). This can sometimes be contacted as an entity as can even bigger composite minds, such as the group-mind of mankind or the Earth. Also animals and plants seem to have a basic mind and intelligence that sometimes can be communicated with telepathically. As a rule this is outside what we go for in DEEP. But it may turn up at our doorstep. If that happens, just use the proper tools and routines contained in this book. These entities are addressed as identities and we will find decisions, thoughts, emotions, efforts and habits in any and all of them using the same questions we use in normal running of DEEP.

Some History and Thoughts

Running incidents and issues from viewpoints is not something new. Novelists and playwriters have done that as a way of working through issues since writing was invented. Actors use their mental characters in their work. They have access to all these archetypical characters in their own subconscious mind. Somehow there is the lover, the villain, the knight, the monk, the nun, the heroine, etc. Using points of view in session with clients has also been around for many years. We learned a lot from Robert Ducharme and his R3X, Advanced Incident Running, where it is used. Also the practitioner Jack Horner used it at the end of 20th century in his therapy called Eductivism. In therapy it has also been used as psychodrama of the 1960s where the clients play out traumatic situations and relationships as roles. Fritz Perls, who developed Gestalt therapy in the 1940s and 50s, used a similar approach in dealing with clients' relationship issues and also their dreams. The client simply had to play all the roles of a relationship or a dream, one after the other. In gestalt therapy the technique is called "the empty chair's technique." You address the fictive person in the empty chair and change back and forth between chairs.

Addressing viewpoints and identities is at the core of the approach in DEEP. When we add to that, finding the DEEP elements in and around these identities and discharge all these elements, you have the short description of what DEEP is all about.

There is one more point that will be covered later and that is the session format. This format is highly disciplined and is codified in what is called the Clearer's Professional Code. Without sticking to this disciplined approach we cannot guarantee that the results will be as stellar as we see them in our practice. The session has to be a safe space where the emotional charge can be brought out and discharged. And the discharge has to result in deep-felt relief and very uplifting results or it isn't DEEP. Fortunately, the format is well codified and described so it can easily be taught to new clearers.

Identities and Living

Our identity is the way we present ourselves to the world. It is the 'Be' in the Be-Do-Have cycle of action (chapter 7). It is choosing a role in the game of life we are engaged in or want to engage in (chapter 9). It is so central to existence that it determines our fate. In society you get punished economically and socially or get ignored if you cannot prove your identity. In some countries you get arrested on sight for this "crime". "Your papers, please!" or else... Education is all about honing one's skills and developing into a qualified and respected identity. Fashion and clothes are all about presenting one's identity in an attractive or respectable manner. Property is often seen as an extension of one's ego. The bigger house, the newest and most expensive car are signals to others about who we are. But all these things may not lead to happiness unless we are in harmony with our inner world and the needs and wants of our heart.

In DEEP you have a priceless opportunity to get your inner world in harmony with your outer world. It simplifies things and makes genuine happiness possible when you truly know who you are and what you want in life. And this is our goal with DEEP: to help you end old and almost forgotten games with their now irrelevant and repressed roles; their now irrational needs and wants. We want to make you capable of successfully engaging in new and more constructive games; bring about a clearer and more flexible state of mind. This enables you to live your dreams and live them in harmony with your heart's desires, your loved ones, society with its rational demands on you, and the world at large.

Chapter 12: The DEEP Package

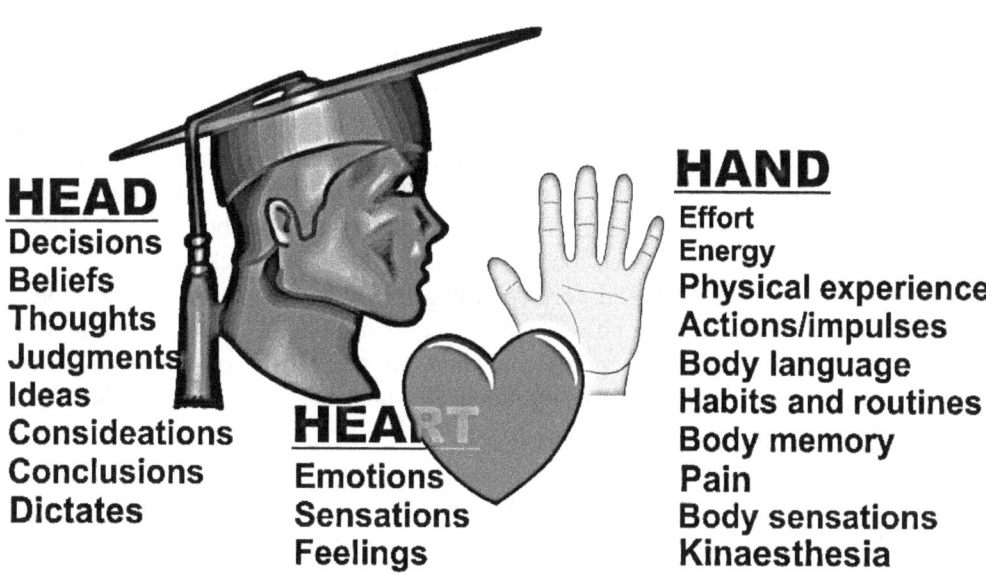

HEAD
Decisions
Beliefs
Thoughts
Judgments
Ideas
Consideations
Conclusions
Dictates

HEART
Emotions
Sensations
Feelings

HAND
Effort
Energy
Physical experience
Actions/impulses
Body language
Habits and routines
Body memory
Pain
Body sensations
Kinaesthesia

As explained in chapter 8, the elements of thought, emotion and effort parallel the classical elements of Head, Heart and Hand. We have the mental band, the emotional band and the physical body band. It is about what we think, what we feel and what we do. Building on this we can say: Life manifests itself through thoughts, ideas and decisions; through emotions, feelings, sensations and pains; through impulses, efforts, behaviors and habits. To this we can add: through alliances and conflicts. Here we have polarities and points of view. Any manifestation of life can be described within this framework. As Beings go along living life and use these faculties and elements, they make recordings of events. They record what they think, what they feel and what they do. They record Decisions; Emotions and Energies; Efforts; Polarities and Points of View. This is what we call DEEP. We live and record our lives in the form of DEEP packages. If we should use two common English words for the DEEP package it would be *subjective experience*. Some of these packages give us power and joy – those that contain valuable moments and experiences. Some of them are charged and hinder our well-being, our success and survival. The charged DEEP Packages are at the center of all DEEP clearing work.

COUNTER-
DECISION
COUNTER-
EMOTION/ENERGY
COUNTER-
EFFORT/ACTION
/IMPULSE

POLARITY

DECISION
EMOTION/ENERGY
EFFORT/ACTION
/IMPULSE

The different actions and overall techniques in DEEP are always to locate these packages of charge as they lock up our spirit and mind, our psyche, in various ways. As explained in chapter 11, "Viewpoints, Identities, Polarities", we have five main DEEP actions we deliver. These are different inroads to the case. 1) There is DEEP Incident Clearing where we start with a traumatic or stressful incident. As we go through the recordings of what happened, the DEEP packages reveal themselves. 2) In DEEP Subject Clearing we have the introspector talk about a troublesome subject or area and several or many DEEP packages will surface and can be addressed. 3) In DEEP Viewpoint Clearing we start with a charged situation, not necessarily an archetypical conflict. We start with the viewpoints of the persons who interacted in the situation. They were engaged in some sort of game of life. We take each player, each viewpoint present, and find the DEEP packages they are operating on in that particular situation. This is of course according to the introspector's recordings of the event. 4) In DEEP Body Clearing the clearing team reviews the introspector's body and the Being's difficulties with the body. Charged or ailing body parts have DEEP packages recorded locally, say, related to a bad back or an ailing stomach. Also, the introspector has a reaction and corresponding DEEP packages to the condition. 5) In DEEP Character Clearing our starting point is an archetypical opposition game. We take up the introspector's perceived opponent or enemy and find all the DEEP packages stuck to that structure. Then we take up the introspector's own behavior and identity in this conflict. These are the five main techniques we use in DEEP.

Once a charged DEEP package is located the routine of handling it is much the same regardless of how we found it. This chapter, then, will give a more detailed description of such a package. The techniques are brought later. There are additional techniques in the technical descriptions of the main actions. For students seeking professional training in DEEP there are additional course materials to study.

Recordings of the Mind

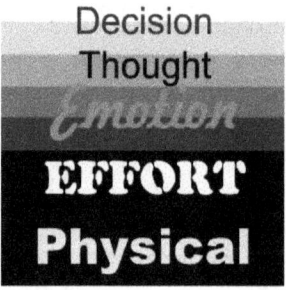

In chapter 10, "Emotional Charge", we illustrated the DEEP package as a scale of physicality. This is a scale of wavelengths with the finest waves at the top and the densest ones at the bottom. The finest wavelength of them all is knowingness. This is shown at the top. Any particular event is recorded on at least eight different tracks. There is probably a near infinity of tracks in the mind's recording systems of events. There are tracks for the five senses plus a wealth of data about the condition of own body, position, motion, state of mind of self and others in the event. It is amazing with what a wealth of details and accuracy a skilled introspector can recall incidents from early childhood and faraway places – including past lives. Add to that, that the introspector can review such events from other viewpoints than his or her own. Critics will of course claim that it is all delusion. Since recalling all these details leads to clarity of mind there is obviously more to it than that. Also, the end result of recalling all these details, after the clearing work is behind us, is that the person is more aware and perceptive of present time. A lot of attention units stuck in past recordings have been reclaimed by the introspector and are available as attention and intention and are now working for the person in present time. In DEEP we are mainly interested in the three tracks of: thought, emotion and effort. These are subjective tracks. It is how the introspector thinks, feels and acts in the situation. How the person manifests him/herself as a Being. By reviewing incidents, subjects and conditions for this subjective content, the person can truly break out of the confines of subconscious and irrational patterns. The person learns what forces and vectors he/she has been up against and gains control over them.

You could see DEEP clearing work as a long exercise in gaining control over own thoughts, emotions and efforts. This adds up to gaining control over one's own being and doing. Having control over being and doing leads to control over one's having. Being in control of one's own being, doing and having truly enables the person to live his/her dreams.

So we concentrate our clearing work on: 1) decisions, thoughts, conclusions and ideas—the thought band; 2) emotions, feelings and sensations—the emotion band; 3) impulses, estimation of efforts and dealing with effort, force and motion—the effort band. Each single element of a DEEP package is called a *DEEP element* or DEEP unit. It is more important to clearing work to sort out this the subjective side than finding out exactly what happened in childhood or 10 lifetimes ago. It is only in DEEP Incident Clearing we go for a detailed account of what happened and the more objective tracks of the 5 senses at the time. Once the introspector is free of all the confines the DEEP elements of the incident imposed on him/her we are done.

Physical Matter

At the very bottom of our scale we have physical matter. This is below subjective experience. Besides 'things', such as tables and chairs, mountains, oceans, clouds, cars, houses, and other non-organic material, we have bodies, animal bodies, plant material, etc.—organic and biological matter in other words. We do not address physical matter directly in DEEP but since life is an interaction between Beings, bodies, organic and non-organic matter we list it here. It is definitely one side of many polarities in life. We live and work to conquer our part of the material world in the form of territory and possessions.

Body: Effort, Impulse, Kinesthesia, Sensation

The way we affect physical matter and physical matter affects us is through Effort. In physics it is called force but we use 'effort' throughout. The effort band is concerned with motion, force and effort, or it *is* motion, force and effort. No-motion, as resistance to change, is of course also part of the effort band.

Efforts have a physical side and a mental side. A physical effort (force) is a property of physical objects and their state of motion or rest. An effort has a direction and a certain magnitude. The physical side is as described by Isaac Newton in his 3 laws of motion. If you drive a car, the speed and weight of the car determine the magnitude of a possible impact. Add to that the direction and you have a physical description of an effort. It is a vector. (See illustration and also illustration in chapter 10.)

Efforts also have a mental side. The mental side is recordings of physical efforts and estimations of efforts. This includes recording the sense of *Kinesthesia*, a sense now recognized by the medical profession (British Dictionary. Kinesthesia: 1. the sense that detects bodily position, weight, or movement of the muscles, tendons, and joints; 2. the sensation of moving in space). A driver must however constantly estimate the counter-efforts he meets and his own efforts needed to overcome them. He keeps an eye on everything: pedestrians crossing the road, dogs on a leash or no leash, barriers like trees and traffic lights, oncoming traffic, etc. Each counter-effort becomes a vector in the driver's mind. It has a direction (possible outcome and impact) and a certain magnitude assigned to it. Through experience the driver has made mental vectors of all kinds of counter-efforts and needed own efforts to overcome them. He uses these data and experiences to estimate situations with their dangers and options.

Should the motorist be so unfortunate to collide with a tree, the impact and injury would be recorded mentally as an own effort colliding with a counter-effort, the resistance or inertia of the tree. In this case it produces pain and injury in the driver.

We can address the mental or psycho-somatic side of this by addressing the two colliding vectors or forces separately. By running the recorded effort of the driver and the recorded counter-effort of the tree, one after the other, the solidity of the injury can be resolved and the pain be relieved. Notice, what we are addressing is the driver's two sets of mental recordings: his recording of his own motion in the car, and the counter-action of the tree, the solidity and sturdiness of, say, an old oak.

Impulses are defined as forming efforts or not executed efforts. They have a subjective existence but they haven't been acted out. The mind can record and play back impulses. (Under 'Impulses' we also include energetic intentions and strong wishes, such as wishing a remote person to get ill. It's a matter of discussion if it should be placed under 'Thought' as it also has characteristics of 'Decision' or 'Postulate'.)

Part of the effort band is body language. In normal social events there may be no effort present to the untrained eye. Still, there may be lots of body language. The introspector will benefit from observing own body language as well as the body language of others in the situation at hand. The introspector can be asked to show it or act it out in session as a way of releasing the tension.

If Effort can seem a little confusing it is simply because it is the band where the spiritual Being collides with the physical universe. And this is one of a Being's basic problems. The solidity and physicality of the universe collide against this non-material Being. The Being can perceive it, imitate and simulate it but it is still very foreign to him. What we do in clearing regarding efforts is sorting out the various vectors by having the introspector clearly perceive the efforts and impulses. When the introspector takes control over own efforts and stops battling recorded counter-efforts from the outside world the problem of the colliding forces ceases to exist. Since there are so many opposing vectors in play in a mental ridge it does take some time to sort it all out. But gradually the person gains more control and gets more exterior to all the commotion and confusion of handling the physical world.

Body sensation is a category comprised of various feelings stemming from the body, such as ache, soreness, itch, thirst, full stomach and dozens of other impulses, good and bad. The body is trying to tell us about its status. By perceiving the range of body sensations we are aware of and in contact with the body and its condition. Pain is of course also a sensation. It can be understood as two efforts colliding. Many odd pains can be relieved by finding the two sides colliding and run one after the other. During normal function and bodily stress sensations are recorded. These recordings can be taken up in session later and discharged.

Sensations can be taken up in DEEP—as long as we are talking about recordings. If a person has an acute sensation or pain in the body, the right thing to do is of course to look for an immediate physical cause and a way to deal with it, such as seeing a health professional.

Emotions, Feelings

Above Effort in our scale of physicality we have Emotions and Feelings. Emotion is a type of mental energy closely related to being alive. There are several types of emotions/feelings. We sub-divide them into 1) Causative emotions; 2) Reflexive emotions; 3) Feelings.

1. Causative emotions: These are emotions generated by the Being and directed at the body or towards the exterior world. These are the emotions of an extroverted person dealing with the environment; the emotions of a hunter, a sportsman, a worker in action, etc. Emotions in this band can have a clear physiological function. They control or influence the body directly through the nervous and endocrine systems.

New research – presented by scientists such as Bruce Lipton and Candace Pert – has shown that emotions even can be directly perceived by the body's cells and thus influence them energetically. Emotions act as commands to the body. Causative emotions are also part of our communication. A skilled public speaker, a musician or artist uses causative emotions to convey his or her messages. The emotions in communication are aimed at influencing the listeners' emotions and behavior. Causative emotions are an outflow.

2. Reflexive emotions: are our emotional responses to things. They comprise a huge amount of luggage; some of it useful, much of it mainly a burden. How big a role emotions play can vary enormously from person to person. It can be a very healthy way to navigate in life. For some it is a curse causing depression or unnecessary stress and general unhappiness. Reflexive emotions are seen as inflow.

3. Feelings: Are closely related to the above. Any given feeling is a complex combination of thoughts, reflexive emotions and impulses. It cannot be categorized into the well-known clean emotions of the affinity scale. It can be a "gut feeling", "feeling sort of hopeful" or "feeling like dancing", etc. In chapter 10 we covered Emotional Markers. They also fit in here. We assign emotional values to things, such as friends, foes, foods, situations, subjects, entertainment, etc.

Using feelings and emotional markers is a quick way of "thinking" about one's situation, about other people, a project, etc. It is a clear manifestation of awareness and a way to know. It is "thinking with one's heart"—some say with their gut. Some call it "an instinctive feeling," such as to what is right and what is wrong. Intuitions fall in this category.

Thought, Decision

Thought is mental activity dealing in ideas and concepts. Thought can be verbalized. There is 1. Rational thought (or reason,) and 2. Repressed thought in bypass reactions.

Decisions are causative thoughts. They can be rational or originate from the subconscious mind. Decisions set a course for the future or they can be causative or final conclusions about the past. A decision has a subjective and final quality to it. There may be hundreds of thoughts, for and against, before a decision is arrived at. The decision finalizes matters even when it's wrong. In DEEP we also talk about Dictates. They are reactive thoughts out of control.

1. Rational thought (reason) is clear thinking with a high ability to differentiate and see tiny differences among very similar things. It is characterized by the ability to discern differences, see similarities and recognize things that are identical. Working with, studying or looking at something using  reason, one can perceive and classify things correctly and work with the concepts of things in the mind. One can combine ideas and arrive at new ones. One can forecast correctly, be aware of consequences by using logic, etc. This is of course a desirable state of affairs and we don't try to run it out. Yet, we can take it up briefly in DEEP as it can act as the positive pole in a polarity where the negative pole is dominated by reactive thought.

2. Repressed thought stemming from the repressed mind and its bypass reactions is a coarser function of the mind. It has much to do with conditioned reflexes, or stimulus response. Certain stimuli will cause a predetermined response. This can be due to upbringing, education and indoctrination. Also physical trauma may cause this. The person seems to "learn" certain lessons during such moments. A girl burns her fingers on a stove and will have an involuntary flinch next time she sees one—even when it is cold. She has "learned" not to touch stoves. The conditioned reflex seems to be in place to make sure it doesn't happen again.

(This is what we could call the "Must-not-happen-again" reaction. If a person has many of those, living a normal life becomes very hard.) When the girl sees a stove the mechanism can be triggered. It will however include much or all of the original discomforts (negative emotion, sensation and pain.)

It will also contain decisions and conclusions made at the time of the injury. They now act as Dictates. By contacting and reviewing the original burning incident this spell can be lifted. In DEEP we make sure to address and flatten thought, emotion and effort contained in the trauma. The girl can now again touch or not touch stoves as she sees fit. The burning incident has been transformed to experience.

The Shock Moment

Of special interest in DEEP Incident Clearing are decisions and thoughts made during traumatic moments. Any thought content has been locked up in the incident together with emotions and sensations. If generalities, destructive, self-destructive, or self-limiting decisions or conclusions were made, they can have a very negative effect on one's thinking and behavior later  on. They become self-limiting thoughts. Also, decisions that made sense in a certain situation may make no sense or be destructive in just about any other context. They are now simply out of place. They were urgent emergency decisions that, apparently, had to be carried out, or reacted out, before the person could act based on reason. A soldier in war, for instance, has to make many decisions of this nature. If he carries them over into civil life he will find himself in a lot of trouble. The same is true for victims of war. 'Instinctive decisions' made under such circumstances can be hard to detect. They seem to live on in the repressed mind without the person suspecting them. Since they are hidden and still have command value we also call them Dictates. They dictate behaviors and patterns. Also due to the high pain and stress content in the trauma, these decisions tend to be avoided consciously. They are unpleasant to get near and thus stay secluded and uninspected. In clearing any locked up, irrational, out-of-context thoughts and hidden urgent responses are isolated and cleared and the person's thinking is again freed up.

Examples of Dictates and Self-limiting Thoughts in Shock Moments

A woman gets raped and decides after the incident of shock and panic that "all men are bad!" and lives by it ever since. Such thoughts can be conceived during the incident or as conclusions afterwards. A man gets injured in a car accident and in a flash decides "I should never have driven!" and agonizes each time he drives a car after that. A boy gets blown to sea in a small boat and gets suddenly very scared and says to himself "I won't make it!" This may act as a self-limiting thought for the rest of his life. Getting these decisions and dictates—these often urgent exclamations and outcries—isolated and run out may turn things around. The incidents were remembered as nightmares. After being reviewed in DEEP such incidents become invaluable lessons of life: on the rational level, on the emotional level and on the behavioral level. They become accessible without any pain or negative emotion. They simply add to what could be called the person's intuitive understanding of the situation—and this is life experience at its best.

Polarity or Points of View

We covered the theory in the previous chapter. Let us repeat here, when the clearer runs the charge out of a DEEP package with its thoughts, emotions and efforts, he/she should be on the lookout for any counter-thoughts, counter-emotions and counter-efforts. If things get sticky and resistive in session it is usually because of the counter-vectors. Ask for them and clear them and things come apart. The Tool-box chapter has detailed descriptions of how to train and run the DEEP packages.

Relative Importance of DEEP Elements

The relative importance of the various DEEP elements was covered in chapter 10, "Emotional Charge". First of all, the DEEP elements are much more important to find and clear than the photographic recordings of events. The recordings of the 5 senses and the records and tracks they produce are truly amazing. Still, they are like thoughts compared to decisions; there can be millions of thoughts but they may just add up to one decision that we keep. When we concentrate on the DEEP elements we deal with the content we keep. Dealing with these elements is the most productive path to positive change.

The most important element to find is *Decision, defined as causative thoughts about self and the future and final conclusions about the past.* What really moves a case is of course to find hidden irrational decisions. Emotion and effort is mainly dealt with to uncover very central decisions of irrational nature. Still, emotion and effort are forces of life we need to deal with in clearing. In practice, the clearer starts with the DEEP element the introspector offers up front and finds the other elements from there. If no particular element is offered, we ask for the emotion/feeling of the moment as the person usually has a clear feeling about a particular charged moment or condition. A very charged moment may have all 6 elements. 1) Own efforts; 2) own emotions 3) own thoughts/decisions. 4) Counter-efforts from an opposing player or force; 5) counter-emotions from the opposition; 6) counter-thoughts/counter-decisions from the opposition. You only take those elements up that are charged so you may only need to run 2 or 3 to be done with the double package. Still, the clearer looks for all 6 possibilities.

Knowingness and Forgiveness

The reason we work so hard on the DEEP elements is so the introspector can rise above them. Once we have worked through all the charge the person has regarding a certain issue or incident he/she is able to rise above it. The person will reach a state of knowingness regarding the subject at hand. In Christianity and Buddhism the remedy for hardships and suffering is to forgive. This can sometimes be very hard to do when the hardship seemed so cruel and meaningless. When all the DEEP elements are worked out of an issue it seems like a natural next step. We can see the issue from both sides and there are no hard feelings to hold onto. Now there is only our knowingness that pervades the situation. We have learned our lesson. We can forgive and move on. But we have also become smarter and wiser. We know how to deal with the situation, should it come around again.

Repeat and Tell

This is our main technique used to deal with DEEP packages. Once we have located a DEEP package we need to discharge it. This should be done in the same session it is found. That is when it is hot and fully accessible. Our basic technique is to take one DEEP element and do some discharge of that with Repeat and Tell. Then add another element from the same package and discharge the two further. We add additional elements this way and discharge the whole package until flat or gone. The introspector confronts and perceives the chosen DEEP elements repeatedly and tells anything that happens. It can be stray thoughts, memories of similar incidents, mental pictures, and similar "pop-ups". The clearer makes sure this communication is flowing freely and can from time to time ask if anything is happening and the like. Usually the pop-ups do not require the clearer to do anything new.

The clearer should just listen to, understand and acknowledge what came up and continue the repeating till the item is cleared. The clearer simply uses 'Communication Drill 5, Pop-ups, to the situation. The endpoint of running a package should be that there is no more change in the area – it's all dissolved. In the Tool Box chapter you will find the exact instructions on how to run the DEEP packages. Chapter 16 contains the full theory of Repeat and Tell.

"Life Is a Pinball Machine"

The reason why Repeat and Tell works so well, compared to just experiencing the effort, emotion or thought on the fly, is well documented and understood. We tend to live our lives as balls in a pinball machine. A person hits a DEEP package in life and is bounced off without seeing or knowing what is inside or what exactly happened. The person is sent on a new course until he/she hits the next DEEP package and is sent in another direction. In DEEP the person has, maybe for the first time, a chance to see what is really inside the thing that bounces him/her around. What is inside is a moment of stress and confusion, a shock moment to some degree. It contains some live energy that is out of control. It takes repeated efforts of the clearing team to get to the bottom of things and see it for what it is.

This does not necessarily happen in traditional clearing sessions. The client may experience relief and feel it's all in the past – just to realize a few days or weeks later that the relief was just temporary. There was reactive energy left in the issue. Now it is a mystery that things 'already handled' aren't really handled after all. What do we do now?

Our solution to that situation is to finalize the handling of the DEEP packages in the first place or run the old clearing procedure again simply to find the DEEP packages that were overlooked first time around. Now we can handle them once and for all. There are three layers or more of subjective recordings, layers of repressed energy, that all need to be released in order to obtain stable results in clearing. When we handle the DEEP packages as we go along, we handle any and all old and irrational reactions bound in the issue.

Life tends to bounce us around – like a ball in a pinball machine.

Chapter 13: Some Questions and Answers

How do I get started on DEEP clearing?

Persons who have read a book or website about DEEP are much more capable of running DEEP. It is important that the person understands the basic principles. A planned series of DEEP sessions with a new client should be started with an intro session given by an experienced DEEP clearer where the DEEP principles are demonstrated in practice on light incidents, such as what happened during the last shopping trip or another non-traumatic incident.

What makes a clearing session different from other methods?

What makes clearing and DEEP different from most other forms of self-improvement and therapy is that it is done under the Clearer's Professional Code (see chapter 14) and that the communication drills (see chapter 3) are applied by the clearer in session. The clearer has to conduct him- or herself according to these standards at all times in session and not violate the trust of the person outside session. These are cornerstones in DEEP training. Similar codes and drills exist in a few other modalities while you don't find such instructions in the majority of self-improvement and therapy systems. They are of vital importance to the uniformly stellar results gotten in DEEP.

Are DEEP packages always charged?

No. DEEP stands for Decision, Emotion, Effort, Point of View. These are basically the factors through which life manifests itself. In plain English it is called subjective experience. If you take a skilled actor, who has the task of bringing a certain figure or character to life on stage, he works intuitively with this. A character comes alive and becomes credible when the actor can equip it with these faculties of life in a plausible way.

We found the following quote on the internet, written by a rabbi named Aron Moss:

"Our personality has three layers to it - intellect, emotion and action; what we think, what we feel and what we do. Intellect: My opinions on issues, philosophies on life and attitudes to myself and others. Emotion: My moods, desires and passions; what I love and what I hate, what I am scared of and what attracts me. Action: Not my beliefs or feelings, but what I actually do, how I live my life, and how I spend my time and energy.

Ideally, these three faculties should be in sync. My beliefs and ideals should direct my passions and ambitions, which should in turn be translated into my lifestyle. But so often we find this is not the case. What I know is right doesn't always feel right, and what I feel like doing is not necessarily what I do."

The rabbi says it very well. What we need to address are DEEP packages where things are out of sync. What we address in DEEP are *charged* DEEP packages where some kind of short circuit has made it impossible for the person to deal with or integrate the content in his or her life.

Can clearing and DEEP be done via the internet?

Much of our clearing work has been done by video-telephony, via the Skype computer program.

This has worked very well. For students who want to do as much DEEP clearing as possible at an affordable price, the best method is to take some training in DEEP together with a designated partner and then do DEEP teamwork via, for instance, Skype. Even people in remote locations from each other can team up and just do DEEP clearing in their free time without having to make expensive and time-consuming travel arrangements.

Does the Ability One Group only deliver DEEP clearing?

No, we also deliver other modalities of clearing tech. DEEP is a new modality and many of our clients prefer modalities they are familiar with or they want to complete actions they have started elsewhere. We are fully equipped to do just that. Also, some clients early in their self-development work will get more benefits from covering all their issues at a faster pace. The strength and power of DEEP is that this modality can handle resistive issues. It can handle issues the person has unsuccessfully tried time and again to get fully handled elsewhere.

Who can benefit from DEEP?

DEEP is intended as an advanced type of clearing. New introspectors may benefit more from other types of clearing, such as a current life-issues program, also called life-repair, and the ability grades. We see the subconscious mind as having three layers: thought, emotion and effort. Traditional types of clearing take care of the thought layer and make a dent in the emotional layer and the effort layer. It may not be that orderly in practice, but it remains a fact that not all people will run the full DEEP procedure with added benefit. DEEP goes more into details with resistive issues. When a person first starts clearing there are obviously many issues that all need attention. Therefore, going over it all in a lighter, faster way is a valid strategy.

We have an approach we call DEEP light, where we ask into emotions and efforts without trying to erase these layers. That is more appropriate for starting introspectors when we talk DEEP.

When do you not recommend using DEEP?

People with heavy issues triggered here and now do not always run DEEP with sufficient ease. Since clearing work should be experienced by the introspector as a relief, where each session ends in a positive mood and relief, we use that as the most important mark to steer by. In some clearing practices the act of reviewing incidents, where emotions and efforts play a bigger part, is placed late in the line-up. This is because it is considered too difficult an action for beginning clients. The same can be the case with DEEP. So the clearer has to make sure the introspector is winning. If this is not the case, the introspector should be put on lighter clearing actions.

Also, if a DEEP introspector is experiencing a lot charge in life, a lot of bypass reactions triggered by the environment, the best approach is to find and indicate the charge. Not just to go into a thorough examination of one particular upset or problem when there are maybe 5, 6 or more. Also, minor upsets and problems that routinely may be needed to be taken up at the start of the session should not be run with DEEP. We just want to get the introspector sufficiently focused to be fully present and with the activity. We just want these disturbances out of the way. We don't want to make them the main subject of the session. One way to get the introspector ready to focus on main issues is to run some Fresh Reality (Havingness) in the start of the session. These are objective techniques and get the introspector's attention off disturbances and problems and onto the present time of the session and clearing work.

How long should a DEEP session be?

The length of a session is not set in stone. Some clients like shorter sessions, such as 30-45 minutes. Others like them long, like 2 hours plus. One client complained about sessions being too short. He wanted sessions of 2 ½ hours straight or more at a time. He said it took him long time to be fully focused on the session and doing only 1 hour was a waste of time.

As a rule, clients new to clearing should be given shorter sessions to start out with. Also, clients who have a lot of triggered charge in the present should be given shorter sessions until things settle down a bit.

A session should always be taken to a good point, to an endpoint and very good indicators. Also extroversion is an important indicator. A client who has extroverted with very good indicators is at a point that can be used as a session end point. To continue, the introspector has to be put back into session, you see.

Depending on the main action, there are usually several or many possible session end points in a normal session. You never end the session if the introspector is in some kind of trouble or has entered something hot and heavy and hasn't come out on the other side. If the introspector is all into it, you have to complete that before considering ending the session regardless of what the clock says.

Can DEEP be done solo?

DEEP techniques presented in this book do not lend themselves well to solo work. By far the best results are gotten when working with a clearer. The clearer helps the introspector to get through and overcome difficult issues. The most economical set-up is to get some basic training in DEEP. We recommend you do training with the developers at Ability One Group. We arrange seminars in person and via net conferences. You should arrange for having a partner to work with during and after this training. The Ability One Group will of course be helpful in finding you a partner. You should also arrange to get a few hours of clearing work done by a professional clearer. This will handle some of your own issues and give you a valuable experience with DEEP. From there you can work with your partner and do as many hours as you possibly want at no extra cost.

Do you recommend the use of bio-monitor?

DEEP was mainly developed *without* the use of these instruments. This was in part due to the fact that we mainly have worked long distance via Skype. At the time of development there was no possibility of transmitting meter reactions via the internet.

We have found that DEEP works very well without the use of bio-monitor. And therefore we teach it as an activity that doesn't depend on this instrument. Instead, we teach the clearer to ask additional questions to find out what is going on and to watch the indicators of introspectors to determine what to run and when to end the running of something.

Part of finding what to run is a simple system of asking the introspector to give a number value between 0-10 to items. Let's say we have 3 items related to an issue of 'Going to school.' We then ask: "On a scale between 0 and 10, where 10 means highly charged and 0 means no charge, how would you rate 'homework?'" "How would you rate 'playing ball?" How would you rate "the bully, Jonas?" etc. You then take up the most charged item first, say the bully Jonas that was rated with 10. Then you take Homework (rated 8), then playing ball (rated 6). If two items have the same rating, you simply ask which item the introspector is most interested in running.

What are the prerequisites to be accepted for DCC?

DEEP Character Clearing is addressing the archetypical opposition games we have played over countless lifetimes. This is actually high level stuff. A DCC program is usually started with addressing the general DEEP case of the person. When it is deemed possible and beneficial, the person will be started on DCC. The preparation may only take about 5 hours. There is no other prerequisite to DCC except making sure the person can run it with benefit. There are no liabilities connected with receiving the program. There is no danger to the case, except that it may not be running well. That said it was developed to benefit advanced students and clients. Clients, who have done lots of other self-improvement work and want to take a major step towards their goals in personal development, are the prime group that DCC aims at assisting.

Can DEEP be combined with traditional clearing?

Yes, it often can. If you for instance take an ability grades technique we have experimented with simply adding a DEEP step *after* we have reached a traditional end point of realization on the subject accompanied by very good indicators—and a free needle, if a bio-monitor is used. The clearer reviews the session report quickly to find any DEEP elements or packages the technique uncovered. There may only be such a DEEP element in 20% of the cases. But if it is present, it is simply addressed using the tools in our tool box. Doing that, some underlying and often heavy charges are removed. This results in more stable gains regarding the subject at hand.

How do you deal with attached live entities or spirits?

In some modalities attached live entities (spirits) play a central role on the higher levels. In DEEP they are not seen as a major factor or dark influence. They are seen as additional viewpoints that we may need to take up as counter-vectors, as repression factors, when dealing with a certain issue or incident. The first viewpoint and issue to take care of is of course the introspector's own. Then secondly the other known players' viewpoints that can be gotten. In the training materials there are more data on this. Our experience has been that once the introspector's issues have been resolved, these additional viewpoints, these counter-vectors, tend to take care of themselves. So it remains a firm rule in DEEP that the introspector's issues are what are important to address and resolve.

How others react to the person's issues, including entities, should be considered but should not be given first priority. It is a well-known fact that once a person has worked through an issue and made up his or her mind, what critics or well-meaning advisers say – or any other "noise" – is of very little importance.

Are these entities simply dead spirits?

Here we are into religion and cosmology. It is outside what this book and the basic subject of DEEP is about. My personal opinion about this is that most of what is contacted as 'entities' are better understood as attention units split off from some Being. Most of them are split off from the person's own psyche, sometimes called sub-personalities. Some of them are split off from relatives' and associates' psyches. These attention units, it appears to me, have similar properties as DNA and holograms. They seem to contain all the traits of their parents. Maybe the phenomenon of 'entities' can be understood in the framework of 'entangled particles'. In quantum physics, entangled particles remain connected so that actions performed on one affect the other, even when separated by great distances. The phenomenon puzzled and upset Albert Einstein, by the way, and he called it "spooky action at a distance."

Whatever the explanation might be, we leave this to others. What we seek to accomplish in DEEP is to make the client's viewpoint stronger, to make the person capable of controlling his/her own destiny. Our approach to this is to spend our time and efforts on doing just that. As the person gets stronger, new counter-vectors turn up and they are then dealt with as such.

Who can be trained as DEEP clearers?

At the time of publishing we have several people in training in a more informal setting. We are planning to develop shorter seminars in DEEP where the participants are teamed up to do clearing teamwork two and two. This will be delivered in Copenhagen and via the net.

To be accepted for training as professional DEEP clearer, we prefer candidates who are already trained in some modality of therapy or self-development. This gives the best possible background.

Who delivers DEEP clearing and how?

At the time of this writing (May, 2015) it is only delivered professionally by the Ability One Group in Copenhagen, Denmark. We have, however, several students in training to become professional DEEP clearers in various parts of the world.

What is your opinion on Emotional Intelligence?

This subject is very relevant to DEEP. DEEP certainly is a highway to develop someone's Emotional Intelligence. EI has several definitions. One definition is: "The ability to perceive emotion in self and others and recognize their importance to well-being as well as to productivity and to social life." In other words, it is about understanding and integrating the emotional side in one's personal life, in one's relationships and in one's professional life. It is about interacting well with others and taking one's own and other people's feelings into consideration and using the power of emotions. Since we work with understanding and integrating the emotional side with thought and action of the client in every session, it is no surprise that tests show a marked rise in EI after DEEP. Social Intelligence is also advanced by DEEP for that simple reason that the client's issues are viewed from all relevant points of view. Scientific studies have shown that people with high EI have greater mental health, exemplary job performance, and more potent leadership skills.

Part 3: DEEP Clearing The Main Actions

This part 3 of the book contains the exact procedures of 4 of our 5 main actions in DEEP. Since the Clearer's Professional Code should be observed at all times when working with DEEP Clearing, we start with bringing the full code. Another equally important pattern of conduct in session is observing the Communications Drills. They can be found in chapter 3, Live Communication. In training it takes a lot of drilling and practice to get the conduct of the clearer down cold. When it has become second nature to the clearer, sessions are easy to do and the clearer may not think much of it. It has become part of his/her professional beingness. Once all the rules and guidelines feel natural they simply add up to excellent session presence on the part of the clearer.

Chapter 14: The Clearer's Professional Conduct

The Clearer's Professional Code

DEEP Clearing work is done under a set of ground rules that has to be closely observed and followed by the clearer in session.

The rules are based on years of practical experience. They have come about through extensive analysis of successful sessions and failed sessions regarding what to do and observe and what not to do. It is a professional code of conduct for clearers.

The common denominator of the rules is to bring about a high level of trust between the client and clearer. This enables the client to drop all defense mechanisms and fully concentrate on his or her case. Optimum results are only possible when this trust is established and the client can dive deep into the caves and tunnels of his/her subconscious and repressed mind or bring sensitive material out in the open without any fear of backlash. Only then can this material be fully inspected, understood and reevaluated by the client.

The clearer's role is to be the guide and rope-holder who at all times makes sure the client is safe and is not getting lost. When the client feels he/she can fully trust the clearer and the session procedures, outstanding results become easily obtainable.

1. Do not evaluate for the client.

The client is the expert on his/her own case and inner world. The clearer should not and does not offer advice or answers to the client's problems. The clearer will of course instruct the client in the procedure and clear up questions and definitions related to this. But the procedures are designed so the client can find his/her own answers to personal issues and questions. The goal of clearing is to make the client more self-reliant and self-determined, to bring out intuitive knowledge and certainty. If the clearer were to step in and offer advice and opinions, the client would become dependent on the clearer to tell him/her what to think about his/her case rather than obtain inner clarity and certainty.

2. Do not invalidate the client's case or data.

The clearer does not tell the client "what is wrong with him/her." Nor does the clearer challenge or contradict the client's personal data or opinions. If the client doesn't fully understand the procedure, the clearer would of course make sure to instruct the client properly. But when it comes to the client's case and opinions the clearer accepts all views and statements as the client's points of view. The clearer lets the client work freely on bringing out and reviewing his/her problems and inner world without any judgment or invalidation.

3. Be interest*ed* in the client's case; avoid being interes*ting* to the client.

Showing a high level of interest in the client and what the client presents can lift the session quality considerably. It sets a friendly and productive tone for the session.

The clearer should avoid being *interesting* as this would place the client's attention on the clearer rather than on the client's own case. A session is effective when the client's attention and interest is on own case and the client is willing to talk to the clearer whenever there is something to tell. In a productive session the client would typically use most of the time looking inward for answers and data. Then, when something is found, the client tells the clearer about it. The clearer then acknowledges the answer in an interested but otherwise neutral way.

The clearer should approach the session in a positive way and be willing to have and experience anything the client says or displays without reaction. Showing an attitude, such as being motherly or sympathetic to the client's troubles is counter-productive. Likewise, being angry with the client, for whatever reason, is counter-productive as it is a form of invalidation.

4. Work with the client's interest.

Attention and interest are the determining factors of progress. Only take up charged issues and items the client has an interest in. If the client's attention and interest is on some situation from daily life, that should be addressed before going into more basic issues.

Also, a client who is not fully with the clearing work in the first place, but, for example, is there to satisfy an employer or relative, should not be engaged in clearing work right away. The client needs to be educated to a point where he/she is willing to do clearing work out of own determinism and interest.

5. Be responsible for the session environment.

A session should be conducted in a safe place and without time pressure. The clearer makes sure to have a room with comfortable chairs, a pleasant temperature, etc. and a session time and place that will not be interrupted.

When conducting sessions via internet video telephony, the clearer is still responsible for a safe environment at the client's end. The clearer makes sure that the above requirements are met by the client before starting the session.

6. Keep your session appointments.

Appointments once made should be kept. Changing appointments introduces disturbing randomness and may make the client feel that he/she is less important to the clearer than someone else.

Part of keeping the appointment is to stay with the client for the length of the session. The clearer should not walk off from the session for whatever reason as that introduces uncertainty and insecurity on the part of the client.

7. Make sure the client is rested and well fed.

The clearer should before each session make sure the client is well rested and not hungry. Also, the client should not be under any influence of alcohol or drugs. Clearing work can be quite demanding on the client's mind and body and the client has to take care of the obvious reasons for being less than fully fit for the task.

8. Always take an action and technique to its end point.

The clearer uses actions and techniques in order to relieve the client from charge. Techniques are designed to trigger a specific charge that subsequently is flattened or neutralized. If the clearer stops prematurely the charge is still active and bothersome. Part of this clause is also to get the client safely through the action to a good point. Sometimes a client gets scared and wants to stop prematurely. The clearer should recognize this as temporary back off and get the client through it anyway. This clause also has the consequence that a session can be longer or shorter than planned. Getting the end point is first priority. Therefore the session length cannot, and should not, be determined beforehand.

Note: There are different types of end points as described in the materials. The smaller steps may simply be taken to no more change (flat) while the bigger, and overall desirable, end points should result in new realizations and a liberated feeling in the client.

9. Never take an action or technique beyond its end point.

If an action or technique is carried on too long it may be hard on the client. The gains that were gotten earlier are not being recognized and thus invalidated. The clearer should recognize when an action or technique has run its course, has produced a change and reached its end point and stop there. Should too long a run occur, the end point can be regained by spotting it and cleaning up any accumulated charge.

10. Maintain good communication with the client.

The clearer should maintain a good communication cycle with the client. Make sure questions asked are understood; give the client time to find the answer or answers; acknowledge the answer; and allow the client to now and then bring up other things that seem important to the client. Such pop-ups should be understood, handled and acknowledged by the clearer but should not change the overall course of the session. If the client feels he/she can tell anything to the clearer and be understood the communication factor is really in.

11. Do not enter irrelevant comments into the session.

The positive and interested tone of the session does not mean it's a social event. On the part of the clearer it is a highly disciplined activity. Any comments on things not relevant to the session should be kept out.

Also, the clearer should not justify any mistakes, whether real or imagined. A simple, "I am sorry" is fine and then the clearer simply moves on from there.

12. Maintain confidentiality of privileged information.

The clearer must not under any circumstances reveal privileged information to anyone other than directly involved professionals, such as a person supervising the activity. The client needs to know that any secrets and sensitive personal data are safe with the clearer.

13. Do not promote or use DEEP clearing to treat medical diseases.

DEEP clearing is a self-development system and is not intended to treat or cure the body from medical diseases.

Possible medical conditions and diseases should be examined by a medical doctor. Only the medical doctor can determine if the client needs medical treatment or not.

Chapter 15: The DEEP Toolbox
Revised February 2019

In the toolbox you will find tools and techniques that help you, the clearer, to deal with all kinds of situations and phenomena in a DEEP session.

1. Clearer's Approach
2. Staying in touch
3. Complete cycles
4. Optimum pace
5. Assessing
6. Repeat and Tell

6-0. Sorting out Step
6a. EF Emot./Feeling
6b. Body sensation
6c. IE Impulse/Effort
6d. TD Thought/Decis.
6e. Notes on Running

6f. Secondary Impulse
6g. Other Viewpoints
7. Create/Replace
8. Hello/OK
9. Identities Dialogue
10. Fixed Ideas

11. Before/After
12. Feel it Back
13. Alternate Confront
14. 6-Directions
15. Unblocking as Tool
16. Positive Recall
17. Fresh Reality

Control, Duplication and Completing Cycles

DEEP and the DEEP tools have a common purpose that can be summed up in three concepts:
Duplication, Control and *Discharge by Completing Cycles.*
Since we are dealing with subtle energies in the psyche and the person's energy field, some of the techniques may seem strange—maybe controversial to some.
However, they are all designed to gain control over these fine energies, to duplicate them and let them complete their life cycles by discharge and thus cease to exist.-
This is routinely accomplished by repeated perception and viewing of the element. Sometimes the person has to demonstrate a DEEP element by acting it out or creating the energy on purpose. This unblocks the frozen energy so it can flow. In both cases, perceiving or acting out, it's important that the person notices and tells what's going on in the mind and body. This is what the central technique, Repeat and Tell, is all about.

Control

The clearer puts in the control factor by guiding the person and giving the needed support to get going. Most of the content we dig up was repressed because it was painful, unpleasant or didn't fit. So it is important that there is an external person that makes sure the instrospector gets through it. This is done in a pleasant and supportive manner.
Some of the tools below stress mainly the control factor. In Six Directions (6-D), for instance, the person is asked to exert control over a DEEP element or a mental object. Since these mental objects typically exert control over the person we are in fact reversing the flow. Instead of it controlling us we now control it. Tools like 'Feel it Back' and 'Fresh Reality' are also mainly working due to the control factor. But all the tools have the important element of control of attention. The clearer helps the introspector focus on unpleasant items so they can be observed and duplicated. This will not happen without control of attention.

Duplication

It is important that the clearer does not interfere with the introspector's endeavors to observe, perceive and duplicate. The clearer skillfully guides the person to the sources. But it is the person's ability to recognize, perceive and duplicate the original sources of charge and let the energy run its course that has the therapeutic effect.
Synonyms to duplication: facing, confronting, maintaining attention and interest, recognizing the source of, inspecting closely, viewing; also *observing with Mindfulness* and *Witnessing* as used in various practices and types of meditation.

Pervasion: is the ultimate form of duplication. Pervasion takes place when the person can fully *BE* something or recreate something in the mind. It could be a scene, an identity, an opponent, etc. When the person can fully be an opponent character, for instance, he/she can recreate, neutralize and dissolve that character, as far as he/she is concerned, and is thus no longer the adverse effect of that character. The polarity that existed between the two sides has been eliminated. The person has taken full control over the area.

Synonyms for pervasion: permeating, fully viewing, being the source of something, recreating.

Completing Cycles

Charge can be seen as incomplete cycles. This is a very useful definition. By taking off the repression of such a cycle stored in the mind and body its energy will come alive and discharge. This is true for single DEEP elements as well as for whole traumatic incidents. We are dealing with so-called blocked receptive cycles. The person simply shut down his/her perceptions and never found out exactly what happened. The person suppressed the emotions and reactions and stored them as incomplete cycles as well. When the content is confronted and duplicated the negative charge will apparently evaporate. We use the DEEP techniques and tools to complete these cycles of perception, of subjective experience and reaction. We bring the stored energies back to life and let them run their course. When an item has discharged we say it has gone flat. (See also Completing Cycles below.)

Four Basic Rules

1. The Clearer's approach: The most basic technique is the approach to the session itself. The clearer has to create a safe space and be a good listener. The clearer "holds the space" so the introspector can safely look inward without risking to be judged, criticized, or given "advice" on the subject at hand. The clearer has to be a good listener, showing attention and interest in what the introspector says, asking into things from time to time. The clearer should acknowledge the person's communications and keep the introspector looking into the energy field and mind until the full answer is found. The clearer has to ensure that the communication line between introspector and clearer stays open. The clearer should be interest*ed*, not interest*ing*. He/she should be very curious about the person and the person's case. The clearer should attract minimum attention to self and hold the position of an interested and understanding operator of the session, who nevertheless holds an external position that ensures staying in control.

2. Stay in touch with the introspector: Another basic technique that is understood to be part of the tools and techniques below, is to ask into what is going on. Ask into the person's reactions to what is being run from time to time. In some techniques we take up other viewpoints, meaning the person sees the event or conflict through, for instance, the opponent's eyes. The clearer should regularly ask into the introspector's own reactions to this. Examples of questions are: "How are you doing?" "What is your own reaction to that?" "How do you think the other side would react to that?" "Is it still running?" "Did it go flat?" "On a scale from 0-10, how would you rate it now?"

3. Completing cycles in techniques: It is understood that all the small steps or techniques are used to produce an overall positive change for the introspector. Doing a step may stir up something unpleasant. This is expected as we are addressing unpleasant things with the aim of permanently eliminating them. "No pain no gain," and "the way out is the way through" are the maxims we work from. We keep using a technique as long as it produces change and no longer—to a point we call a *flat point* where any discomfort is gone or the technique is producing no more change. That means that that particular cycle has been completed. Quite often these small steps produce big wins as well.

Note: Running a specific DEEP package is considered one technique, one cycle, so you can e.g. shift from running Emotion to running Decision before Emotion is 100% flat. You are still working on the same short moment of some degree of overwhelm, confusion or shock and are just taking it up from another perspective that may be more productive and faster. (See also #6, DEEP Packages, below and then re-read this paragraph.)

4. Find the optimum pace: There is an optimum pace in clearing. When the introspector changes mood according to the material reviewed and is OK and winning when something goes flat, the session is running well. Showing the full scale of emotions while running DEEP means the energies are being contacted and are running out. As a result the person should feel great at the end of the session.

If the clearer demands more than the introspector can find or assimilate, the introspector will react to the session itself. The person is being overwhelmed by the action. This is also known as getting re-traumatized. The solution is to use a lighter approach; to get there using more but smaller steps. Maybe the person needs another program entirely (see #16, Positive Recall, below.) But first of all, let the introspector address the DEEP items plainly visible and go easy on digging things up. Also emphasize the "Tell" part rather than the "Repeat" part in Repeat and Tell. Remove the charge in plain view. The charge comes off in layers and if the team just continues removing charge from an issue it will eventually be fully handled. Also, the client gets better and better at doing DEEP as he/she gains more experience. So start easy and increase the intensity when the introspector is ready. (See also chapter 3, Live Communication "Two Rules for Good Communication": 1. Be willing to experience anything; 2. Cause only those things which others can experience easily.)

The Tools

5. Assessing for Items

To get started on clearing, the clearer interviews the introspector about issues he/she is bothered about. Issues found are made into a list. The clearer then goes through the list of items and issues with the introspector to determine which item has the most charge and interest. This is simply done by asking: *"On a scale from 0-10, where 0 is no charge and 10 is unbearable charge, how would you rate Item A? Item B? Item C?"* etc. The clearer then takes the most charged item up first. If two items both are rated 10, let's say, the item with the longest history is preferred. An item like 'mother' has a much longer history than a 'co-worker', for instance. There is a lifetime full of experiences with 'mother' and only two years, 9-5, with the 'co-worker'. The clearer can also ask which of the two items has the greatest interest to the client to break a tie. Interest is always an important factor. It is the plus side of protest. Interest ensures the client's engagement which is the key to excellent results. If the person is protesting to take up the item or issue it is never taken up.

This action is called 'Assessing for Items'. The item can usually be taken up with DEEP Subject Clearing (DSC). The DSC will give a lot of data about issues, incidents and identities that can be listed out and assessed after the DSC is complete.

6. Repeat and Tell

Repeat and Tell is the workhorse in DEEP. When a DEEP package is encountered the package needs to be discharged. There are four formal versions according to the DEEP element the introspector offers. If we just have a charged moment and no particular element, the clearer starts with emotion/feeling as that usually is a good starting point. It is important to inform the introspector to tell about ideas, images, old incidents, etc. popping up, the so-called Pop-ups. The telling part ensures optimum discharge. The clearer listens to and acknowledges pop-ups but usually takes no further action. Each time the introspector does the instruction it is acknowledged. That makes it more real to the introspector and helps put it in the past. The general instruction is "Get/experience/feel that (DEEP element)" ["and tell me what may come up."] We add the 'Tell Me' part, shown in [ ] above, when needed. It helps get the client going on the Tell part that is so important for effective discharge.

Note: sometimes pop-ups are very significant. What is popping up can be a heavy traumatic incident or an earlier similar incident to what you are running. You have uncovered some underlying charge. So the clearer may have to shift to what popped up. But as a rule, most incidents and pictures just fly by and all that is needed is to notice them, mention them, get them acknowledged, and let go.

6-0. The Sorting Out Step

The Repeating step is not always appropriate. Often the person brings up a very confusing picture with emotions, sensations, thoughts and impulses sticking out in all directions and in conflict with each other. The conflicting elements were never resolved and that is actually why the person is still carrying them around. Here it is more important to sort out this confusion. After all, confusion/ overwhelm/ shock/ indecision is what we are trying to overcome. It was, and still is, an unresolved conflict. So the best thing here is to have the person talk it out; put some order in and get an overview of the situation. You can ask "What were your emotions or state of mind?" (Emotions) "What thoughts/decisions/intentions did you have at the time?" (Thoughts) "What actions/impulses/body language/gestures did you have at the time?" (Efforts/energies). You give the person as much time as needed to get it all out in the open and then sort the conflicting emotions and thoughts out. If no clear DEEP element stands out you may leave it at that. If a clear and charged DEEP element emerges you can go ahead and do the repeating and full Repeat and Tell. It would be an error to do Repeat and Tell on every little or volatile DEEP element mentioned, but if you have two sides in obvious conflict you should pay attentions to both sides.

When sorting out a single element to take up you are looking for the dominant ingredient to take up. An element that has some energy tied up in it. When you sort out thought, for instance, make sure it is a causative thought, one that could shape reality; a thought that could affect the person's behavior, way of thinking, feeling or even health. We sometimes use the word Dictate – that is if it comes from an unconscious or subconscious source. In sorting out emotion or body sensation, make sure it isn't just a brief reaction but one that seems to remain when thinking back on the package.

You may, however, also find several elements in the same category, such as conflicting emotions of fear, anger, despair, revenge, that all should be run, one after the other. For each emotion taken up you can in turn ask in for connected body sensation, impulse/action and thought/decision. But don't push it if the person cannot find anything. Maybe nothing got stored. You are dealing with a confusion. Cleaning it up can be delicate business.

In the Sorting Out step you can still ask in to emotions, body sensations, thoughts and actions/impulses, etc. But especially with new and inexperienced clients you may not want to take it further than that. If you use this method throughout (and are not using the Repeat step at all) we call it DEEP Light which may be the right pace for inexperienced clients. But most often we sort out the content of the DEEP Package and then pick a dominating DEEP element and flatten that with Repeat and Tell. We then take the next Element and do the same, etc. (Read also the versions of Repeat and Tell below and then re-read this Step 6-0.)

Even though verbatim instructions are given here, it is expected that the clearer adapts questions and instructions to the situation. It is just not possible to cover it all with canned instructions. The way to learn DEEP is to practice many different situations beforehand with an accomplished instructor or partner. This prepares the clearer to be capable of thinking on his/her feet in real sessions. (Also see chapter 12, The DEEP Package, for further theory.)

6a. Version E: Starting with Emotion, State of Mind (E)

You start with Emotion/State of Mind when the package is obviously emotional. You also start with Emotion if there is no clear dominating element. Some kind of emotion or special state of mind will be there or it isn't charged.

1A. "What are the emotions/state of mind in that moment/package?"
Sort it out further, keeping instructions under "6-0 the Sorting Out Step" in mind. You have the person talk about it until an obvious dominating emotion stands out.
1B."Get that..."/"Experience that..."/"Feel that..."/"Contact that…"/ "Witness that…" etc. is used repeatedly until relatively flat.
Then the next element, usually body sensation, is asked for and added. When this combination is relatively flat, Effort/Impulse/Action/Body Language is asked for and added. Then the thought is found and flattened. The whole package is then taken to flat. In the example below the emotion is "Desperation."

1B. *"Experience that feeling of (desperation)." [- and tell me what may come up]*
Use this till relatively flat.
2A. *"Is there a body sensation in the situation?" or "How does it feel in the body?"*
Sort it out. Get it located in the body and have the person describe it a bit. "Where does it sit as an energy?" and "how does it feel?" are good questions.
We use 'tension in body' as an example.
2B. *"Get the sensation of (tension in body) and at the same time get the desperation (and tell.)*
Run this till relative flat.
3A. *"Is there an impulse, effort/ action/ body language in that package?"*
Sort it out and run together with (1 and 2)
3B. *"Get the impulse of (pushing) and at the same time the body tension and the feeling of (desperation)."*
Note: If a clear action, physical reaction or impulse cannot be found there is at least body language and physical posture which should be taken up. You can ask to position of body, limbs, hands, head, facial expression, tensions, gestures, etc.
4A. *"What are the thoughts/decisions/intentions connected with the emotion, sensation and impulse?"*
Again, have the person talk about it and sort it out. If there is a thought that could shape reality; a thought that affects behavior, way of thinking or feeling, you take it up. You leave stray and fleeting thoughts alone.
Sort it out and run together with (1) - (4)
4B. *"Express: I can't make it!"...and feel the desperation, the tension and the impulse to push."*
Note: You can at each step ask into where the DEEP item is located, its shape, energy, vibration, etc.
"Where is that desperation located? What is its shape? What is its energy or vibration?"
We want to establish the physicality of the item.
If you cannot establish clearly if an item is flat, use "Create/Replace that (desperation)" until the item is flat for sure.
Use various questions to ensure the client tells what's going on during the run. The Tell part is very important. That's where the person for sure gets rid of the charge.

6B. Version S: Starting with Body Sensation (S)

This version is used when a Body Sensation is obvious, such as in past illnesses and accidents. Pain is part of body sensations. Also strong smells and other remembered perceptions can be dealt with. If the person is sick or in pain here and now, the right tools may be medical attention followed by assists, such as DEEP Body Clearing. Here the body sensation may well have a physical cause and that should be attended to first. So keep this in mind.
1A. *"What are the body sensations in the situation?"*

Sort it out further, keeping instructions under "6-0 the Sorting Out Step" in mind. You have the person talk about it until an obvious dominating sensation stands out. "Where does it sit as an energy?" and "how does it feel?" are good questions.
(We use body tension as an example.)
1B. "Get the sensation of (body tension) [and tell what may come up]".
Run it till relative flat.
Then add the next element, usually Impulse/Action/Body Language. When this combination is relatively flat, ask for the emotion and include that. Then we look for the central decision/thought. Now the whole package is taken to a flat point.
2A. *"Is there an impulse/action/body language in the situation?"*
Find it and run (1) and (2) together.
Note: If a clear action, physical reaction or impulse cannot be found, there is at least body language and physical posture which should be taken up. You can ask to position of body, limbs, hands, head, facial expression, gestures, etc.
2B. *"Get the action of (pushing) and the sensation of (body tension) at the same time."*
3A. *"Is there an emotion or state of mind in the situation?"*

Find it and run with (1) and (2).
3B. "Get that feeling of desperation, the action of pushing and the sensation of tension at the same time."
4A. "Is there a thought or decision connected to the sensation, impulse and emotion?"
Get the thought that could shape reality; a thought that affects behavior, way of thinking or feeling.
Find it and run together with (1), (2) and (3). (Example: 'I will never make it.')
4B. "Say: 'I will never make it' and at the same time experience the tension, the desperation and the action of pushing." [And tell.]

Note: You can at each step ask into where the DEEP item is located, its shape, energy, vibration, etc.
"Where is that desperation located? What is its shape? What is its energy or vibration?" We want to establish the physicality of the item. (Sometimes this action develops into running Body Sensations.)
If you cannot establish clearly if an item is flat, use "Create/Replace that (desperation)" until the item is flat for sure. Use various questions to ensure the client tells what's going on during the run. The Tell part is very important. That's where the person for sure gets rid of the charge.

6c. Version IE: Starting with Impulse, Effort, Action (IE)

What we are dealing with here is the physical side of things. It may start as a mental impulse or effort but it is aimed at the body or the physical world. It is sometimes called the Effort Band. It is the realm of body memories, physical experiences and actions. It is the band where Man meets the World and the World meets Man. While Thought and Emotion are mainly mental phenomena, the Effort Band is about putting things in motion and action or receiving physical motion and action from the outside.

We use this Version IE when the situation is obviously physical. The situation contains body action, motion, impact or physical experience.

1A. "What are the impulses, efforts or actions in that moment/package?".
Sort it out further, keeping instructions under "6-0 the Sorting Out Step" in mind. You have the person talk about it until an obvious dominating element stands out.
1B. "Get the effort of (running for your life)." [- and tell me what may come up]
There may several efforts in conflict, including impacts from the outside that can be run.
1C. Is there a behavior or pattern that stems from that package?
Here we are looking at the behavior that may be contained in the package. It may unfold to a behavior pattern that the person tends to re-enact or dramatize. It may take some sorting out. It is a Show and Tell action. You can invite the person to tell about it at length and you can have the person reenact it knowingly by going through the motions, while remaining seated in the chair.
When this is sorted out and gone through, ask for emotion/feeling:
2A. "Is there an emotion/feeling while running?" Answer: "I feel terrified."
2B. "OK. Get the effort of (running for your life), and at the same time get (feeling terrified)."
3A. "Is there a body sensation?
3B. Find it, include and run it in a similar fashion. When relatively flat, ask for thought.
4A. "Is there a thought connected to the situation?" Answer: "I must reach the house!"
Get the thought that could shape reality; a thought that affects behavior, way of thinking or feeling.
4B. "OK. Express: 'I must reach the house' and at the same time get (the whole package.)

Note: You can at each step ask into where the DEEP item is located, its shape, energy, vibration, etc.
"Where is that desperation located? What is its shape? What is its energy or vibration?" We want to establish the physicality of the item. (Sometimes this action develops into running Body Sensations.)
If you cannot establish clearly if an item is flat, use "Create/Replace that (desperation)" until the item is flat for sure. Use various questions to ensure the client tells what's going on during the run. The Tell part is very important. That's where the person for sure gets rid of the charge.

6d. Version TD: Starting with Thought, Decision (TD)

Often the introspector will express the thought in the package right away. Thought is the most important element and it is taken up first when available. Make sure it is a causative thought you take up – one that could shape reality; a thought that could affect the person's behavior, way of thinking, feeling or even health.

1A. First, make sure it's the central thought or decision. Some are important, many are not. We assume you have sorted it out, using the 6-0 Sorting out Step, and have found a central statement or sentence.

1B. Have the introspector repeat the statement a few times.

"Express that statement." or "Say...(verbatim statement)." "Thank you."

Each time the person says it, it is acknowledged as all executions of instructions are.

We often use *"Express that"* rather than *"Say that (verbatim) statement"* as some persons like to rephrase the thought continuously. That by itself shows they are very engaged. Also, you may often run into thoughts and decisions that were never put into words so expressing them now takes some work.

1C. Check if the wording is correct. It may change during the procedure. It is the person's own formulation and wording we want to address.

"How does the wording seem to you?"

2A. Get the original emotion/feeling of the statement.

"Is there an emotion or feeling of that statement?"

Have the introspector say it in that tone of voice.

2B. *"Say the statement in that tone of voice." [- and tell me what may come up]*

3A. Ask for any body language, impulse, etc. and have the person duplicate it or act it out while doing (4).

"Is there any body language, impulse or effort connected to that statement?"

You can ask to position of body, limbs, hands, head, facial expression, tensions, gestures, etc.

3B. Have the introspector show it or act it out.

"Say the statement in that tone of voice and show me (the effort)."
or *"Say the statement in that tone of voice and, at the same time, show (the body language/effort)."*

Note: we don't expect clear action, physical reaction or impulse here. Usually we find body language and physical posture and that is taken up. You can ask to position of body, limbs, hands, head, facial expression, tensions, gestures, etc.

4A. Ask for body sensation.

"Is there a body sensation?"

4B. *Find it, include and run it.*

Run the whole package until it goes flat. Sometimes the charge contacted will blow suddenly and the introspector feels happy. If so, the package is completed for that statement.

Note: You can at each step ask into where the DEEP item is located, its shape, energy, vibration, etc.

"Where is that desperation located? What is its shape? What is its energy or vibration?" We want to establish the physicality of the item. (Sometimes this action develops into running Body Sensations.)

If you cannot establish clearly if an item is flat, use "Create/Replace that (desperation)" until the item is flat for sure. Use various questions to ensure the client tells what's going on during the run. The Tell part is very important. That's where the person for sure gets rid of the charge.

6e. Notes on Running DEEP Packages

It is not always that you get to do all the steps of the above procedures. Your objective is simply to get the stored energies released. Once that is accomplished you are done. With some experience you will know what to work on and what to skip. Some elements may blow as you run others and when you formally get to that element it is already handled. (Also, some elements may never have been recorded.) One element may dominate. In an accident the physical and body elements dominate and you may have to run a number of physical reactions, sensations, including pain, impulses and actions. Also, impacts from the outside can be run from their point of view. In losses and break-ups the emotions may run high and need a lot of detailed work. There may not always be a clear thought, except the instinctual reaction to the situation or accident. You can still get the person to express it in words, such as "Run!" or "Get out of there!" - or such dictate.

Especially Impulses and Energies can be repressed and "invisible". Energies, such as to push another away or pull another in without physical action, can be very important to run. Here it is a strong "wish" that runs under the surface. There are other types of invisible energies, such as feeling a constant pressure from the outside. This may be the receiving end of another person's (or an object's) push or pull. You take it up as an Impulse/energy and run it with Repeat and Tell. In such cases it is especially important to also run the opposing point of view, since the energy is created from two sides and will dissolve only when the act of creating it is addressed (duplicated) on both sides.

In some incidents there seem to be no action or impulse; yet there is body language and body attitude that can and should be picked up and be demonstrated or "shown" by the person. You can ask to positions of hands, head, posture, gestures, tensions, etc. When running Effort, Action, Body Language, etc. the person usually remains seated in the chair but goes through the motoric energies – as an athlete does before a jump or other physical performance.

6f. Secondary Impulse: Also, the person may be repressing or stopping an impulse from being expressed. This is quite common in social situations where a certain impulse is socially unacceptable. It can be "politically incorrect", a sexual impulse, too violent a move, or other behavior that does not fit. If that is coming up, ask the client "is there a secondary own impulse that represses or stops that primary impulse?" Run the secondary (own) impulse as part of the package.

Children

With children you can make it into a game where the child draws the incident while telling. Then illustrates what happened with toy figures while telling the story and demonstrating how the figures felt. Then the child may reenact the incident in the various roles. The clearer may take on a supporting role. The child can also be asked to work out the incident in clay, showing the drama. The point is to get the child engaged and replaying it as a game. This usually takes a special setup.

Different Types

You will find different types of people. Roughly you could say there is a type for each element. There are action/effort persons, such as artisans, skilled workers, engineers, etc., who mainly understand the world through motion, action and physical manifestations. They may have a hard time with emotions and abstract thoughts.
There are emotional people, such as artists and caretakers, who largely understand the world through emotions. They may be strong in intuition and compassion but have a hard time doing practical things or solving abstract problems. There are "thought people", intellectuals, accountants, scientists, "nerds", etc. who may have a hard time relating to others (emotion) or deal with practical problems (action/effort). Finally we may have to do with "body-people" (body sensation). They are mainly aware of what happens to their body, their health and fitness, their looks, their age, their physical performance, etc.

Each type will have easy access to the DEEP element that corresponds to their type but have a harder time accessing one or more of the other elements.
The clearer must take this into consideration. Don't try to run elements that are totally unreal to the person; just discuss the content of such an element and move on. The person will eventually catch on and run all the elements.

Some DEEP packages with little charge may fizzle out and fall apart before you get very far. You can ask into it or check for charge on a scale from 0-10 to find out if it is still worth working on. The tools below can also be taken in use, such as Six Directions on a significant object in the package, Create/Replace, Identities Dialogue, etc. If the introspector is engaged in the session but loses interest or extroverts from a specific package it is safe to say it is flat regardless if all formal steps are run or not. But always ask into things to find out what is going on. If the person was simply running away from the content there is more Repeat and Tell to do,

As with any set of tools, it takes practice and experience to know which tool to take out next. The saving grace is that you can follow the basic instructions step by step and still accomplish great results. As you get more experience and master your tools you can accomplish miracles in half the time.

6g. Other Viewpoints

When you run Other Viewpoints than the person's own, they may run much lighter and the Viewpoint may fall apart quickly. So don't push it if that is the case. The charge and viewpoint dissipated and that is it. It has gone flat. Viewpoints that routinely are run in DEEP Incident Clearing are opponents, perpetrators, bystanders, sympathizers and antagonists. In very physical incidents the Body's Viewpoint can be run separately. Also the "Viewpoint" of an object or animal can be run, such as a car, a sword, or a fly on the wall. Sometimes dominating people in the person's life can be run with benefits – even though they were not present in the incident. A child doing something wrong may think "what would my mother say to this?" Well, find out! Run the mother's viewpoint. If running the opponent's viewpoint seems to be disgusting and thus impossible to take, you can run the viewpoint of a fly sitting on the opponents shoulder, etc. If you are running out a rape, for instance, it may not be possible for the victim to run the rapist's viewpoint. But if you use the trick with the fly, etc. the woman will gradually get enough courage and confront to run the perpetrator's viewpoint.

When looking for other viewpoints to run, always ask the client for "relevant viewpoints" to the incident or material in question but run only those that are charged.
"Higher Viewpoints" is a special category that can be very beneficial to run. You are asking the person to take a step back and occupy a multi-determined view; to see it all from above. Clients may have different names for this, like "helicopter view", "a reporter's viewpoint", "God's viewpoint", "the viewpoint of the higher Self", etc. Our generic name is the "Outside Observer", but we prefer to ask the client what name he himself would like best. In any event use an expression that is real to the person. Even though these viewpoints are somewhat abstract they are very beneficial to run. The person is asked to step out of the turmoil and take a detached from-above look at "those funny puppets down there." The truth is that the person can take any viewpoint in or around the situation. This is a basic ability – not always developed we may add. But the essence of running viewpoints in the first place is to develop this ability as it enables the person to rise above the situation and learn from it. So you can even ask, after running a higher viewpoint, "What could or should [character] learn from this incident?[if s/he were willing to learn]" This question is asked several times until no more answers, and it is asked about each of the main character in the introspector's "movie". We are not asking the characters, we are asking the "Outside Observer" about the characters.
In DEEP we use the slogan "DEEP turns trauma and stress into Life Experience!" Taking a higher, detached viewpoint and sort of analyzing what happened, how and why for sure accomplishes just that.

7. Create/Replace

This tool can be used on any resistive DEEP element. Also, if the client cannot clearly say if an item went flat or not, we can use the two instructions or just the first one ('Create'). 'Feeling terrified' is used as an example.

1. "Create (or generate/act out/flow) that 'Feeling terrified'." The person is asked to self-determinedly turn that DEEP element on - like an actor would do.
2. "Now, place it where you felt the 'Feeling terrified' before."

By doing this Create-Replace step repeatedly, the introspector is asked to take control over 'Feeling terrified.' If he/she gets the idea that it can be turned on at will the person will sooner or later realize, he/she can also stop it or turn it off at will. The Create-Replace step is repeated until it produces no more reaction, the item is blown, or the person has a win.

8. Hello/OK

Hello/OK is used to establish a communication. Once the line is established we shift to 'having a conversation'. It has proven to be a very effective tool to discharge former and existing relationships and conflicts. It can also be used to establish communication with ailing body parts and other phenomena in or around the introspector, for example a resistive mental mass.

1. "Say 'Hello' to (item)."
2. "Have (item) say 'OK' to that hello."
3. "Have (item) say 'Hello' to you."
4. "You say 'OK' to that hello."

This should turn into a conversation or exchange. It can be in words or in flows.

5. "Is there something (item) wants to say to you?"
6. "Acknowledge that."
7. "Is there something you want to say (in response to that) to (item)?"
8. "Have (item) acknowledge that."

To keep track of what to say next in session, it can be written like this: the clearer makes an arrow for each delivered communication that shows who speaks and who receives.

<u>You</u> ----> <u>Item</u>
<----
---->

9. Identities Dialogue (2ID)

This is a variation of the above. Often we run into a situation where the introspector is recalling an old situation that had a lot of unexpressed communication in it. We have two known people, the introspector and the other person. Or we have two persons different from the introspector. We simply have the person imagine the situation and complete the unsaid or unfinished communications. Make sure the introspector uses direct speech directed at the other person and vice versa. It is not enough to use indirect statements such as, I would tell him so and so. No, we want verbatim statements like, "You don't know how it feels", etc.

1. Is there anything that (A) wants to communicate to (B)? [(A) talks to (B)].
2. Have (B) acknowledge this.
3. Does (B) want to reply anything? [(B) talks to (A)].
4. Have (A) acknowledge this.

The whole cycle is done in a loop. When the introspector has nothing more to say, the communication is turned around and the receiver now has the chance to say his/her piece. The loop is continued until both parties have no more to say. You may stay on one side (1-2), for several or many rounds if A mainly has something to say to B – such as a child having a lot to say to a parent and not necessarily expecting an answer except acknowledgement.

10. Fixed Ideas Handling (FIX)
A fixed idea has popped up during session. By Fixed Ideas we mean stuck or limiting beliefs. In DEEP we also use the words Dogma or Dictate. It is an idea the person has been operating on in certain situations without inspecting it for rationality or usefulness. Such ideas are often very irrational or harmful. The idea is being dictated to him/her from the subconscious mind, from the culture, the group, the morphic field, or whatever.

The Fixed Idea or Dictate is statement A. This is noted down and taken up later in the same session

Ask: To your mind or in your universe, what is the opposite of (statement A)?
That is statement B. Make sure you have a positive and a negative. Not 2 negatives or 2 positives. Use the following and keep the introspector reporting on the ideas:

1. Get the idea of (statement A).
2. Get the idea of (statement B).

Theory: Fixed Ideas Handling is a simple, yet very effective tool that can be used in many contexts. It can be used when the person expresses some idea or statement that seems to be at the core of a problem. This may be expressed as a realization in an end point. "Oh, yes! Ever since that day, I always thought that salesmen should be avoided." You can take such a realization one step further, using FIX, and broaden the realization considerably.

FIX can also be used on ideas expressed during unblocking or two-way communication. You take the statement up after the action at hand is ended. It is sometimes an alternative tool to Repeating.

The person holds a certain datum or dictate as true and it has caused endless problems ever since. Such a datum is not necessarily false but it doesn't fit present time. A fresh look is needed. It can of course also be a totally illogical dictate or dogma such as a generality like "all men/women are bad." "Never talk to a stranger," "Eating fish equals death," etc.

Another version of dealing with fixed ideas (used in DEEP Viewpoint Clearing) is:
How has (the idea) helped you?
How has (the idea) harmed you?
This can be used as a general tool in other contexts.
This can be followed by asking:
Can you find a less stressful idea of your own that would fit in the situation?
Then you can go back and forth between the old fixed idea and the new idea and in this way loosen up the person's thinking. When this is flat, do some rounds with the new idea alone to a good point.

11. Before/After
1. Recall a moment before the incident/shock moment.
2. Recall a moment after the incident/shock moment.

Theory: If the introspector is stuck in a shock moment or stuck in any other past event, the above will unstick the person. The introspector should be told that it can be any moment before and any moment after, including when the person was 5 years old (before) and yesterday (after). Often introspectors think it has to be moments closely connected to the same incident, but that is not the case.

12. Feel it Back
1. "Put that emotion/feeling into the wall."
2. "Feel it back."

Theory: This is a simple tool used to handle strong emotions, feelings and sensations. If the person experiences such an element that is too strong to endure, use "Feel it Back".

Also, if we are dealing with a strong emotion the person wants to hide or hold back in a social situation, Feel it Back is one way to deal with it.

The clearer can pick other big and solid objects than walls in (1), of course. One example was a situation where the client was sitting in his parked car during a telephone session. We used the motor block as the solid item. Buildings or mountains in sight could also have been used.

13. Alternate Confront

1. What part of [item] could you confront?
2. What part of [item] would you rather not confront?

Theory: This is a great little tool. It can be used on anything the introspector finds difficult to confront. For example, if one of the other tools hasn't worked all the way, try Alternate Confront. When asked for something he/she would rather not confront, the person still has to take a peek and identify it.

Note: "Confront" in this sense is a receptive action. Synonym are: duplicate, facing, confronting, maintaining attention and interest, recognizing the source of, inspecting closely, viewing; also *observing with Mindfulness* and *Witnessing* as used in various practices and types of meditation.

You may have to clear this up as another dictionary meaning of Confront is: Standing up to something or someone in an aggressive or accusative way.

14. 6-Directions (6-D)

1. Put (item) above you.
2. Put (item) below you.
3. Put (item) out to the right.
4. Put (item) out to the left.
5. Put (item) out in front of you.
6. Put (item) to the back of you.
7. You may add: Put it far away.
8. Bring it in and place it at a comfortable distance.

You can end off (after many rounds) "Stick it deep in the ground" (or similar).

The distance the item is put from the introspector can be changed from time to time. "Put the item 1 meter above you", etc. for several rounds, then 2 meters, etc.

If the person finds it difficult you can use: Put it on the ceiling; put it on the floor; put it on the wall to the right; put it on the wall to the left; put it on the wall in front of you; put it on the wall behind you.

Theory: In Six Directions the person takes control over these items in mental form that have influenced his/her life and way of thinking negatively. Once the person can take control over such mental items by moving them around at will, their command value soon becomes zero. Instead of being pushed around by items and concepts the client is pushing *them* around at will.

The person is asked to get the concept of a charged item, be it an incident, a time-period, a person or identity; or even a resistive energy phenomenon the person has encountered in his energy field. Then the person is asked to place it 'Above him', 'Below him', 'To the Right', 'To the Left', 'In Front of him', 'Back of him' (6 directions). This is done over and over to a flat point or to some kind of shift. When dealing with own identities it's advisable to first ask the person, "assume a higher/exterior viewpoint". When addressing incidents with 6-D you can use: "Take that experience and roll it into a ball" or "Imagine that incident being on /a spool of film/ a memory stick/ a printed page, etc." You can also pick significant items from the incident: persons, vehicles, weapons, trees, houses, etc. even when it runs well. Some clients find this system easier than taking the whole event. (See also below.)

Another use of 6-D is as a repair tool if things have become all confusing, say, in incident clearing. Simply take an item from the incident, the car you were driving in, the weapon the soldier held in his hand, the opponent identity, or whatever, and use 6-D on that. Take some item you are sure is in the incident and flatten it with 6-D. You can do several items like that, each to a flat point or shift, and at some point the whole event sorts itself out and you can return to the original action. This can also be useful when the person just can't remember what happened nor has too many "versions" of what might have happened. You take a solid reference point and move it around and things loosen up—either in the form of remembering what actually happened or the energies simply dissipate.

A special use of 6-D is when the person has a stuck or random picture. One handling for that was (and still is) to find the exact time and place (date and location) when the picture was formed. This can sometimes be difficult to establish. Instead, use the 6-D on the picture or a significant part of it and it will resolve.

Note: If you have a stuck sensation or pain or other DEEP element, you can ask the person to move it, just a little bit. This can be done as a preparation for 6-D.
"Can you move that pain/headache 2 cm to the right?" "2 cm to the left?" etc.

15. Unblocking as a Repair Tool

Unblocking, as given in the chapter on DEEP Subject Clearing, can be used as a repair tool. If a session or action seems to go nowhere and the clearer doesn't know what went wrong, doing unblocking on the session or action can loosen things up. The introspector is made to look at the session problem from many different angles. This helps get any charge off the situation. Sooner or later the team will find out what went wrong and the clearer can now correct it. When Unblocking is used in repair you don't run DEEP packages. Just let the person talk it out.

16. Positive Recall

A useful technique, when ending sessions, is to run Positive Recall. Most often we have run out unpleasant and negative things during session. Any lingering of a negative atmosphere can be countered by recalling positive things. "Recall a time you were happy." "Recall a time you enjoyed life." "Recall a time when you proudly had accomplished something." "Recall a time you enjoyed your family" and the like can be used. If you have run out something like 'trouble in the family' it's a good idea to finish off by recalling moments when the family (or **a** family) was a happy and smooth functioning unit. You would use this technique before you use Fresh Reality to end off a session. You have the client recall happy moments and then you bring the client to present time using Fresh Reality if needed.

Positive Recall is a powerful technique all by itself. For persons who find DEEP too demanding it can be used as an independent action in a series of sessions. There exist lists in DEEP (and also in Applied Metapsychology, for instance) that consist of a long series of questions to positive experiences and the perceptual content in the incidents (such as sight, smell, sound, touch, etc.). Running Positive Recall for hours on end will help a frail personality to get a better confront and more energy and optimism—and generally a more positive outlook on life— even without addressing trauma and stressful situations directly. So if DEEP in itself is too steep a hill to climb for a person, Positive Recall Lists as the main action are one way to get the person in better shape. There are also many other actions that can be done to this end as a tailor-made program. The simplicity of Positive Recall is that the person exerts some intentional control over the past and its memories rather than being controlled and pushed around by them. This rationale is valid for all the tools. We are dealing with the Duplication and Control factors in a simple form.

17. Fresh Reality
Choose one line and ask it 10-20 times:

"Look at that (room object)," vase, table, picture, wall, etc., etc.
"Pick a random object in sight." "How could you make that object more interesting?"
"Point out something."
"Where is the (room object)?" (introspector points.)
"Look around here and find something you would like to remain in place."
"Point out something in this room you could keep looking at."
"What else is that (indicated object)?"
"Duplicate something."
"What is the condition of that (room object)?"
"Find an object you are not in (inside)."
"What scenario could (that object) be part of?"
"Look around the room and find something that you like."
"Look around and find something that is round."

(You can use Round, Square, Rectangular, a certain color, etc. – any visual or even tactile characteristic, the point being to extrovert the attention.)

Theory: This is a class of techniques that helps the introspector become alert and grounded again when the going gets a bit tough in session. Symptoms like grogginess, sleepiness and the like, point towards the need for using Fresh Reality. It is also routinely used at the end of the session to get the introspector extroverted and back in the present again. It can be used in the middle of session after an action is completed with a proper end point. The clearer takes just one of the above lines and asks it maybe 10-20 times—until the introspector feels more alert and present.

Chapter 16: Repeat & Tell

This chapter was written one year after the original publishing. It was part of 2nd edition but has now been revised and illustrated in this 3rd edition. The biggest difference to the original text was that the effort band is now divided into two DEEP elements: 1) Body movement, impulses, action (kinesthesia and motoric systems). 2. Bodily sensations (sensory systems). This is now reflected throughout the book. But this chapter still offers an in depth description of Repeat & Tell and additional data on the DEEP package.

Repeat & Tell is the core technique in DEEP. When a charged incident has been found, we use this general tool to discharge the central DEEP packages in the incident. We use it to dissolve and integrate those elements that cause the incident to produce charge when it is triggered (activated). We need to get hold of *the original recordings* stored in the memory systems: in the mind, in the heart and in the body. We are interested in 1) thoughts and decisions; 2) emotions and feelings; 3) action and impulses to move and body language; 4) and in bodily sensations. These four categories are what we call *DEEP Elements*.

Once we have found a DEEP package we can use Repeat & Tell. Of the above mentioned elements we start with the one that is most present in the package. There is a drill for each category. The drills, teaching you to use Repeat & Tell, was given step by step in the tool box (chapter 15). What we give here is a comprehensive description of the theory. It is noted that the clearer, in real sessions, must be able to adjust his tools to the situation, and especially the sequence in which he/she runs the DEEP elements. But during drilling the models given in the tool box are used. It often happens that some of the elements have

That's the essence of Repeat & Tell

no or little charge. This may cause the client to jump the sequence. Adjust to the client as much as possible. Go back and check the skipped elements afterwards as needed. This chapter explains how and why the technique works. It also explains how you get it to work optimally.

How 'Repeat & Tell' works

What we are after is the dissolving and integrating of the *original recordings* of thoughts, emotions, feelings, impulses/movements/ energetic action and body sensations. We work with one DEEP element at a time. Doing it this way makes it easier to handle and experience. One of the problems with stressful and traumatic experiences is that they are too overwhelming. They overwhelm the person and take the power from him/her. The overwhelming also causes the elements to be repressed and stored in some kind of physical form. If we had been able to experience the elements fully in the incident itself, we would probably be able to remember what happened without the negative aspect of storing them as charge. It seems that overwhelming incidents go straight into the subconscious and repressed mind or lodge in the body's tissue. They are stored there until we get an opportunity to experience and integrate them fully. One could wonder if the idea is that we shall experience and learn. If we do not experience and learn when something happens, or shortly after, this mechanism apparently takes care of storing it in the subconscious systems for a later occasion. Luckily we have that opportunity now with DEEP Clearing. We can re-experience and transform stress and trauma into live useful energy and life experience!

It is, as said, easier to handle a charged incident when it is divided into its elements. We have already gotten a distance to the experience. We are beyond danger and risk of physical overload. Now, as we have divided the incident into its DEEP elements, it is even easier to handle and dissolve. The client can maintain an important 'curious interest' in what is happening to his/her case when we are dealing with only one DEEP element at a time.

Curious, positive interest

Curious, positive interest is a key ingredient in Repeat & Tell. We must be able to observe the DEEP element consciously in a calm and inclusive way. It is hidden somewhere or other in our subconscious systems, including the body. By calling the element up and observing it in an inclusive way it will be transformed from being mental mass into being live energy. The method does not erase the remembrance of what happened. But the automaticity, which caused that the negative element could be triggered out of our control, has been dissolved. When all elements in a traumatic or stressful incident have been dissolved in this way, they will no longer be a source of stress and discomfort. All elements have been made conscious and been integrated; and through this technique their negative influences have been broken.

The Sorting Out Step

The Repeating step is not where you start. Often the person brings up a very confusing picture with emotions, sensations, thoughts and impulses sticking out in all directions and in conflict with each other. The conflicting elements were never resolved and that is actually why the person is still carrying them around. We need, first of all, to sort out this confusion. It was, and still is, an unresolved conflict. So the best starting point is always to have the person talk it out; put some order in and get an overview of the situation. You give the person as much time as needed to get it all out in the open. It would be an error to do Repeat & Tell on every little or volatile DEEP element when it is first mentioned.

When sorting out a single element to take up, you are looking for the dominant ingredient; a central element that has some energy tied up in it. When you sort out Thought, for instance, make sure it is a causative thought, one that could shape reality; a thought that could affect the person's behavior, way of thinking, feeling or even health. We sometimes use the word Dictate – an automatic, uninspected thought that has command value. In sorting out emotion or body sensation, make sure it isn't just a brief reaction but one that seems to remain when thinking back on the package.

Finding the DEEP Element and integrating it

When we have found a charged DEEP element it is important to be able to perceive the element taken up. If there is a bodily sensation like a distinctive discomfort, tiredness, soreness, smell etc. it is a good place to start. An obvious body sensation would be the physical pain from an injury, illness, etc. Physical pain is always taken up first. When the person finds the original recording of this sensation it is usually experienced as being located in a specific place in the body. The person is asked to focus on the sensation; use their hand to point to the place it is perceived to be. Then kind of taste it as if it was something pleasant. Some nice food you could say. Instead of repressing or destroying the sensation/feeling the drill is to experience and include the feeling, let it come up, unfold, and express itself.

Imagine playing the lead role in an exciting movie and going through some fantastic experiences and perceptions. This positive inclusion of the feeling is important. The person must overcome all the defense-mechanisms that were used against the experience. We typically try to renounce responsibility and involvement. We try to flee from or deny the discomfort and the pain in the experience. But the outcome of that would be that sensations and impressions were stored as recordings, a multi-track recording containing several layers of the occurrence. And this multi-track recording was stored in the person's body and energy field.

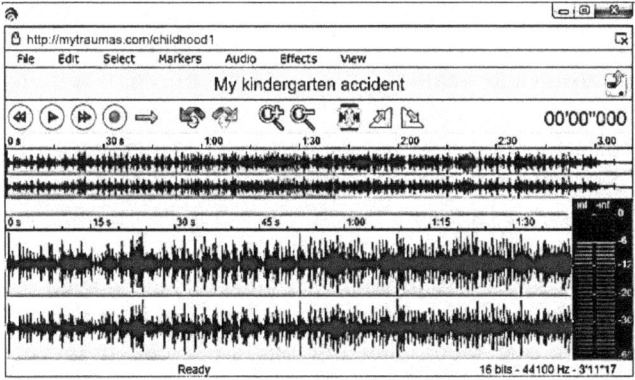

The recordings of an experience contain many tracks, as explained. The four tracks that contain most energy and power are thought, emotion, effort (kinesthesia) and body sensations. In trauma and stressful situations the potential energies contained in these tracks are our primary target. Each track is contacted and the charge is resolved. Rather than "noise from the past" we now have Life Experience!

When we find this stored recording in session, the experience of the element will go through a cycle. First it becomes stronger and clearer. Then it becomes weaker and finally it becomes difficult or impossible to find. The person can be asked to **create it knowingly**. In the same simple way the person would do it if she was an actor. Being able to create it on demand and knowingly

means that full control over the element has been obtained. Now the person can for instance decide to feel the pain or decide to stop the pain. This goes for the psychosomatic part of the pain – not for pains caused by acute injury, of course.

It also often happens that a specific feeling for instance, changes character after a few moments. It is like the original feeling has been dissolved and a new layer appears under it. Fear can change to anger. Sorrow can reveal an underlying suspiciousness, etc. When that happens you naturally follow up on the most pressing aspect and maybe just check if the original feeling disappeared; that the original element" went flat" as we say.

When an element like a body sensation has gone fairly flat we ask for the next, for instance the feeling. We cannot expect that the body sensation will disappear completely isolated and on its own. It is of course connected with the related elements. But when the body sensation has eased off and can be looked at then we include the next DEEP element. We ask:"what is the accompanying feeling?" Now we run the two elements simultaneously. "Sense the feeling and the body sensation at the same time." This way we add more and more of the DEEP package that was formed at the moment we are focusing on.

Regarding pain: Of course, a new blow to the same area will cause a new and real pain. Experiencing a real pain has a survival function. It is a clear signal to get away from the source of the pain. That this signal is then stored and can be triggered much later is not always understood. Why is it stored?

A likely theory is that we hold on to these recordings in body and mind so that they can serve as automatic danger signals if we should get into similar situations again. We burned the fingers once and now shy away from fire. A conditional reflex has been installed. Even though this may seem useful from a survival standpoint we can very quickly build up so many conflicting conditional reflexes that our freedom of action gets heavily reduced; we get tied on hands and feet.

The purpose of DEEP is to transform all these automatic reflexes into useful energy and life experiences. In other words, we can learn a lot about ourselves and life and at the same time get rid of all these heavy moments with their automatic reactions, dictates and ties.

It should also be mentioned that another reason they get stored is that they simply are hard to look at; they are painful and disturbing. It's a "fear of the dark" reaction. But when we have the support and courage to do so the fixation, the life force, the attention and energy which were tied into the traumatic and stressing incident or subject are freed up.

What Works and does not Work

The purpose of DEEP is to dissolve automatic reactions, thoughts and action patterns. We dissolve them by becoming aware of the small and big moments of overwhelm by looking at their creation. The attitude to maintain as a client is that of clear interest, a willingness to experience, maintain an inclusive curiosity, a wish to understand and embrace the phenomenon. You know it is an expansion of your personal life experience. Look at it as such and integrate the experience and its DEEP elements as another valuable lesson in being human—in being you!

We are all fascinated by film and TV where all kinds of situations are played out in front of us. A good movie contains a lot of strong feelings and situations which we would rather not experience ourselves. But when we see them play out on the screen it is very interesting and stimulating. We revel in murder, violence, treason and disasters. In sorrow, fear and anger, etc. And also of course in the more positive sides of life, like heroics, exiting travel experiences, wild car chases, falling in love and having sex and participating in huge parties. These films have such a big effect upon us because they trigger similar experiences and moments in our subconscious. The film plays against this subconscious material and makes us feel that we experience them ourselves—without the negative consequences to our health and wellbeing.

In DEEP Clearing, however, we focus directly on our *own* small or big experiences in our *own* subconscious systems and on all those DEEP elements these moments  consist of. To dissolve and discharge these elements we have to look at them in the clear light of our awareness. We must show Mindfulness – to use a Buddhist concept that has turned mainstream. So we do not focus on the big screen or the TV but inward towards the original sources of these elements of thoughts, feelings, sensations, etc.

Such elements are not discharged by for instance 'letting off steam'. 'Letting off your angry steam' might give a momentary relief, at least until next time you feel exactly the same way. We can express our anger towards the government or politicians, time and again without getting any special change in our mood. But if we look at specific incidents which involve politicians and observe our own recordings of the evoked feelings etc. directly, then we can actually dissolve these DEEP elements in an effective way. Our repeated angry outbursts can for instance now be replaced by constructive criticism. We have freed ourselves from automatic thought and action patterns and from emotional reactions that just run in the same groove.

Repeat & Tell as Communication

Another way to understand the core of Repeat & Tell is to view it in the light of communication. The discharge of a DEEP element itself can be understood as a communication between the element and the consciousness. There is actually an exchange of microscopic, but measurable energy between the element and the consciousness taking place. Figuratively speaking you could look at consciousness as a grounding and the elements as a positive charge.

A DEEP element from a situation of overwhelm is a signal generated in our systems that never arrives in the consciousness. It has been denied access as being too overwhelming – it hangs up and solidifies into mental mass. When we later consciously perceive that same DEEP element, it changes back from mental mass to live energy, to a live communication. When this communication arrives at the consciousness level and is received with an open mind and open arms, so to speak, the circuit has been completed. The charge is neutralized. The communication, whether it was a feeling, a thought, a body sensation etc., has fulfilled its purpose of informing the consciousness about what exactly is going on. When the communication arrives at the consciousness its cycle has been completed and its energy becomes neutralized. The mission has been accomplished successfully and body and mind no longer need to store the energy or content.

Let us underline that when we talk about DEEP elements we are talking about energies that are stored in the person's body, mind and energy systems. *It is recordings and impressions* formed for instance during an unpleasant or traumatic incident. We are not talking objective reality like in a car crash and the broken arm the driver got. We are talking about *recordings* of what happened and especially recordings of thoughts, feelings and body memories.

We can delete these because they were created by the person him- or herself. Even though a trauma comes from the outside, it only fixes itself because mind and body, at some level, create recordings of what happened and store them somewhere. Naturally, there are many detours and relay stations involved in a process like this. The person's own body and other people and the surroundings are needed ingredients in the forming of such a trauma. But the only effective way to discharge a trauma is by the consciousness looking at the stored recordings with a loving accepting attitude, change them from "frozen" to live communication and energy which is then received and discharged in the bright light of consciousness and 'grounding'.

We must underline that a significant reason for such trauma to persist is that we tend to fix our attention towards external factors. Like the spider, the assailant, the unhappy event, the drunken driver who caused the accident, etc. *We tend to overlook completely that our own recordings and storing of incidents are the factors that in the long run are the sources of our difficulties, sufferings and discomfort.* It is our own recordings and repressions and storing of these 'messages' that cause the permanent damage. Only when we, aided by DEEP Clearing, are able to find and discharge these stored communications and recordings, does the communication arrive fully, and a significant change in the situation occurs. We must use introspection (i.e. looking inwards, into our own mind and recordings) rather than blame the drunken driver if we really want to get over the accident and start anew. As long as our attention is fixed at external factors no significant change in wellbeing and condition will take place. Just "being a victim" is a very unproductive state of mind.

Looking at Repeat & Tell as based on communication is meaningful in several ways. You have to establish a live connection, an open communication line between the DEEP element and the consciousness; because as explained, this allows the repressed and incomplete communications to complete their cycles. Likewise there must be a good and free communication between the person and the clearer. This ensures that the discharge is not only occurring between the element and the person's consciousness, but also between the person and the clearer. Especially the Tell part needs an interested listener to be able to flow towards a natural completion, of course.

Some Tips

It is important to help the person sort out the feelings, sensations and clues coming up. If the person says that he/she is confused, then you can't just ask him/her to feel the confusion. Fact is that the different DEEP elements are recorded and stored in very different layers of awareness and are not always coordinated. It is a well-known fact that there can be conflicts between feelings and thoughts. Just like conflicts between intentions (thought) and actions often are experienced. Overwhelms and confusions are partly a result of the conflicts existing between the various DEEP elements. Part of the art in Repeat & Tell lies therefore in finding the original DEEP elements that underlie the confusion and overwhelm that arise when the elements appear simultaneously in disharmony. This requires that we do the Sorting Out step properly. Only when that is done can we isolate each individually recorded track in this multi-track recording and be able to dissolve or release the original recordings.

Likewise, you should be aware of the fact that the incident taken up can prove to be the top layer of a layered structure of a sequence of incidents. Ideally you should get to the very first incident where the feeling or sensation in question was created. We call it the basic incident. Naturally it is covered by several later incidents and layers that have placed themselves on top. It can be compared with archaeology. We can uncover the story layer by layer. But there is also a difference. Normally DEEP elements can be discharged without knowing or tracing back their entire history. But of course, you need to get a charged incident in order to have something to discharge.

If you have an original issue like "afraid of spiders" you should ask for incidents where the person was scared of spiders, several times, until one with considerable emotional charge appears. Just don't take the first offered but be on the lookout for a deeper layer—ideally the basic incident. As it is not possible to establish objectively what incident is the basic incident, we use the criterion that there has to be enough charge in the incident we pick, to create a result in the form of obvious relief when it is run. This incident can then lead to another one with even more or new charge which is earlier. If there is charge, but the incident is later, we can still take it up. The most important criterion is to find and discharge relevant charge rather than try to reconstruct a chain of incidents. We are completely finished when the subjective distress is gone to 0 (on a distress scale from 0 – 10) and the person experiences relief from the item.

Incidents, subjects, characters

In the examples above we have especially discussed *incidents* containing the DEEP element we wanted to discharge. This is the best approach, if possible. But as mentioned, it is definitely possible to discharge DEEP elements without knowing their exact history—and especially without knowing the basic incident. It is also possible to discharge elements to a large extent without connecting them to a specific incident. After all, it is about thoughts, feelings, sensations and reactions being present now. They are elements that we, to a greater or lesser degree, nourish and supply with new energy right here and now where we perceive them. Therefore, even when there is no obvious incident we can still work directly on the DEEP elements. It could for instance be a person, a character, as we call it in DEEP, who seems threatening and fear-provoking. We could tell the person to: 'Feel the fear that the Devil is provoking' – provided of course that the person brought up fear of the Devil as something to handle. The person perceives the fear repeatedly and notices where it is in the body, etc. But during this, a real incident might appear. It could be a hell and brimstone sermon in church. Now we have a real incident with time and place.

Typically we will shift focus to that incident where the fear possibly was created or was significantly present.

It is a matter of judgement when to pick up a new incident or just let the person give detached associations containing that same fear. But if the starting point was a fear which was hard to place in time then, when such an incident surfaces, it is of course a better point to work from. Again, the criterion would be, if the fear suddenly is perceived to be more intense it is because we have moved closer to the point in time where it was created. It is like playing the children's game 'Object getting hotter'. (This is a game where a small object is hidden and another person has to find it. When the person gets closer to the place where the object is hidden, you say: It's getting hotter', and in this way the person will finally find the object.)

Description of the DEEP Elements

Let us look at the different DEEP elements more extensively. They are also explained in other places in the materials, but a summary would fit in here.

In DEEP, as mentioned above, we are interested in: thoughts and decisions; emotions and feelings; impulses to move or body language; and body sensations. With some clients, also in non-physical (energetic) actions. These are our DEEP elements. They form a scale starting from something mental and non-physical and move towards more and more physical phenomena. The borders are: non-physical awareness upwards, and physical body downwards. As mentioned, we find that the stored DEEP elements have a physical existence, even though it takes special electronic equipment to measure them. The best way to see their existence clearly is by the subjective experience of "before" and "after". How does our subjective wellbeing and perception of the world change when we dissolve distressing DEEP elements?

The reason we first and foremost are interested in these four elements of our mind and subjective experience is that they belong to four different systems. These systems are storing the most energy and effect. The content of these four "brains" or memory systems have a lasting effect on our behavior and wellbeing. They affect how we perceive the world.

The effect each of them can create is illustrated by the following concepts: We have the 'power of thought' (problems, obsessions); passions, cravings and urges (emotions, feelings); the power of habits and panic reactions (behavior, movements); and an ill body and unbearable pain (body sensations). Obviously these are the most important forces in our internal systems. Therefore, only when all four systems have been contacted and examined and "emptied out" for content can we say that we have dissolved the available charge in a trauma. We could also have chosen, for instance, to stick to the five senses as the five recording tracks of interest. Or we could have worked only with those thoughts and ideas that existed around trauma or stressed situations. These methods were also tested in the development phase of DEEP. But it became evident very quickly that strong forces in mind and body were overlooked. When we turned to the traditional model of man consisting of head, heart and body (mental, emotional and physical), it became evident, that this model was a lot more relevant, as it led to faster and more stable results. It should be noted that we now consider perceptions as part of body sensations. Especially smell and taste can be stored in trauma. We can investigate them and run them as bodily sensations and/or perceptional impressions, when needed.

Impulses as Non-physical Actions

It has also become evident in sessions with many clients that non-physical actions like pushing somebody away, hitting him with "laser beams" of mental energy, or the intense pulling action of a desire or craving can carry considerable charge, without any body movement ever becoming visible from the outside. We could attribute these forces to what is called the "subtle bodies" in ancient eastern systems – or the "energy body" in modern language: subtle energy structures that surround the physical body. It helps a great deal to let the client make the non-physical actions visible in the session by acting them out physically. Instructions taken directly from the client's content, like "hit her", "strangle him" etc. allow the client to burn up all the fuel he has put into the "tank" for this specific impulse.

Secondary Impulse: In this context, it should be repeated that often the client has an additional impulse in place, which is to hold such actions back in order to avoid dire consequences that range from losing loved ones to being convicted as a criminal. Holding back is basically an act of self-discipline – technically we call that a "secondary impulse/effort". Please note that both the primary and the secondary effort have to be discharged for the whole package to dissolve. It is also necessary to ensure that the opposing pole is discharged; because the recording of the opponent's force in confrontational situations is what is holding our client's charge in place.

The Elements of the DEEP Package

When we discharge a DEEP package we move, as a rule, from the more physical elements to the more mental ones. But it shall be noted that not all DEEP packages have preserved all four elements as recordings. If we take a complete DEEP package it has the four elements. Lowest on the scale we find body memories including pain caused by physical impact. Going further down, we would find ourselves in the physical world, including the physical body. But here we move into the medical realm and we will rather leave that to our competent medical profession. If we talk about acute damage or illness we recommend seeking medical help. DEEP can come in handy afterwards as a way to recover faster or to remedy chronic conditions which the medical treatment didn't fully handle.

Body sensations (instinct, physiology – physical experience)

This includes bodily signals that tell about the body's condition and needs. Examples are: physical pain; pressure; soreness; itch; perception of own energy; smell; taste; warmth; coldness; dryness; humidity; hunger; satiety, etc., etc. There can be different forms of cravings and urges, including hunger, thirst and sexual drive. The list is long. It is an intricate part of the body's life seen as an individual organism and with all the signals and instinctive behavioral patterns going on. Bodily sensations are, especially in the brain, connected to the brainstem (medulla oblongata) and the little brain (cerebellum), but also to other places in the brain. There are, however, many signals that are stored directly in the organs 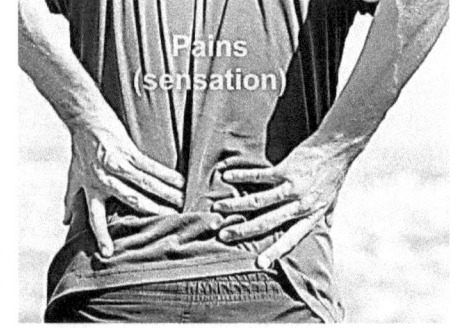 in question and in various parts of the nervous system. Perceptions like vision, smell, taste, etc., are stored in different places in the brain. There are also recordings and storage which cannot be located in the body or the brain. We assume that they are stored in the energy body, the field of subtle energy around the body.

Technique: First you sort out body sensations. As a result you have the person name one charged body sensation. Then this is integrated (run flat) by feeling it several times or by guiding the person's attention and awareness into it in order to experience it. The clearer never forces anybody into pains or discomforts. We are trying to overcome the original overwhelm, so it has to be done with a feeling for how much the client can handle without being overloaded.

It has to be done gradually in such a way that the person takes one bite at a time and experiences getting better and better at it. When the person can "be" inside the body sensation fully, the remembrance of it will disappear magically. The fully or partly blocked communication of the signal has been lifted. The body sensation has been integrated or gone "flat".

The "Tell" part of Repeat & Tell consists of getting the person to tell which thoughts, incidents and pictures are coming up. These are the so called 'pop-ups'. The clearer often needs to remind the person to tell about it. Use questions like "what is happening?", "any change?" etc., or the clearer can simply say something like, "Gently feel that again and tell."

If there are acute present time sensations, like pain or hunger, they, of course, have to be remedied by mundane means, such as first aid or good food. What we can handle is the *recordings* and the storing of DEEP elements. Body sensations and actions/movements are often combined as they both belong to the body. When the body sensation has subsided an underlying feeling often appears. It is closely connected to the memory of the pain, etc. and is taken up when it is readily available.

Action, Movement (physical experience)

This is partly awareness of own body's position and movements and partly awareness of other objects' positions and movements. Using a medical term it's called Kinesthesia (British Dictionary: 1.

the sense that detects bodily position, weight, or movement of the muscles, tendons, and joints; 2. the sensation of moving in space). It appears that this type of memory records physical efforts and movements and also body language. This is very interesting as these recordings are part of the entire stress- and trauma-picture. What we get hold of is of course the recorded impulses, movements and muscle tensions. These deeply rooted impulses are the core of our action patterns, our habits. (A whole therapy, called Somatic Experiencing by Peter Levine, is formed around releasing this side of trauma alone.)

Aggressive movements are often suppressed in stressed incidents, but the impulses are still there—for instance the impulse to hit the opponent or worse. Because they were suppressed in the incident itself it is more likely that they got stored. When we re-experience these impulses, or even exaggerate them in session, they are freed up and dissolved. Usually one would also run Secondary Efforts – the effort to hold self back.

> Note: These energetic impulses of primary and secondary efforts are often so extremely charged because the primary impulse had to be held back with super-human force for social reasons. Another example of this would be sexual impulses that in our culture often have to be controlled by the individual in order to keep the social peace. Asking, "Is there a secondary effort or impulse to hold the primary impulse back?" can quickly resolve this.

An interesting side effect of running a lot of old body sensations and kinesthesia is that we experience an increase in physical energy, and activity level. We get all the contradictory impulses and vectors cleaned up; all the conditioned reflexes that are triggered at the same time, but unfortunately counteract each other. Stored body sensations and kinesthesia add up to bodily memories. The body "thinks" in movements and survival and this form of "bodily logic" can be in conflict with the same person's impulsive feelings and sensations; which in turn can be in conflict with what the person's

common sense (or lack of same) tells him/her. These internal conflicts can all by themselves be a source of stress and charge. Part of the gains from DEEP is that these different systems get to work together and pull in the same direction. This alone increases one's energy-level, power and life quality. Agreement, harmony and synergy between the four systems occur.

Body sensations are stored in different parts of the brain, in the nervous system and in the organs that were injured. Thus it is possible to create contact to a damaged body part and get to know many incredible things through direct communication and introspection. We use this in DEEP Body Clearing. You can also find blocked body sensations in the body's energy systems. This invisible field holds a lot of information.

Technique: First you get the person to express the movement etc. in words. Then the person has to go through and show the movement or the body language. The instruction is something simple and encouraging like: "Show me!" or "Act it out!" Normally the person does not need to leave the chair but remains seated. Some clients however get so agitated and excited that they have to get out of the chair and stand or walk or run around in the room. If that is the case, you let them do that, of course. Most often the person goes through the movements physically as if he/she was preparing to actually do them. By just indicating and going through the movements in this way, the person can get access to the kinesthetic and motoric memories.

Suppressed, aggressive or defensive movements or facial expressions may be exaggerated in session so they get clearly communicated and made known. Motions where the client felt out of control - like attacking somebody in a blind rage – can be run through a little drill where they are started and stopped as with a switch, until the client feels he can comfortably control them. This goes for both physical motions and energy attacks that the client perceives like a laser beam or lightning flash – during that drill, the client is also encouraged to bring out all verbal content, anything he wanted to say or scream at the time but was forced to hold back or "swallow". Again, the person has to be able to observe his/her acting out with interest, be able to introspect and show mindfulness. It is not enough just indulge in the automaticity that normally controls the element.

The body's logic and way of thinking is like an animal's. It avoids pain and sources of pain and seeks survival in terms of food, shelter and procreation. Its logic is usually black and white. Things are dangerous or friendly; edible or inedible; pleasant or unpleasant. The body lives in the moment and is very dependent on instincts and conditional reflexes.

Emotions and Feelings

Emotions and feelings are "the heart's logic". This logic causes us to be drawn to or repelled by things, to like or dislike things—be it different people, situations or objects.

Normally we make emotional conclusions from positive or negative experiences. If we have for instance burned the fingers in an open fire, we are later typically scared of open fire. We can become enthusiastic about for instance a teacher and thereafter all he says is "truth". We can fall in love and everything the loved one does, is of heavenly quality and should only be explained as admirable. When we check our "gut feeling" it means that we consult our emotional logic. We try to evaluate the situation with our heart and feelings. Throughout our history of experiences we have built a database of emotional conclusions that form the core of our emotions. This type of experience can quickly and spontaneously be translated into action. This is an important advantage in pressed situations. To first arrive at a rational conclusion before acting will too often mean that we react too slowly to survive a dangerous situation. To act based on feelings makes the reaction time very short. But, naturally, this may also cause mistakes, as this form of 'logic' doesn't do any rational analysis of the situation.

Thoughts and emotions can easily be mixed up. Emotions and feelings are felt bodily or energetically. They usually sit in a specific place in or around the body, especially in or around the torso. Thoughts are mostly perceived around the head.

Emotions and feelings are connected to the limbic system in the brain. In traditional psychology it is connected to the heart and the chest. In Eastern psychology the feelings are connected to the heart and the part of the aura called the emotional body. Feelings have a great impact on our endocrine system (glands) and prepare us through that to meet dangers (fight, flee, or freeze reactions).

Emotions and feelings play an important role in our communication. Through our emotional life we seek community, friendship and love. We avoid sources of fear and hate. When we use the 'logic' of emotions and feelings we see positive or negative; good or bad. Emotions are not suited to register fine differences between similar things and phenomena. But feelings, in the form of intuition, can be a reliable compass.

Technique: We are looking for distinct emotions and feelings. It is the emotions themselves we are after. It is not unusual that the person will offer a situation or a thought. "That looks dangerous to me" is a thought. The feeling would be fear. Likewise "confusion" is not a feeling but a condition, a conflict. But there are feelings inside which we shall find. First, have the person freely tell about the emotional content. The Clearer guides the person. Confusing emotions can be an indicator of that the person had numerous options, numerous strategies in play: to attack, to flee, to hide, to appeal for sympathy, etc. The team sorts it out to find central emotions that are charged. The person must find a charged feeling and name it. There are thousands of words in the dictionary describing feelings. The person is however welcome to use own expressions like "a red feeling" if that's what gives the best meaning to the person. The feeling is then contacted and sensed many times. You can have the person send his attention and awareness into it where it sits. The person should contact it several times or "be" in the feeling until it integrates (goes flat). Part of the technique is to ask where the feeling is located; "do you experience it in a specific place in or around the body?" is the usual question. You can ask about things like energy, solidity, intensity, color, vibrations and similar. But this is usually not needed. The emotion may change as it is has layers. The Clearer would reflect that and take up the new feeling that surfaces. You get the person to experience the feeling and tell about the thoughts, pictures and memories coming up. The clearer can also ask, "Feel (the feeling) and tell me what comes up." Or say something like, "Experience that again and tell." This is Repeat & Tell.

> **Note:** A special case of confusion is when the client is apparently divided into two conflicting people (opposing "sub-personalities", "identities" or "characters"). This resolves quickly when an observant clearer asks if there is a feeling of being divided or split into two very different and contrasting personalities. Once the client confirms this, the chaos of feelings typically can be sorted out by fully defining the two characters, each of whom will be found to own several of the colliding elements that made up the initial confusion. The two opponents are then run through a special procedure (the dialogue tool) that reconciles them with each other and integrates them with the main personality. Sometimes each of the two have to be run on their own DEEP package - spectacular things happen in sessions when two sub-personalities of the same person are starting out in a bitter fight and end up as the best friends and partners!

Thoughts, Decisions (dogmas, dictates)

It is not the logical explanations we are interested in in Repeat & Tell. To help the person we seek the stupid, the unpremeditated, the short sighted or outdated decisions and beliefs—the now automatic thoughts, the dictates. In DEEP we talk about decisions and judgements; about beliefs, dogmas, dictates and prejudices. It is the unfortunate and the unconsidered judgements and decisions that have the biggest power to perpetuate traumas and stress situations with their negative feelings and unfortunate habits and behavior.

Ideas and thoughts like that can prolong unwanted physical conditions and illnesses. Often there is an ocean of thoughts appearing in connection with a specific incident. Let the person talk freely. But as clearer you look for a specific type of thought or idea that kind of sums up the incident. We look for generalities ('always', 'never', 'all', 'no-one', etc.). Because expressions like these tend to get general validity for us. We look for emotional outbursts (for instance: "I hate you!", "It goes to Hell for sure!", "I am lost!" etc.). It is what we call emergency thoughts; they were expressed as fast judgements and emergency solutions in a pressed situation. When we have run an incident through the previous steps (body and feeling) we have a pretty good idea of the incident. As clearer we keep an eye on the expressions the person comes up with in order to catch one of these self-limiting expressions that kind of sums up and explains the incident in one short statement. It can be as short as one word (example: idiot!) up to 7 – 10 words (example: this goes bad – I think I die!). The core of the wording or idea will match the emotional content of the incidents.

"You are no good!"

Dictate
(Limiting belief)

If there are several such charged expressions in an incident you can handle them one by one. You may want to assess them on the distress scale from 0 – 10 to find out where to start. Then you start with the most charged expression. But usually there will be one central expression that stands out after the first turmoil of recounting the incident has settled down. Ideally you get one that determines the person's future, or reduces his or her energy level, self-esteem, perception of self (size as a being), or even blocks particular skills and abilities. Remember, a person's decisions regarding self are the law of the land - the have power like the decree of a king! When we think rationally we think in sequences; in planning; in what pays off the best. We use analyses and logic. We can differentiate fine shades and see similarities and differences. But in the category of dictates, prejudices and judgements we usually find primitive and stubbornly held ideas that are easily triggered. In clearing we are more interested in unreason than reason. The dictates and judgements we are looking for limit us—and those around us as well.

Thoughts are anatomically connected to the brain and especially neocortex in the forehead. The neocortex is seen as the seat of rational thinking. In Eastern psychology thought is connected to the part of the aura called the mental body.

Even though we touch on the anatomy of the psyche in our theory, it shall be stressed that when we work with DEEP it is about the person's own subjective understanding and perception. We simply ask where the element is experienced to be—in or around the body. We personally believe that the brain, the nervous systems, muscles, organs, consciousness, and the energy body all play a role in recording and storing incidents, impressions and conclusions. It seems like these systems overlap each other, are back-up systems. But we are clearly talking about systems that are far more complex than we can understand and describe scientifically. Therefore we trust the person's own perception when it is about self-understanding and therapy.

Technique: First the Clearer gets the person to tell all the thoughts coming to mind: "What thoughts did you have at the time?" Once that is somewhat sorted out, the Clearer goes for the dictate or the causative thought at the center of the package. The Clearer asks something like: "Is there a thought or decision in the incident which sums up the feelings and event?" or "Is there a causative dictate?" or "is there a decision that could shape yourself or the future?" Answer: "I will never make it!" (Fear).

Clearer: "OK, say, 'I will never make it' and feel at the same time the fear in the incident."

The wording is repeated as all the elements are added one by one (body sensation; body language and movement; any energetic action; emotion and feeling; and the spoken expression).

The "Tell" part of Repeat & Tell is again about getting the person to tell which thoughts, incidents and pictures come up. The clearer also has to ensure that the wording of the expression is correct and that it hasn't changed. The clearer corrects the wording as needed before continuing. The clearer can also use something like: "Repeat the thought and tell what might come up."

The stored elements and recordings make up our DEEP Package. It is an emotionally overwhelming moment that has been stored in the body, heart and mind. It locks up attention units and it can be triggered. When it has been integrated it is dissolved. It is no more a burdensome luggage but freed up energy and life experience.

A Sequence of the DEEP Elements

In theory the elements should be picked up in the sequence of the most physical first, then going to the less physical ones—as mentioned. In other words, we start with body sensations; then movements and body language. Then we get to emotions and feelings; and finally arrive at thoughts, decisions and beliefs.

This is however just a loose rule. As mentioned it is not always we find that all four elements have been recorded and stored. In practice there will be one dominant element which the person finds and shows at once. Here the type of incident also plays a role. Is it a physical incident? Is the incident mainly emotional? Or is it the belief and the thought content that dominates? The clearer evaluates this and starts at the most logical place.

The best approach is to take up the first element offered by the person or the one the person is effect of when he/she contacts the incident here and now in the session. We often start with the emotion/feeling. But it often happens that before we really get into it, the person gives the central thought in the incident. The clearer can now pick up the thought using Repeat & Tell on it—but at the same time ask the person to experience the emotion/feeling. It could go like this:

Clearer: "Repeat, 'I will never do it again!' and feel the annoyance at the same time."

Both the feeling and the thought might change during the running. The clearer adjusts accordingly. The clearer has to make sure he is still working on the same DEEP Package. In incidents this means we hold onto the same point in time in the running.

If the clearer doesn't have any clear manifestations telling him where to start, the best way to get going is to ask for the emotion/feeling. All the incidents of interest have a feeling content. If you get the person to recall the emotion/feeling in the incident, you have opened the door and can now find all the elements of the subject or moment that are present.

There are of course situations, as mentioned several times, where all the DEEP elements are not present. This can be because the different types of consciousness not necessarily "think" the same way. They can be out of sync. If the person was unconscious, recordings were still made by the body's two awareness centers. There could also be some emotional content. But actual thinking is limited to before and after the unconsciousness. However, words said to the person during unconsciousness can act as hypnotic dictates and commands. This kind of thoughts can have a very negative effect.

It is theoretically possible that a traumatic incident only appears in one or two of the four layers of energy. It could happen that there was no movement, or that there was no bodily sensation, or no real thoughts happening. But an incident with no DEEP elements at all means, of course, that we should not have taken it up in the first place. If we have an incident with charge we check all four to make sure nothing is left behind.

When first learning to use DEEP we say, "Ask for the feeling first." But of course, if the person is readily offering another element there is no need to ask. Pick up that element which is offering itself and take the remaining elements afterwards.

Rounding Off

So this is Repeat & Tell which is the "central processing unit" (CPU) in DEEP. The technique takes into account the four different kinds of logic and four kinds of memory. It can be compared to recording music in a professional studio; there are different tracks. In a recording studio there is a track for each instrument and one for the singer. In DEEP we concentrate on those four tracks that taken together make up the central part of the traumatic incident.

This is the reason that it is not enough just to make the person talk about what happened, let alone suggest to "just forget it" or give the person a pill. Getting the person to talk about it is of course a big step in the right direction. But unless we can gain access to the original recordings we cannot finish the job. To dissolve a traumatic or stressful incident it is important to get in contact with the original tracks and carefully convert the stored recordings into live energy which can then easily be discharged.

This is the essence of DEEP: We need to work up our courage and contact the original recordings. There are four different kinds of memory, four tracks of interest. Each track has to be inspected and handled for charge. Before this is done we cannot say that we have fully cleaned up and completed a stressful incident or subject. In DEEP in general we also take opposing points of view into account. It's a hidden form of repression and counter-force that stopped the natural discharge. By establishing contact to all the DEEP elements, including those in opposing viewpoints, and discharging them we free the energy and life force that was locked up in the incident or subject.

We have converted trauma and stress into new vitality and life experience!

The dissonances of the past are deleted –now it's time to enjoy the music!

Chapter 17: DEEP Subject Clearing (DSC)

In DEEP Subject Clearing we combine the action of Unblocking (see below) with the tools in the DEEP tool box. Using the unblocking buttons we uncover charged elements. These elements are then fully discharged using the DEEP tools.

The unblocking buttons by themselves are designed to get the introspector to really duplicate and look into a subject. Let's say a person has all kinds of reactions to cats. A characteristic of a charged subject is that we cannot simply comfortably look at and duplicate what is in front of us. Instead of looking at a cat for what it is, the person in our example meets 'cats' with all kinds of defensive actions and attitudes; with a wide variety of emotional responses, reactions and thoughts. The unblocking buttons are designed to get the person to look at all these bypass mechanisms and pop-up ideas and clear them away on a mental level. Once all these bypass reactions and repressions are cleared out of the way, the person can simply look at and duplicate 'cats' without all the irrationality and commotion. In normal unblocking this is accomplished by back and forth communication. The clearer asks questions, the person simply answers.

In DEEP Subject Clearing (DSC) we take it a step further. We take up and clear the underlying DEEP packages and items. To do DSC the clearer has to be familiar with the DEEP tools, of course. They are used in the same way as in DEEP Incident Clearing and other main actions. Below is described the normal procedure for unblocking. Then we describe the additional step of DEEP Subject Clearing.

In training, DEEP Subject Clearing is considered an easier subject to learn than DEEP Incident Clearing. So DSC is a good starting point for new trainees once they have learned Repeat and Tell and other basic DEEP tools.

Unblocking

Unblocking is a technique where we use a series of button questions to expose all aspects of a subject. Each button question is asked repeatedly to get all possible answers. When there are no more answers, we move onto the next question and use it the same way. If we unblock the subject of 'cats', the first question is, "On 'cats,' has something been suppressed?" As another example, question (4) 'Careful of' is: "On cats, is there something someone has been careful of?"

The questions are formulated in this open-ended way. A question does not define 'who is doing what to whom.' Anyone and any way it comes to the introspector's mind is valid. The important thing is to get the person to talk about the subject any way possible. If the person cannot see an answer in an area where there most likely is one, the clearer may poke around a bit, such as saying "have you suppressed anything on cats?" "Has your mother suppressed anything on cats?"—say just enough to cover the obvious.

Each question is asked repetitively until the person runs out of answers or has an endpoint for that button. Then the next button is taken up. This is kept up until a full endpoint for the overall action occurs or the button list is finished. In the shown version there are 28 Buttons. Other versions exist and can be used. Once a question is embarked upon, the clearer has to make sure to use the same question to get another and another answer until the introspector says, there are no more answers.

(s/t=something; s/o=someone.)
1......has s/t been suppressed?
2......has s/o expressed their opinion?
3......has s/t been invalidated?
4......is there s/t s/o has been careful of?
5......is there s/t s/o didn't say?
6......has s/t been denied?
7......has s/o's communication been cut off?
8......is there s/t s/o has been angry about?
9......has there been a conflict?
10....has a mistake been made?
11....has s/t been protested?
12....has s/o had a grudge?
13....has s/o been mocked or ridiculed?
14....has s/o had a worry?
15....has s/t been decided?
16....has s/t been avoided?
17....has s/t been abandoned?
18....has s/t been finalized?
19....has s/t been ignored?
20....has s/t been insisted upon?
21....has s/t been pretended?
22....has there been a lack of help?
23....has s/t been misunderstood?
24....has s/t been altered?
25....has s/o or s/t been resisted?
26....has there been a failure?
27....has s/o or s/t been rejected?
28....has s/t been helped

Normal unblocking, without the DEEP step added, is used as a repair tool. We can unblock items like a situation at work, a bad day with the children, a session that didn't go well, etc., etc. When a person is upset or worried about something and out of balance, it is a better idea not to use the DEEP step as we want to cover as much ground as possible lightly rather than go for an in depth handling of just one aspect.

DEEP Subject Clearing (DSC)

When the student clearer is comfortable with doing normal unblocking and using the DEEP tools, DSC is an easy combination of the two.

First you ask a button until no more answers, like in unblocking. Mark DEEP items in your worksheet as you go along. If an obvious DEEP package shows up you can however take it up right away. You have found some charge. Once that is handled, you can move on to the next button. If nothing obvious, you can quickly review the marked answers given for that button and maybe ask into one that has potential underlying charge. If nothing in particular is found, you move onto the next button.

You take up any DEEP elements, be it self-limiting or repressed thoughts, emotional content, or physical/effort content. Also charged persons can be taken up. If a charged emotion, effort or thought shows up it is dealt with using Repeat and Tell. An irrational thought could be taken up with Repeat and Tell.

Also Fixed Ideas Handling can be used. Fixed Ideas Handling can also be used without first using Repeat and Tell if the situation isn't highly charged. Should a charged person from the past come into the foreground, tools like Hello/OK and Identities Dialogue are good choices.

If there hasn't surfaced any DEEP element during the run of a button, you simply go on to the next button. A certain subject may only have a few DEEP elements that need to be taken up. This can vary greatly from subject to subject and from person to person. Just take the obvious ones and leave the borderline or doubtful elements alone. If they are of importance they will most likely come up in a more obvious version later on the same subject.

DEEP Subject Clearing is used as a planned action to get to the bottom of a subject that may have been addressed several times before with lighter techniques. The unblocking format is simply used as a door by which we can enter the DEEP case related to a certain subject, such as 'cats'.

Adding a DEEP Step to other Clearing Techniques

DEEP Subject Clearing is unblocking with a DEEP step added, as explained above. This strategy can be used to get more out of many other clearing techniques such as ability grades. Each ability grade technique is based on a set of printed instructions or questions that should be used as they are written. You take a charged subject and ask the questions over and over until you get to an endpoint of very good indicators and a realization. But again, if an obvious DEEP package shows up you can deal with it right away and get your End Phenomenon that way.

It is our observation that the DEEP step can be added once the endpoint is reached by normal means. The clearer looks over the notes and picks out items suited for further DEEP handling. Often even the endpoint itself is some kind of realization where the introspector suddenly sees an irrational idea that has run a part of his/her life. If that is taken up with DEEP tools, such as Repeat and Tell or Fixed Ideas handling, a much broader understanding is reached.

It should also be noted that endpoints often read on a bio-monitor with charge suddenly blowing off and a free needle. This is a large reaction pointing to more available charge! When we have explored such endpoints with DEEP, we have many times found that indeed there was much charge available that still could be gotten off the issue. When asking into it revealed it wasn't charged or the introspector wasn't interested, we simply left it alone.

Some of our own clients are happily doing the ability grades as they are. So we do just that as that is how they want it. Others would not do ability grades techniques without the DEEP step added.

We have several clients who did all their ability grades elsewhere years ago. Now they are here, wanting to have their ability grades addressed all over again with the added DEEP step. It does make sense by itself to review the ability grades again after for example 10 years. The person's issues have shifted a lot from being a 20 years old bachelor to a grown man of 30, for example. The person is now married with children and has a demanding professional career. The introspector faces new relations, new problems and upsets; new challenges. To review these issues through the medium of ability grades expanded with the DEEP step is what we recommend.

While normal unblocking is often used as a repair tool DEEP Subject Clearing is NOT used as a repair or patch up action. In a patch up you want to cover a lot of ground and do it lightly. Using the DEEP tools is done to get to the bottom of a narrow area or subject.

Chapter 18: DEEP Body Clearing
Basic Version

Note: There now exists a more comprehensive action, called DEEP Body Clearing – Professional Version. It is included in the professional training materials.

In DEEP Body Clearing we view the body as an organized collection of organs and body parts under the person's command. The body works like a human organization. There are local command posts that need to be in touch with levels of commands above it and below it. All too often we have body parts and organs that have local problems. We address these trouble spots and view them from the body part's own point of view as well as from the person's senior point of view. The introspector can actually have a conversation with an ailing kidney, find out what the kidney is complaining about and hopefully remedy the matter. DEEP Body Clearing, Basic Version (DBCB) is mainly intended to get the person in better communication with his/her body. It is neither a medical procedure nor a body work procedure – just a light first aid based on communication that should be followed up by an examination and treatment by a health professional if something is found wrong. It was developed so we could deliver assistance to introspectors with light body troubles via Skype video telephony.

In DBCB we first address trouble spots and when we have done that, we go over the whole physical body to restore a feeling of vitality and well-being.

New Biology

Dr. Bruce Lipton, an American biologist and stem cell researcher, explains in his book 'Biology of Belief' (2006) the science of how each and all of our body cells have their own independent life. Each cell has its own perception and intelligence, its own system of communication and defense. Moreover, based on his research, Lipton explains the mind as a data field that assists in controlling the brain and body (in addition to automatic and instinctive systems). The mind controls the body through instructions to the brain that activates the nervous system and the endocrine system. The mind as an energy field can also directly influence the organs and cells. The 50 trillion cells in our body, explains the professor, are influenced by our mind and by what we think. Here is a quote: "Your mind is the government of your body's 50 trillion cells."

DEEP Body Clearing by Steps

We use 'bad back' as an example below.
1. The clearer asks the introspector: "Is there any part of your body that is ailing, bothering you or has been acting up from time to time?"
The answer here is 'lower back'.
2. Tune in to the (lower back). "Do you get any messages or flows from there?"
3. If you do, clarify it and use Repeat and Tell on it.
4. If no response, but there seems to be some kind of problem with the back, you use Hello/OK on it.
"Say 'Hello' to your lower back."
"Have the lower back say 'OK' to that hello."
"Have the lower back say 'Hello' to you."
"You say 'OK' to that hello."

This may turn into a conversation or exchange. It can be in words or in flows, such as certain sensations and pains turning on. The clearer would try for getting it expressed in words but shouldn't insist on this.

"Is there something your lower back wants to say to you?"
"Acknowledge that."

"Is there something you want to say (in response to that) to the lower back?"
"Have the lower back acknowledge that."

5. If something now gets stirred up it is handled with Repeat and Tell and other tools from the DEEP tool box. This step may lead to painful and traumatic incidents that may have to be taken up with DEEP Incident Clearing or DEEP Viewpoint Clearing. In general, if a DEEP package turns up, all the tools and actions of DEEP may be considered.

6. Once the trouble area has been handled, we do an additional step. "Feel the aliveness of the lower back." This is asked repeatedly to its end point.

7. When lower back is handled, we ask for another trouble spot. The procedure 1-5 is then repeated on that body part.

8. Once all the trouble spots of the introspector's body have been addressed this way, we add this wellness step, going from toe to top of the person.

   A. "Feel the aliveness of your right foot" to an end point.

   B. Then "Feel the aliveness of your left foot," etc., taking all the main areas and body parts of the person. Skip body parts that may embarrass the introspector.

   C. This is kept up until the whole body has been worked over, from feet to top of the head.

A case example: the author had by accident cut a deep wound in his hand. It took some surgery to fix the damage. After the surgery and some rest, the author got about four touch remedies for two days. Here the clearer simply touches the introspector's body from top to toe. At each touch she asks, "feel my finger." After a week the hand had healed well and it was time to address the subjective side of the damage. The introspector subsequently got clearing work on the accident and operation. First the ordeal was addressed with DEEP Incident Clearing. This went very well and most of the charge came off. Then he was given DBCB on the hand. Here the hand had quite a story to tell that didn't surface during the DIC session. The hand was upset with the author for being so clumsy. The hand was also upset with the nurse, who had made five injections to apply local anesthesia to the area. The dialogues were discharged. Also the doctor, who had used scalpel and needle and thread, was a cause of upset. And again, the hand now had the opportunity to tell its side of the story. After the damaged hand was cleared, the other hand (the right one) was given Step 8, ("feel the aliveness of your right hand") to balance the two sides of the body. Subsequently the hand healed up very fast and at check-up at the hospital, the medical staff was very surprised over the unusually fast healing process.

Transparent Body

Transparent Body is an independent tool that can be used on areas which seem painful or troublesome. It is a form of body work—except it can also be administered over the telephone. It can be used in connection with DBCB as described above.

Let's say the left knee is causing problems.

1. Ask the client to place one finger or hand on the knee.
   "Place your left hand on your left knee."
2. "Close your eyes."
   "As a spiritual Being look from the inside and through the bones and tissue of your left leg."
   "From the inside, look at the area where your hand touches."
3. The instruction is repeated many times while the client covers the area with his finger or hand. The other side of the body (here right knee) is covered as well to ensure balance.

Transparent body can be used to cover the whole body from head to toe. Areas with pains or other symptoms are given extra attention. Transparent Body is originated by Heidrun Beer. Also the original form of DBCB was developed by Heidrun Beer and later refined for DEEP use.

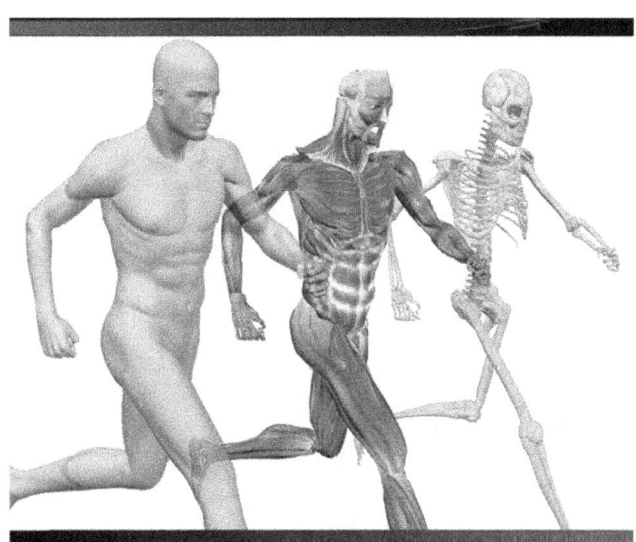

Chapter 19: Deep Incident Clearing

It is a well-known fact that our personal history will leave us with emotional and physical scars. Past generations had no real answers to this beyond the medical patch up—and maybe a "sympathetic ear" of a friend. Maybe some professional would advise to "let time heal the wounds" or to "make a change of environment" to get over it.

Today there exist a number of alternative or cutting edge therapies that are quite effective in resolving these traumas. Among the ones we are familiar with and have studied can be mentioned, Traumatic Incident Reduction by Dr. Frank A. Gerbode, Routine 3X by Robert Ducharme, Transformational Processing by Flemming Funch, Clearing Tech by Hank Levin, and Somatic Experiencing by Peter A. Levine. These methods are all quite effective. That does not mean there is no reason to look for improved methods of dealing with trauma; because traumatic incidents, severe or light, play an important—if negative—role in most people's lives.

In Deep Incident Clearing (DIC) we define Trauma as an overwhelming of the person. This overwhelm can happen on three levels. It can be an overwhelming of thought, of emotion, or on a physical level—as in physical trauma. The overwhelming can be on just one level or on all three levels at the same time. The degree of overwhelming determines the severity of the trauma. Trauma as overwhelm is described very well by Peter A. Levine in his bestselling book "Waking the Tiger."

The basic concept of DIC is to address all three levels and convert any overwhelming found into experience. In "D.E.E.P." we have <u>Decisions</u> on the thought level. Decisions are causative thoughts about one's options or situation. We have <u>Emotions</u> and feelings on the emotional level.. <u>Efforts</u> and forces can be expressed as vectors on the physical level or mental level. This level also includes body sensations. Pain is a result of conflicting vectors and is in this band. Finally we have <u>Polarities</u> on the inter-personal level. It covers the situation that led to the trauma. It was a confrontational situation: it could be two persons in a fight of some kind. On the thought level it could be an argument. It could be an emotional impact, such as from a severe loss or bad news. Finally it could be a physical impact leading to a physical trauma, such as a car accident. See also chapter 12, "The DEEP Package", and chapter 16, "Repeat & Tell", for the full explanation of the DEEP elements.

If you want to translate the DEEP elements into two common English words it would be 'subjective experience'. They cover the important elements we keep after we 'have been through something'. There may be thousands of other impressions and facts one could pick but they all tend to fade away. But the lessons and conclusions we draw from an experience, the emotional content (good memories or emotional scars) and the habits and routines and reflexes we take with us are what we keep long after the details have faded away. The basic concept of DEEP Incident Clearing is to concentrate on these more permanent elements of incidents, the subjective experience we keep. Our task at hand in DIC is then to convert a repressed subjective experience into life experience.

Any situation that leaves the person in an overwhelmed state, rationally, emotionally or physically, is recorded by the person. It is recorded in the mind and energy body on all three levels. It ties up the person's attention and interest and steals some of the person's energy, vitality and joy of life. In case of physical trauma, the first thing to do is to make sure the victim is given proper first aid. Then we have to make sure the person gets competent medical treatment. What DIC addresses is not medical situations. The ambition is to help the person, after medical treatment is well under way, to recover faster and overcome lasting negative effects of the accident or injury.

In DIC we take experiences of overwhelm (traumatic experiences) and convert them from being subconscious 'beatings' to intuitive and integrated experiences. Through working with DEEP Incident Clearing the trauma gets assimilated as part of the person's life experience. As a result the person has a new and better chance of succeeding in that field or endeavor and, through reviewing many types of incidents with DIC, the person has a greater chance of success and happiness in life in general.

Defining the Complaint

We can address and clear different types of incidents and complaints:

Incident Complaint: The person can have a complaint about a certain and known traumatic incident. The incident will be addressed as a known event of the personal history. It can be loss of a loved one, an accident, an assault, an operation, a severe illness in the past; a period or situation of extreme stress like a bankruptcy or divorce, etc. It can be loss of any kind; emotional or physical trauma of any kind. Such incidents can be addressed directly.

General Complaint (Themes): The person can also have a general complaint of unpleasant emotion and reaction to certain things. It can be "stress" in general or an inexplicable physical ailment, such as a pain, a soreness, itch, etc. with no immediate or medical explanation. One starts out by making a list, asking for the various aspects of feelings, emotions, sensations and pains. These items are also called Themes. Once the list is established the themes are rated for charge. The clearer now takes the most charged one and asks for an incident containing this unpleasant complaint; be it negative emotion, unpleasant feeling, a pain, odd body sensation, etc. An incident containing this complaint is found and taken up with DIC. If needed, another incident can be found and taken up, etc. This is done with all the charged aspects. A person suffering from "stress" may be able to list a dozen aspects that make up the condition. Clearing key incidents and then list for remaining aspects (themes) that are then taken up as thematic complaints can be kept up until the overall condition is gone.

Subject Complaint: The complaint can also be about the person's feelings and reactions towards a certain subject or an area of difficulty. One would first find and review key incidents related to the area. Then one lists for remaining emotions, sensations, feelings and pains connected to that subject or area and review them as general complaints. It is done in a similar fashion as described above. Examples of area complaints could be "feeling bad about one's time in middle school," "having troubles with study," "having troubles in one's marriage," etc.

The Main Difference from Earlier Methods

Compared to the techniques mentioned above, the DEEP techniques take a greater interest in the person's subjective emotions, feelings and reactions. This is based on the repeated observation that the same or comparable incidents (such as loss of a loved one) can have a very different effect on different people. Different individuals have different thresholds for being overwhelmed. A paramedic can arrive at an accident scene and just consider it "business as usual" while a bystander, a little girl for instance, just seeing the same scene, can be horrified and traumatized for life. We conclude that it is not the incident itself that does the most damage. It is actually the person's spontaneous reactions and decisions and perpetuated reactions to the incident that seem to be the permanent damage. By concentrating on that subjective side, the subjective experience, the emotional and cognitive damage can be repaired relatively easy.

Relief and significant case improvement also happen routinely using the older techniques; but the end goal of DIC is to exhaust and clear the person's reactions to the event rather than have the person look at all the bad things that happened to him or her. The person, in other words, gets an intuitive lesson in his or her own participation and unknowing cause of subsequent troubles and sufferings. These are the subjective elements the person can do something about—and the clinical records show that this is the fastest and most complete way to overcome such trauma.

DIC is still regression therapy, is still incident running. But once an incident with the complaint is contacted, the clearer works directly on the discomforts contained therein by having the person re-experience and intensify them and even recreate them in the session using various techniques. The theory is that the person basically continuously, though involuntarily, generates these unwanted sensations him- or herself. By using the DEEP techniques the person can be made to gain control over them and then turn them off.

The DEEP approach is less tasking on the person's ability to recall incidents in detail. The unwanted emotions, sensations, etc. are what bother the person and that can be addressed directly. The method, thus, makes the need for a detailed recall of past incidents, including past lives incidents, less necessary. Many introspectors have had problems finding very early incidents and getting all the details of for instance childhood incidents—or even finding an earlier similar incident when that was called for. The DEEP method emphasizes the many sensations, pains and feelings that bother the person, also in present time, and clears and exhausts those under competent guidance in session. We have less use for dramatic scenarios and long stories. The efficiency of DEEPs approach, contacting and reviewing the subjective experience, has been supported by plenty of clinical research and case stories. The basic experiment has been to take up incidents that were already reviewed with other modalities and see if there was any important charge left. In all cases there were.

It is, however, remarkable to note in how many details any given incident is recorded. One can find many other perceptions than the classical five of sight, hearing, touch, smell and taste. As examples of additional perceptions recorded, we can mention sense of motion, emotion, pressure, pain, relative position of body, sensation of weight, condition of body and its organs, etc., etc. Recalling all these perceptions and all the details of what happened is possible with some persons, but others find it very tasking or outright impossible. It is therefore of great practical value that the elements that directly bother the person can be addressed head on without having to depend on whether the person has perfect recall or not.

Main Spheres of Interest

The objective content of an incident, as outlined above, is recorded in great detail and with a remarkable number of distinguishable perceptions. The subjective experience of an incident can be reduced to four main elements, 1) decisions and thoughts; 2) emotions and feelings; 3) body sensations 4) effort (and anything 'motion'). These elements make four bands or layers of subjective recordings.

Together, these four layers make up the subjective experience. If you compare the experience of the paramedic working on an accident scene with the traumatized little girl standing by, you will find that the girl's traumatic content is mainly thought and emotion. An injured person, say the victim in the car accident, will have traumatic content consisting of effort or energy in the form of bruises, wounds, broken bones, etc. and added to that, thoughts, emotions and feelings.

If we concentrate our work in session to address the decisions and thoughts; emotions and feelings; body sensations, efforts, forces and the various effects of energy vectors – if we address these elements effectively they will cease to affect the person negatively and the person will have gotten rid of the traumatic content permanently. (Again: we are talking about an accident victim that has already been attended to medically and has somewhat recovered.)

General Principles of DIC

First of all, the clearer has to find an incident to take up. As mentioned, we can take up *an incident complaint*—be it a physical or emotional trauma or simply a situation of extreme stress. Often we will find that the emotional trauma is sitting on a hidden physical trauma. If that is contacted during the reviewing of the emotional one, the clearer should take up the physical one as well, immediately after the emotional trauma has been well discharged.

We can also work from a *general complaint or Theme*, such as an unwanted emotion, sensation or pain the person wants to get rid of. We find incidents, one or several, which may have caused the condition and review the incident. The interest factor is important. If the introspector has a strong interest in doing something about the complaint the chances for success are much greater. The introspector is motivated and has a good awareness in the area. When the interest factor is high, the chances of finding other incidents containing the same complaint are much greater too. Once the first incident has been discharged, we can simply ask for another incident containing the same complaint. This is only used if the introspector at this point still seems preoccupied with the complaint. The clearer would guide the person to finding another similar incident. It will typically be earlier but since we are mainly dealing with the subjective experience the apparent similarity is more important than it being earlier. So we accept any similar incident the person may bring up. Going earlier is not stressed as much as in some other modalities of incident running as our main objective is to fully discharge the pain or discomfort, the complaint itself, rather than learning all about the person's past.

Sometimes the first incident the person can find is not the charged one but helps uncover earlier (or later) more charged incidents. In such case there is no reason to stay with the first incident as it only served as a lead-in to the real charge.

Reviewing an Incident

When an incident is contacted, the person is first returned or regressed to the time it took place. Then the person is sent through the incident as if it were happening right now, re-experiencing it. This is by the book of the other methods of regression therapy and incident running. The person is sent through the incident two or several times until the story line is sorted out (what happened.) As long as new details and changes of events are coming up it is actually beneficial to do such passes-through. Some introspectors can develop an amazing number of details. It could be compared to developing photographic prints in an old-fashioned darkroom. For each pass more details become clear and sequences of events are sorted out. So we don't set a number on times of passes that are needed. But an important aspect of this is that there is a large group of introspectors who don't have perfect memories. Here we can only get the rough outline of the story and anything after that seems to be guesswork. The person provides answers, simply to satisfy the clearer's continued questions. This is what we don't want. The objective story step is completed even though it seems to be lacking in details. It is time to embark on the subjective experience, the DEEP package.

Locating DEEP Packages

Once the objective story is in place per above, we go into DEEP mode. In DEEP *Subject* Clearing, the clearer would have listened carefully to how the person described own and others' reactions to a button question and made notes all along. He would then take up the DEEP elements that had surfaced.

In DEEP *Incident* Clearing this is of course not forbidden but the recommended and most streamlined method is different. Once the objective story step is complete, the clearer sends the introspector through the incident once again. But this time the person is asked to look for a moment of charge. We can ask for *"the first moment of emotion, reaction or charge"* or some such question. The introspector will easily find it. That is our first DEEP package in the incident. It is taken up with Repeat and Tell and possibly other techniques from the tool box. Once the package has been discharged, the next moment of emotion, reaction or charge is looked for. This is then taken up with Repeat and Tell, etc. Once the clearing team is through the first pass and the DEEP packages are found, the procedure is done all over again. On this second pass there may still be charge on some of the DEEP packages and others may have surfaced. This is kept up until no more charge is found from the introspector's point of view on a final pass.

Polarities and Points of View

We have the 'P' in DEEP meaning 'Points of View.' That is what we address next. We explore the other charged points of view related to the incident at hand. We typically start with the opponent's, the wrong-doer's point of view. The introspector is asked to take the wrong-doer's point of view and go to the starting point of his/her incident. It typically starts a little differently and at a slightly different point in time. We can do a single objective story pass but here mainly the DEEP content is of interest. Other points of view in the incident can then be reviewed; bystanders, a policeman, a supporter, a supporter of the wrong-doer, etc.

The introspector may sometimes have a hard time taking the wrong-doer's viewpoint. The person has become so disgusting to the introspector. The clearer first tries to coax the introspector to do it. If no luck, the clearer can ask the introspector to take the viewpoint of a fly sitting on the wrong-doers shoulder, for instance. At some point the introspector will be willing to see the incident through the eyes of the wrong-doer and that is of course what we are aiming for.

Sometimes the clearer chooses to start at other viewpoints than the wrong-doer. This is another gradual approach. These viewpoints should in any case be checked and if charged, they can be taken up with benefit. In some cases objects can be taken up as viewpoints. Say, someone got hit by a branch from a tree. It can be taken up and somehow be run as a point of view or a colliding vector. In very physical incidents the body's viewpoint, as separate from the Being's, can be checked for charge and run.

Finally we can take up viewpoints exterior to the event. The clearer can ask the introspector to take a multi-determined viewpoint or God's viewpoint. Doing this as a final pass for significant traumatic incidents gives the introspector a chance to see it all at a distance. It brings it to a peaceful closure where the colliding viewpoints are seen interacting from above. Other exterior viewpoints that can be used in special situations include a guardian angel, a leader of a company or activity; a moral or religious leader, such as Jesus or Buddha; the prime minister, etc. It should be someone above the activity in a serene but informed position.

The Shock Moment

In chapter 12, The DEEP Package, it was stressed that it is important to find and review any shock moment in a traumatic incident. The whole trauma may be locked up in just one such moment. In most cases the shock moment will soon surface and be one of the DEEP packages the person offers. The clearer should still recognize it as being the crucial moment to clear. The clearer should make sure to get any and all self-limiting thoughts, dictates, emergency decisions without an expiration date, generalities, etc. Often, they are the pivotal elements that hold all the misery in place. We are interested in decisions rather than random thoughts: Decisions about self, about the future and conclusions that maybe were made after the shock.

Note: The technique of running viewpoints can also be used to specifically discharge the shock moment. Each viewpoint present in the shock moment is simply taken up. The person is made to review the moment or short sequence through the eyes of each principal person, group or viewpoint present, one at a time, and the confusion in the shock is reduced or it evaporates.

DEEP INCIDENT CLEARING BY STEPS

Assessing for the Item

The first step is to sort out where to start. Usually the person will present an issue he or she sees as a major problem or block in his/her life. It can be a traumatic incident; it can be stress in general, a certain environment or subject, a disability or body problem. Each type of issue will have some unique steps. The outline of questions to use is found above in the section "Defining the Complaint". Now we assume that the clearer has obtained a list of items pertaining to the issue.

The clearer goes through the list of items with the person to determine which item has the most charge and interest. This is simply done by asking:
On a scale from 0-10, where 0 is no charge and 10 is unbearable charge, how would you rate Item A? Item B? etc. The clearer then takes the most charged item first. If 2 items are both rated with 10, for instance, the clearer simply asks: "which of these 2 items seems most interesting to take up?" Another way to settle a tie is to consider which item has the longest track record. A parent has a much longer history than a colleague at work, for instance. Finding an item to address is called 'Assessing for the Item'. Before the clearer actually takes up the item it should be checked for interest by asking the introspector:

"Are you interested in running...?"

You only take up items the person is interested in taking up. That ensures success. If you take up items the person is not interested in you may run into various difficulties. For one thing, there will be another item the person would have preferred and it will now act as a distraction.

Once you have the item to work on there are two possibilities.

1) You can have an <u>incident complaint</u> (such as an accident, loss or stressful situation);
2) or a <u>general complaint (theme)</u>, be it a negative feeling, emotion, sensation or pain.

(You can also take up happy moments or events. This is mainly used in training, but does have some good effects and is sometimes used to stabilize or cheer up a person. You would not ask for negative thoughts or decisions. You simply ask for thoughts. You can also use, "Recall a happy moment" repeatedly.)

1A. Incident Complaint: Locate the incident when (you fell off the bicycle.)
(We take a known unpleasant incident, in other words: a loss of something, a traumatic or stressful incident.)

1B. or General Complaint (Theme): Locate an incident that contains (the chosen theme.)
(A theme can be an unwanted feeling, emotion, sensation, attitude or pain)
You get the person to briefly state what the incident is. We are just looking for a headline, such as "mother angry at me."

2. Where was it?

3. When did it happen?
The person may already have given this in (1). You may ask for exact time and location if it still seems a little vague. Finding time and place are basic actions to get the incident more present so the introspector can be returned to it and run it. If it still seems vague to the introspector, don't push it. Go to (4).

4. Go to that incident.
The introspector is sent "back in time" to the incident. It is reviewed (re-experienced) as if it happened right now.

5. How long does it last?
Getting the exact time and length helps turn on perceptions of the incident, especially visual perception. The clearer takes whatever the introspector can get.

6. Go to the start of the incident and tell me when you have done so.

7. (Close your eyes) what are you perceiving (in the incident)?
We just want a snap shot, not the whole movie. We want the opening scenario. Typically we get a scene or one principal person in a situation. Sometimes we may only get an odd detail (like "I see a bed post") a vague impression and the feeling of the moment. What comes up may not be a visual impression but maybe "a sense of danger," or the like. Take whatever is offered.

8. Go through the incident to the end.
Here we ask the introspector to start "playing the movie" of going through the incident. Usually the introspector likes to tell what happens while going forward; that is what we want on the first pass. The introspector sometimes goes through it rather silently. We then have him/her tell about it under (9). If the introspector just comments during the run, reassure that you are following it closely and get him/her to continue. The formal instruction is to say "OK, continue."

9. Tell me what happened.
If the introspector already told you while going through the incident, this question is omitted. Otherwise let the introspector tell what happened without any additional questions. The way you get more accurate information is to send the introspector through again.
Steps 1-9 establish the introspector's reality of the incident by contacting his/her recordings of the event in the mind. One does not ask for more than the person can give.

The incident may need additional passes to sort out what happened. As long as the story changes or new details surface the action of getting the objective story is of benefit. Use the following instructions for the additional passes:

A. Go to the start of the incident and tell me when you have done so.
B. Go through the incident to the end.
C. Tell me what happened.
The steps correspond to 6, 8 and 9 above and the same comments apply.

DEEP Mode

Once we have a good idea of what happened, we can go into DEEP mode.
D1. Go to the start of the incident and tell me when you have done so.
D2.-EF. Go forward in the incident, and look for the first moment of emotion, reaction or charge.
We are searching the incident for repressed subjective recordings, the so-called DEEP packages, from start to end. When we find the first charged package we discharge it before going forward to find the next package. An incident, even a severe one, typically only has a few of these DEEP packages. They are our target when we are in DEEP mode. One of these moments will be the crucial Shock Moment. (In lighter incidents, there may not be an actual shock moment, of course.) Often we will find that the DEEP package that contains the shock moment is practically identical with the whole traumatic experience. So we are very interested in these DEEP packages. Once they all are cleared the incident is handled or discharged completely. It is exhausted for traumatic or repressed content.

"A moment of emotion, reaction or charge" can be replaced with "a moment of charge," "a charged moment" or similar. Regardless of wording, it is important to make sure beforehand that the person understands what we are looking for.
D3. We work over the DEEP package found using Repeat and Tell and other basic DEEP techniques and tools.
Then:
D4. Continue forward through the incident, and look for the next moment of emotion, reaction or charge.
In this fashion we work our way through the whole incident, discharging the DEEP packages one by one. In the process we will encounter any shock moment as well—as explained above. It should be recognized as such and given extra care and attention.

Usually we have to do several passes using the D1-D3 steps before we are done. It is kept up until it's all discharged and dissolved or another similar and more charged incident has turned up. It is often possible to discharge any given incident completely without formally going earlier similar—as long as we allow the person to talk freely about any incident that turns up. We call these other incidents for Pop-ups. However, if we are reviewing a light incident and a heavy one turns up, we would shift to the more charged one instead. Below, we will explain in more detail when to take up another incident.

Discharging the DEEP Packages

Once we have found a DEEP package to work on we use the Repeat and Tell procedure. Repeat and Tell can be found in full in the tool box. We can also use other tools.

Other Points of View (POVs)

The general theory explains the basic principles of taking up other viewpoints (see "Polarities or Points of View" above.)
There is, however, another approach that is often used if there isn't a clear cut opposition in sight. It simply consists of checking for resistance or opposition as we go along doing the DEEP packages. Say, we have run an effort; now we check for any opposition.
Clearer: "To the effort getting the thing done, is there any opposition or resistance?"
Answer: "Yes, my colleague thought it was a bad idea."
Clearer: "OK, what was the counter-effort?"
Answer: "It was to keep me quiet."
Clearer: "OK, from the viewpoint of your colleague, get this effort to keep you quiet."
This is then flattened using Repeat and Tell.
The same pattern can be used when dealing with thought/decision and emotion/feeling.
"Is there any thought or decision conflicting with your decision?"
and *"Is there an emotional response directed against yours?"*
and similar questions would pick it up.
It may, however, also pick up conflicting thoughts and emotions our person had at the time, which is fine. Whatever is charged is taken up and from the viewpoint of the originator.
Especially in clear-cut fights and conflicts between two parties, the clearer would review the incident from the opponent's viewpoint as well.
We use instructions that are slightly different from A, B, C above.

P1 Assume the viewpoint (VP) of (opponent.)
P2 From that VP, go to the start of the incident.
P3 From that VP, what do you see or perceive?
P4 From that VP, go through the incident to the end.
P5 From that VP, what happened?

One pass is usually sufficient. The clearer can then shift to DEEP mode and use steps D1-D4 above, just reminding the person regularly to hold the point of view of the opponent.

It is not uncommon that the person finds the opponent's viewpoint so disgusting or hostile that he/she will not assume it. The clearer can try to coax the person to assume it anyway. But if the person is still unwilling to do so, don't force it. Just note, that it is an indicator of something highly charged. Work with the first method given above or try the tool (see also tool box) of "seeing it from a fly's viewpoint sitting on the opponent's shoulder" or similar. Eventually the person should overcome own resistance and now the charge is addressed for real.

God and Bystanders

On heavily charged incidents the clearer would work all the viewpoints present in the incident. This includes other persons watching or participating. One could also review an incident "from the body's viewpoint." This is beneficial if the incident is very physical. In case of an ambitious marathon runner there may be quite a conflict between runner's dreams of glory and what the body is willing and ready to endure.

Reviewing incidents from a higher viewpoint or the viewpoint of God is also used routinely. This is a good way to round off when an incident was heavily charged. The clearer would say, "Assume a higher viewpoint," or "assume an exterior viewpoint," or "assume a multi-determined viewpoint," or "assume the viewpoint of God." You find out beforehand what the person prefers. The person is now watching the events unfolding and gets some distance to the scene. Especially if the incident appears to still be rough after much work has been done, seeing it all in exterior mode helps smooth it out.

Using the viewpoint of God is the best instruction if the person is an active Believer. If not, use one of the others as covered earlier, a guardian angel, the local leader, etc.

How much is enough?

Obviously using as many tools as described here is not done on every incident. The amount of work put into reviewing one incident has to be adjusted to the amount of charge present. The rule is to work an incident as long as it produces good change. If it becomes boring routine, tends to drag out without much happening, it is time to find another relevant incident—relevant to the issue at hand.

Going Earlier

Using enough DEEP tools on an incident it will usually resolve all by itself. The available charge has been flattened and handled. There is no more charge to be found. The whole issue may resolve as well. The reason for this is that we are flattening the DEEP elements, which are at the core of the problem.

Still, there may be more charge on the complaint or issue. Major issues that clients present go way back in time. The person may have had the same or similar situations happening for ages and ages. And if the issue or complaint persists it's time to look earlier.

Checking for an Earlier Starting Point: It can simply be an earlier starting point of the present incident or another incident entirely. The first thing to ask for is an earlier starting point: *"Does the incident we are running have an earlier start?"* is what you ask. Sometimes the introspector went to the dramatic climax of the incident but skipped how he/she got into that situation. Getting the very start can be crucial if the introspector is mystified by the story line.

Once any earlier start is taken care of and it didn't handle the issue completely the clearer would guide the person towards finding an earlier similar incident. If that doesn't seem available, ask simply for another incident related to the issue. In DIC we accept any similar incident the person may bring up—also later ones. Going earlier is not stressed as much as in some other modalities of incident running. Our main objective is to fully dissolve the pain or discomfort, the DEEP items of the complaint itself, rather than learning all about the person's past.

Sometimes, however, the first incident the person can find is not the charged one but helps uncover earlier (or later) more charged incidents. In such a case there is no reason to stay with the first incident as it only served as a lead-in to the real charge. The clearer would finish up what he/she is working on, not leaving any DEEP element taken up unflat, and go to the more charged one. In other words, the clearer would not ask for additional DEEP elements in the lighter incident.

Flattening DEEP Elements

Earlier incidents typically turn up when flattening an emotion, effort or thought. Initially the clearer does not do anything about it or stop what he/she is doing. The clearer keeps up "Get that emotion" (flattening the DEEP item at hand) *and lets the person freely express memories and pictures from other incidents, the pop-ups. The clearer encourages the person to tell but simply acknowledges what the person brings up.* The clearer keeps asking "Get that (same) emotion," etc. Much of these pop-ups flare up and disappear quickly so changing gear and focus is not what we want to do.

If a certain incident seems to persist in the person's thoughts, it means it contains a major amount of charge. Maybe the story of that incident needs to be uncovered. The story line, of course, is a fascinating aspect of any incident. And some issues won't resolve until the person can see exactly the context and circumstances under which it was initially formed. The person's "fear of dogs" wasn't just due to the neighbor's dog when he was a child. It goes back to him being killed by a pack of wolves five lifetimes ago. So if an incident keeps coming up during repeating, it means it's time to finish up and shift to working on that incident. The clearer makes sure to flatten any DEEP item he/she is working on. Then the newly found incident is taken through all the steps, starting with 1-9 and A-C to sort out the full story.

Ending Sessions

A DIC session should result in a positive result, a positive endpoint, for each session. The person should feel happy and free of the negative incident. The incident can be gone for good or it may need more work in a later session. One can simply check at the onset of the next session, "How does the incident we ran last time look to you now?" If it still needs work, you do it now; or you may find an earlier similar (or another related) incident per above.

The session length is not done by the clock in DIC. The determining factor is to get to a result, to complete what one is doing to a good point. On the other hand, DIC does take a lot of concentration and mental energy when it runs at its best. So the clearer also has to be aware of the introspector is still being fresh enough to continue. But the rule is, take each session to a result, to a good point and to very good indicators. A good length for most experienced persons is 1- 1½ hours. Some persons routinely get a session EP after half an hour and the clearer must respect that.

Also new persons and less robust persons may only be able to do shorter sessions to keep progressing. Too long sessions are just more than they can take and still be winning. There are others who insist on real long sessions, such as 2-3 hours.

The ideal session end point is when the person is "blown out" meaning having new realizations about self and the item addressed. The person is brightening up, extroverting to a point where looking inward seems almost impossible. This is what we call a big win. That is always a session end point, the most desirable one.

It may not mean that the issue is gone forever. But the person is free from it now and going past such a point is counter-productive. Let the person enjoy the win. Then in the next session the clearer can check if that was the end of the complaint.

This phenomenon of the person extroverting from the incident is always an important point to watch for. Unless the extroversion is caused by an external disturbance or other type of distraction, it means the person is done with that incident. There is no more stuff to view so to speak. The incident has been dissolved, has been erased as a cause of bypass reactions and a repressed force.

Exploring Earlier Lives

We have stressed in this write-up that our main objective is to handle the complaint presented by the person and we don't need to go way back to do so.

There is, however, value and a special quality to simply going way back in time into earlier lives, other cultures and planets, etc. and being guided through all these experiences by a skilled and competent guide, the clearer. It expands the person's horizon and scope of life ("Wow! I have lived before? Maybe I am an immortal soul!") It sheds light on many mysteries. It adds a new personal perspective to history. If the person expresses the wish to do this type of exploration, there are two ways to go. The clearer may take each incident to completion and then in the next session ask for an earlier similar incident containing the complaint. This can be taken way back, maybe further than the clearer finds strictly necessary.

Or the clearer may do only the steps 1-9 once plus A-C once or twice on an incident and then ask for an earlier similar one. Then, when an incident from the distant past reveals itself and is found heavily charged the clearer will shift to DEEP mode and get all the charge off using all the tools.

Both methods are completely safe. Of course, flattening each incident encountered on the way back in time is the most thorough but may take more session time than some persons are willing to spend or pay for.

One person that insisted on going earlier and earlier using the thorough method, even after the complaint was gone, was as an experiment taken down this path. The team ended up before this planet, then before this universe, and finally at a series of incidents the person described as separation from Static—'Static' being used for the original soul body of godly nature that split off parts of itself. These parts being described as eternal souls or spirits, as US!

However fascinating and mind boggling such an odyssey may seem to some, it is reassuring to the rest of us that it is not necessary to run or believe in the scenarios that unfolded. It is also a fact that some persons cannot easily be taken into past lives.

The good thing about DIC is that there is no technical reason to push the person further back than what he/she feels comfortable about. An issue like 'fear of dogs' can usually be resolved to a good point long before the person encounters the pack of wolves incident.

The Flows

Issues usually resolve by reviewing incidents where the person was the receiver of the complaint, such as a pain. The person is hit by an angry man and feels the pain, etc. Since we also address it from the viewpoint of the angry man as well, we get all aspects of the mental side of the injury.

There is, however, an additional angle that can be used. That is to take up flows. Once we have addressed the incident where the person is being hit, we can address incidents where the person hits others. It is a fact that incidents and issues may lock up in an introspector due to him or her having been the perpetrator, the wrong-doer, the one that did it to others.

It is even claimed that we cannot experience the bad effects of others' actions unless we have done a similar misdeed ourselves. This may sound like a philosophical discussion. But in some resistive case situations it is also a very practical and technically correct truth. If a pain or other DEEP item won't resolve running the incident and earlier similar ones, it's time to take up the other flows.

We operate with four flows in DIC. Flow 1: something done to self. Flow 2: the person doing it to others. Flow 3: another/others doing it to another/others. Flow 4: the person doing it to self. Flow 1 and 2 are explained above.

Flow 3 is typically being traumatized as a bystander. What one sees is so horrible; yet, one is powerless to prevent it. It's the little girl being traumatized by seeing a car accident. Flow 4 (sometimes called flow 0) is interesting. Often it uncovers a prior decision to get injured rather than bluntly hitting oneself with a hammer. It may uncover what led up to the injury one way or the other and the decisions uncovered may explain why a person gets the same injury over and over; why the person is accident prone in a certain area. If we embark on a long program of DIC, it is advisable to include the four flows. One would only take up those flows the introspector is interested in per the procedure. The steps are much the same. Just the first instruction (1a or 1b) in 1-9 is different. Here is the outline of the flows:

1A. Incident Complaint:
(you start with the known incident on flow 1, such as an accident, operation, loss, etc.)
Flow 1: Locate an incident when another caused you (to fall off the bicycle.)
Flow 2: Locate an incident when you caused another (to fall off the bicycle.)
Flow 3: Locate an incident when another caused another (to fall off the bicycle.)
Flow 4: Locate an incident when you caused yourself (to fall off the bicycle.)

1B. General Complaint (Theme Complaint)
(A theme can be an unwanted feeling, emotion, sensation, attitude or pain)
Flow 1: Locate an incident when another caused you (pain in the toe.)
Flow 2: Locate an incident when you caused another (pain in the toe.)
Flow 3: Locate an incident when another caused another (pain in the toe.)
Flow 4: Locate an incident when you caused yourself (pain in the toe.)

Fresh Reality

As a little supporting action we use a class of techniques we call Fresh Reality. It has in other modalities been called 'Grounding' and also 'Havingness.'

The most basic function is to bring the person up to present time at the end of session. When reviewing past incidents the person is sent back in time and may have lost his/her orientation when the action is over. So the clearer orients the person back to present time. This can be done by pointing out objects in the room. *"Look at that (room object),"* vase, table, picture, wall, etc., etc. This is kept up for about 10-15 items and the person will now be in the present and ready to go back out in the real world. A trained clearer can see the introspector suddenly extroverts – from introspector to "extrospector", if you will.

If the person during the session gets groggy or dopes off it may also be useful to remedy for that condition. If that seems to be happening often, the sessions should be made shorter and lots of Fresh Reality should be used at appropriate places. That means to use it after some item is flattened. If it happens in the middle of reviewing an incident you would always finish the action started. It may be content from the incident that is being triggered.

> **Note:** Fresh reality is also found in the tool box. What happens during clearing is that the tiny mass the DEEP elements and mental pictures contain may be important to the introspector. After all, they explain the person's world. So the introspector may become a little unsettled when this mass disappears due to the clearing work. Fresh Reality replaces this loss with new impressions.
>
> Another useful technique at session end is to run Positive Recall. As a rule, we have run unpleasant and negative things in session. It can be countered by asking the client to recall positive events. "Recall a time when you were happy." "Recall a time when you enjoyed life." and the like. This is done before just running Fresh Reality.

DIC Light (see also Appendix for an easy to do procedure.)

The question has been asked, is DIC for everyone? The answer is that the material addressed is certainly found in everyone and if it can be contacted, reviewed and discharged using DIC it will be highly beneficial. Some persons, however, find it too hard to take up. It takes too much of their mental energy or they get overwhelmed by the content.

With new people we have successfully used what we have dubbed 'DEEP Light mode.' We don't go into full DEEP mode when reviewing incidents. We go through the steps 1-9 and A-C, and when it comes to doing repeating on thoughts, emotions and efforts, we do ask for them; but we have the person tell whatever there is to tell and leave it at that. The fact is, with new persons there is plenty of material to deal with without going into full DEEP mode. Just contacting past incidents and telling about them may be a major breakthrough on the case. It will result in so much material and mental action so there is no need to 'stir the pot' so to speak. Also, with new people the clearer can start off with picking light incidents—even positive events. Taking up positive events is quite therapeutic as the person is accessing his/her own past in a causative way.

There are also many techniques in existence that we use, that may be needed to prepare a case to embarking on DIC. This includes recalling positive moments. Here we don't take up incidents; we simply ask the person to recall a moment of a positive event. We also address charged subjects, situations and persons *in present time* with lighter methods. Instead of looking into the past we focus on here and now. The aim of this approach is simply to greatly reduce the stress and pressure of the present on the person. So if a person doesn't feel comfortable or helped by DIC, there are many other possibilities within the DEEP modality. We also use a series of techniques developed by others in order to service our public professionally.

Being Ready for Session

One factor that helps in any clearing work is that the person is fully rested and fed. Before each session the clearer makes sure the introspector is well rested, isn't hungry, hasn't drunk alcohol the last 24 hours and hasn't used mind altering drugs for the last week. These factors, if out, would all reduce the efficiency. The introspector has to do what he/she can to be fully alert and comfortable in session. Also, any distractions that can be easily removed should be out of the way before session start. Any pending phone calls, the car safely and legally parked, etc.

Session Venues

Deep Incident Clearing can be delivered in person. The clearer and client would sit across from each other at a table, like in an interview situation. This is the preferred set-up.
We have, however, for a number of years delivered DIC via internet telephony. The person may sit in London or Los Angeles while the clearer sits in New York or Copenhagen. We have found Skype video telephony to be an excellent venue. This saves time and money and allows many persons to practice and receive DIC who otherwise wouldn't have any access to this new and exciting subject.

Chapter 20: DEEP Viewpoint Clearing (DVC)

DEEP Viewpoint Clearing was originally developed as a shorter version of DEEP Incident Clearing. We used it mainly with experienced clients who did not need to go through an incident in the smallest details in order to discharge it. Instead we concentrated on the conflicts in the incident and ran the different persons' viewpoints, their DEEP packages. This developed over time and we found new uses for DVC.

In the version we present here, the thought content of the conflict is the focus—the two viewpoints' attitudes, judgements or preconceptions in the situation. This method has proven to be very effective and powerful when it comes to finding the fixed ideas that the person holds onto; ideas that lock up the person's way of thinking and acting—the freedom of choice; ideas with which the person isolates him/herself and uses to justify mistakes and wrongdoings towards others.

It is a well-known fact that we humans love to be right. Being right is after all equal to doing well in life. This however often develops into insisting that we are right, even when everybody else clearly sees that we got it wrong. This kind of fixed ideas and insisting on our own infallibility are at the root of many human conflicts and lost friendships. It can lead to long lasting feuds, even wars.

There are other types of fixed ideas that cause us to not develop personally; to not get promoted professionally nor make it in other important parts of life. In all these areas DVC can be used to loosen up the situation and make growth and expansion possible.

DVC is not the first technique one uses in clearing work. DVC is only taken into full use when the client has gotten most of his life in order and handled the most obvious traumas and stressed areas and situations. Therefore you will typically start a longer DEEP program with the use of DEEP Subject Clearing, DEEP Incident Clearing and DEEP Body Clearing in order to handle the person's issues and different incidents and case problems. But sooner or later these are handled.

Apparently the same kind of problems and difficulties return again and again—only now in new disguises. It is time for a new approach! It is time to look at oneself deeply, look into the mirror and examine if we can find something to change in ourselves in order not to run into the same situations again and again. It is time to apply a magnifying glass on situations where we run into problems and overwhelms. It is about finding those self-limiting fixed ideas, dictates, prejudices and values we operate on. Maybe, if we could re-experience these critical situations and interactions and their mechanisms clearly, it would be possible for us to revise our way of thinking, feeling, and behave—and make it possible to upgrade our expectations and results in life.

Below, you will find the exact sequence of steps that make up the procedure. The steps should in practice be taken as guide lines and not as an end-all exact recipe. The reason for this is that clients have a tendency to jump around themselves, or to explain points not asked for. The clearer must observe this and adjust his pace and approach. Likewise, we have a Dialogue Tool which is not always relevant to use. As a new clearer you can follow the procedure to the letter as long as the client agrees and understands that it will all end up with a good result—but maybe not as elegantly as if done with an experienced professional clearer.

DVC Procedure with explanations

We find a person with whom the client repeatedly has conflicts and problems. We typically use a list of possible persons, collected from earlier sessions or we can ask the client directly:

0."Is there a person with whom you have had repeated conflicts or problems?"

1. Can you find a specific situation or problem with (the other person) where you ran into trouble?

Give the client time to find a negatively charged situation. It is not always the first one he/she can remember. If the client feels that a situation cannot be used, then simply ask for another conflict as per (1) until the client finds one that is negatively charged and seems worthwhile working on.

2. Get a short description, time, place, what happened, persons, etc.

We only need what the client easily remembers without digging deeply into the memory.

3. What were your feelings or state of mind? (Repeat and Tell = R & T)

Get the client to sort it out and word the one you take up. When the client does this, the feeling becomes 'a thing', a temporary condition rather than a part of his being. Thereafter the client focuses on this feeling and state of mind and sits there experiencing it. The clearer uses Repeat and Tell on the feeling. The situation could contain several feelings per sort-out step. Run them possibly one by one.

4. How did it feel in the body? (R & T)

Get the client to describe the body sensation in words. Then focus in on this body sensation and the condition the client experiences. Clearer uses Repeat and Tell on the body sensation.

5. What was your body language? (Show it)

Get the client to sort it out, word it and to show it physically until it is relaxed and is no longer disturbing. Clearer can use Repeat and Tell. Here you use:"Show it again!"

6. Were there motions or actions you carried out or wanted to do? (Show it)

Again, get the client sort it out, word it and show it. Client does not need to leave the chair but shows it as much as possible in the chair. Work with it until it is natural and relaxed.

7. Was there any thoughts, decisions or ideas buried somewhere in that condition?

This is an important step. We look for and sort out the idea that maintains and holds onto the feelings, impulses, attitudes, action patterns etc. It is often a quite simple prejudice or evaluation about one self, the counterpart or the situation. A special type of idea is *self-righteous ideas* where the person insists on being right and others wrong. It usually reveals itself as an arrogant or mocking attitude. Those ideas run very well in step 9. But take whatever is available and don't look for a clever explanation or a longwinded wording.

8. Repeat that thought aloud whilst you show the attitude and the condition as it was (R & T)

This is done several times until it is relaxed and does not change anymore. Clearer can use, "Repeat (the thought) and tell me what might come up." This wording is effective with clients who are not very communicative. The clearer acknowledges each time it has been carried out, by saying "Thank you","OK" or similar.

9. If the thought found in (7) seems negative, irrational or self-righteous, ask:
   A. How has (the thought) helped you?
   B. How has (the thought) harmed you?

Ask (A) and (B) repeatedly until the client has no more answers or until he/she has a realization regarding that idea. The client will typically bring up many similar situations where the same prejudice was used. Listen patiently to these Pop-ups and acknowledge each of them.

10. Can you think of a less stressful idea you could use in the same or a similar situation?
Here the client is to come up with a realistic thought or idea. An idea the client in fact would be able to use next time. Normally the client will test a few. Some get discarded as unreal, some as too optimistic, etc. But finally a useful solution is found.

10 A. Imagine the situation we just looked at - using (the new idea)
10 B. How does it feel?
10 C. How does it feel in the body?
10 D. Say the statement and experience the entire package. (Give the client the time needed.)

THE COUNTERPART OR ANOTHER (A=another)

'A' (another) could be a direct opponent, but could also be another character appearing in the situation – or even a person in the clients thoughts ("what would your mother think?")

a 1. Take (A's) viewpoint

The comments above are also valid for the points below, where the client looks at it from the opponents' viewpoint.

a 2. (As A) Describe the situation.
a 3. (As A) What were your feelings or state of mind? (R & T)
a 4. (As A) How did it feel in the body? (R & T)
a 5. (As A) What was your body language? (Show it)
a 6. (As A) Were there motions or actions you carried out or wanted to do? (Show it)
a 7. (As A) Was there any thoughts, decisions or ideas buried somewhere in that condition?
a 8. (As A) Repeat that thought aloud whilst you show the attitude and the condition as it was (R & T)

a 9. If the thought found in (7) seems negative or irrational, ask:
   A...(As A), How has (the thought) helped you?
   B. (As A), How has (the thought) harmed you?

a 10. (As A) Can you think of a less stressful idea you could use in the same or a similar situation?
a 10 A. (As A) Imagine the situation we just looked at - using (the new idea)
(as help, ask: "You may be able to find a similar situation you have experienced yourself")
a 10 B. (As A) How does it feel?
a 10 C. (As A) How does it feel in the body?
a 10 D. (As A) Say the statement and experience the entire package. (Give the client the time needed)

Dialogue:

If the situation and the relationship are still charged, use the Dialog Tool from the Toolbox.

11. Get the client to imagine the other person in question and ask:

11 A.   Is there anything you would like to communicate to (A)?
11 B.   Get (A) to receive (acknowledge) the communication.
11 C.   Is there anything (A) would like to communicate to you?
11 D.   Receive (acknowledge) that communication.

Above is expressed as direct communications given to the counterpart. Not as explanations to the clearer. The dialogue is continued until there are no more comments, questions or answers – both ways.

New Vitality Lists

There are a number of lists in the appendix called *New Vitality Lists*. These are lists of "buttons" (key-words that might be charged). Each list is about a specific area of life, like 'Work', 'Family life', 'Relationships and sex', 'Fear of people', etc. They are used in connection with DVC. First you chose an area the client has troubles with. Then the clearer assesses the list with the client to find some charged buttons. When a 'hot button' has been found you start using DVC as described above.

DVC versus DCC

In the next chapter we will go through the basics of DEEP Character Clearing (DCC). The two techniques are similar as both address polarities. You can use the short description of DCC to explain new clients what we are doing in DVC. There are however important differences as we in DVC focus on many small situations connected to a specific subject, while we in DCC focus on specific roles and characters which are very central in the client's life. We speak of archetypes – like a dominant parent or a main opponent such as a 'dominating boss', 'environmental pig', 'religious fanatic', 'atheist', etc.

With DCC we can also focus on roles the client feels fixated in. It could be a father role, mother role, female role, male role, the penitent son's role, lover or mistress' roles, doctor's role, minister's role, etc. etc. In other words, here we start with the client's own fixated roles in life, rather than starting with the opponent's role or character. In DCC we have a long list of special techniques that get into all the nooks and crannies of this. It gets into all the oddities that create such fixed games conditions with their roles that seem to stick to us. ***The roles*** have taken control and set limits for our life and life expression.

Chapter 21: DEEP Character Clearing Basic Concepts

This short chapter is used with clients before they start on DEEP Character Clearing. It is an illustrated introduction. The exact procedure of DCC is not included in this book. It will be published in a later book. The below is also a good introduction to DEEP Viewpoint Clearing.

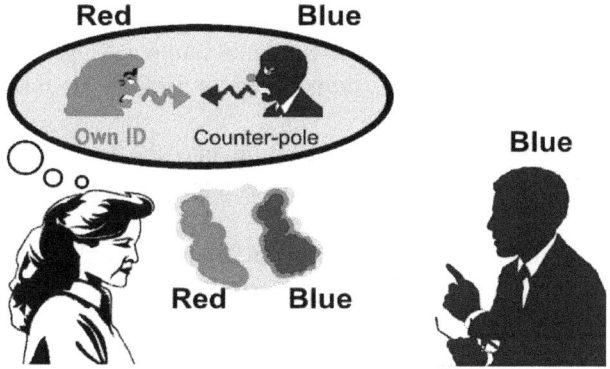

In a troubled relationship there are some hidden factors that make the situation worse. We tend to slip into roles and respond irrationally. One could of course look at each upset or conflict separately to sort it out. In **DEEP Character Clearing** we are, however, looking for one of the root causes. In the illustration above we see what happens in the woman's mind. She has a package of images, energy-masses and ideas about angry men and one of herself responding. Each package is called a *Character* or *Identity*. In certain types of conflicts, these two repressed characters or identities are at work. The woman will project her negative 'blue angry man character' onto the person in front of her. He appears 'all blue'. She will react to this 'blue man' according to her own 'red angry woman character'. Using *DEEP Character Clearing* the woman can have her own mind cleared of the two irrational and clashing characters or identities. Once that is done, the actual relationship will change dramatically as well.

In *DEEP Character Clearing* we find these identities as energy-masses (mental ridges) in the mind. We address each of them separately. The first step is to find the troublesome character in opposition (the counter-pole). The woman can be asked to think of a specific conflict with the man. She is asked questions in order to locate the apparent energy-mass that *represents* the man in the conflict. She is asked to describe or draw its shape and impact on the body as it appears to her. She finds a few characteristics to describe how that role feels. The energy-mass can be perceived to be anywhere: inside or outside the body; near or far away; around the head or elsewhere. Once the basic characteristics of this mental energy-mass is established, the clearer can help the woman to find the decisions, emotions, feelings, energies and polarities that role operates on.

The name DEEP derives from that—as it stands for: Decisions; Emotions; Efforts and Energies; and Polarities and Points of View; and these are the elements the clearer can isolate and discharge in these identities or characters. This results in the two characters losing their hold and power to irrationally control the woman. They will no longer interfere with the relationship.

Finding and discharging the "blue man" counter-pole is thus the first step. Once that is done, the woman can even occupy that role without losing her temper — or leave it alone at will.

Next, we find the energy-mass that represents herself in the conflict (Own ID). A *Character or Identity* contains a whole package of experiences and incidents going way back in time. All this has been organized into an Identity to make it quickly and easily available. It became an identity as the woman adopted a whole set of emotions, responses and fixed ideas to use in similar situations. It has to some degree taken on a life of its own. This can be very subtle — yet it can be found in the best of us without fail. One reason the two identities persist is that they hang up against each other in an unresolved conflict or games-condition. They are both "right" and are blind when it comes to seeing the situation from the other point of view.

There is a series of steps in *DEEP Character Clearing*, all designed to dissolve the two identities as energy-masses. Once the steps are successfully done, the woman can suddenly see her counter-pole for what he really is. She can now communicate directly with the person. She has no need to use or project the blue energy-mass onto the man. It acted as prejudice and mental name calling. As a rule the counter-pole is a dehumanized, demonized or grossly distorted version of the actual person.

Likewise, she can be herself without slipping into the red side of the problem. She can therefore *take the lead in resolving problems* between them in a rational manner.

By using the various *DEEP Clearing techniques*, all kinds of new and old conflicts are being addressed. Also turbulent periods of a person's life can be addressed as the confusion contained therein, consisted of viewpoints in conflict.

The Super Problems Action

One technique within DEEP Character Clearing is called *the Super Problems Action*. Here we take up a subject the client is passionate about. We find all the goals and identities in conflict or opposition to each other within that certain area, be it "marriage," "study," "religion," "collecting stamps," "football," "health," "enforcing the law," etc. We can address any subject the client is passionate about, one after the other. Clearing the area has a powerful outcome — just like it happens in an Italian opera if the plot comes to a happy ending: All the efforts and characters come together in the grand finale having learned to live and work together. They can sing as a quire with one powerful voice.

As a result of the various DEEP techniques, unwanted conditions, physical and emotional, are routinely alleviated. Often forgotten or innocent looking conflicts from childhood are found and may reveal heavy disturbances in the energy field. Clearing them, using *DEEP Clearing*, can turn the key and unlock troubled relationships and unwanted conditions. New circumstances in life may reveal dormant energy-masses that can be addressed right away. At some point all available energy-masses have been resolved *using a number of DEEP Clearing actions and techniques*. The woman will have reached a state of clarity of mind, of having thoroughly cleansed her energy field. She will have grown as a spiritual Being as a result. She will be much more able to enjoy life. She can meet any adversity with an open mind and a resolve that makes it into a game she is willing to play and can succeed in.

Chapter 22: Happiness and DEEP

"Happiness is when what you think, what you say, and what you do are in harmony."
Mahatma Gandhi

Happiness seems to be the thing we all want in life. As Aristotle put it over 2300 years ago: *"Happiness is the meaning and the purpose of life, the whole aim and end of human existence."*

I won't go into a long, philosophical discussion of what happiness is. For one reason, it seems that there are many ways to happiness. I stop short of saying that there are as many ways as there are human beings—because it is obvious that many people live unhappy lives and apparently don't know of any way out of it.

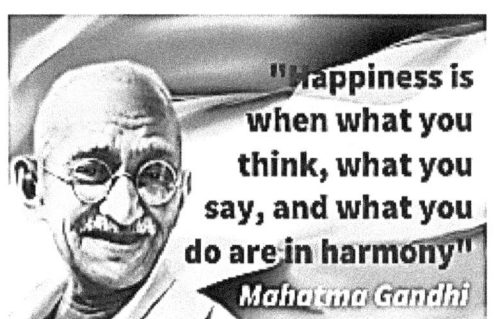

I *do* think that the Mahatma Gandhi quote above gives an important aspect of what happiness is. Without harmony and balance in our lives any happiness is short-lived.

Harmony of Thought, Emotion and Action

In DEEP we would say: there has to be a harmony between what we think, what we feel in our heart and what we do. When our head and heart guide our actions we are on a course that leads towards wholeness of heart and mind. We can reach out to other people in a sincere way, create lasting friendships and alliances; build lasting love relations and families—even build commercial companies and other successes in society that will last.

Happiness versus Misery

The Merriam-Webster dictionary defines Happiness as: state of well-being, pleasure and enjoyment because of one's life, situation, etc.

So obviously Happiness is tied to joy and other high levels of emotion and affinity and—we may add—the absence of the opposites: suffering, pain and misery.

In DEEP we work directly on eradicating suffering, pain and misery. We work directly on helping the client to obtain wholeness and integrity in his or her mind and heart.

Paving the Way

Let's take a closer look. Let us begin at the negative end of the spectrum where we have suffering, pain and misery. In terms of 'state of mind': suffering and misery resides in the negative end of the affinity scale. That's where we find fear, grief, apathy and more complex states of mind, such as depression and neurosis. By addressing these states of mind with DEEP techniques we can help the person the first few steps towards a happier life. Pains, if not stemming from physical or medical causes, have routinely been alleviated using DEEP techniques as well. We have seen that many times.

Much misery and suffering in life stem from conflicts. In DEEP we have a unique set of techniques that can transform conflicts and hostilities to a higher level of understanding, to closure and forgiveness—even to a point of renewed cooperation and friendship with former enemies.

When it comes to finding a balance between one's head and heart, between rational thought and emotion and intuition, we are talking about the very core of what DEEP is about. We discharge any imbalance between thought, emotion and feeling. Sometimes we find irrational thought dominating the scene. It may be prejudice or self-limiting thoughts. Sometimes we find strong negative emotions around an issue that make it impossible to even look at it. We can only react.

In DEEP we restore a state of mind where thought, emotion and feeling can work in unison to achieve power of action and resolve in a given field. Remember: happiness is basically enjoyment, an emotion. But it has to be worked for and defended. To make it last, the person needs to use common sense and rationality to avoid pitfalls. The person needs foresight and perspective to navigate safely in life. As Thomas Merton puts it:*"Happiness is not a matter of intensity but of balance, order, rhythm and harmony."* The quote underscores that the liaison between rational thought and emotion is important.

DEEP and Happiness

We cannot guarantee clients "to live happily ever after" DEEP. Life is a journey and to arrive safely, you have to make countless choices on the road. We can help you remove some scary and unpleasant sceneries of yesteryear; we can remove some stones from your shoes. But life is full of choices and crossroads. When such choices need to be made, you need your emotions, intuitions, rational thoughts and your ability to act to work together so you can make your own choices and carry them out. And that is the direction we take you in when you embark on your journey with DEEP.

Appendix

The Expanded Affinity Scale

Tone 400 to 3.0	Tone 2.9 to 0.0	Minus Scale 0 to -400
400.0 Sovereignty	2.9 Mild Interest	0.00 Death
320.0 Life that is not being	2.8 Contented	-0.05 Failure
160.0 Volition, Coexistence	2.6 Disinterested	-0.1 Pity
120.0 Individuality	2.5 Boredom	-0.2 Regret
110.0 Awareness	2.4 Monotony	-0.3 Accountable
100.0 Truth	2.0 Antagonism	-1.0 Blame
90.0 Decency	1.9 Hostility	-1.3 Shame
80.0 Ideas	1.8 Pain	-1.4 Punishing bodies
75.0 Ethics	1.5 Anger	-1.5 Controlling bodies
70.0 Aesthetics	1.4 Hate	-2.2 Protecting bodies
60.0 Inspirationon	1.3 Resentment	-3.0 Owning bodies
50.0 Amusement	1.2 No Sympathy	-3.5 Approval from bodies
40.0 Serenity of beingness	1.15 Unexpressed Resentment	-4.0 Needing bodies
30.0 Postulates	1.1 Hidden hostility	-5.0 Worshiping bodies
28.0 Considerations	1.05 Anxiety	-6.0 Sacrifice
26.0 Apparencies are Reality	1.0 Fear	-8.0 Hiding
25.0 Flows	0.98 Despair	-10.0 Being objects
24.0 Universes	0.96 Terror	-20.0 Being nothing
22.0 Opinions	0.94 Numb	-30.0 Can't hide
21.0 Games	0.9 Sympathy	-40.0 Total Hiding
20.0 Action	0.8 Propitiation	-60.0 Should Hide
16.0 Sensation	0.5 Grief	-80.0 Surrender
8.0 Elation	0.38 Making amends	-100.0 Destruction
6.0 Thrill	0.3 Undeserving	-120.0 Evil
4.0 Enthusiasm	0.2 Self Abasement	-160.0 Delusions
3.5 Cheerfulness	0.1 Victim	-320.0 Individuation of self
3.3 Strong Interest	0.07 Hopeless	-360.0 Being entities
3.0 Complacency	0.05 Apathy	-400.0 Spiritual death
	0.03 Useless	
	0.01 Dying	
	0.00 Death	

DEEP Subject Clearing, Short Form

Each question is asked repeatedly until the client has no more answers or has gotten an endpoint for that button. When a button is completed this way the clearer looks through his notes and takes up any DEEP material. If there is none, you go onto the next button. If obvious DEEP material turns up on a button, you go directly into a handling. When that is done, the clearer moves on to the next button.

(s/t=something; s/o=someone.)
1......has s/t been suppressed?
2......has s/o expressed their opinion?
3......has s/t been invalidated?
4......is there s/t s/o has been careful of?
5......is there s/t s/o didn't say?
6......has s/t been denied?
7......has s/o's communication been cut off?
8......is there s/t s/o has been angry about?
9......has there been a conflict?
10....has a mistake been made?
11....has s/t been protested?
12....has s/o had a grudge?
13....has s/o been mocked or ridiculed?
14....has s/o had a worry?
15....has s/t been decided?
16....has s/t been avoided?
17....has s/t been abandoned?
18....has s/t been finalized?
19....has s/t been ignored?
20....has s/t been insisted upon?
21....has s/t been pretended?
22....has there been a lack of help?
23....has s/t been misunderstood?
24....has s/t been altered?
25....has s/o or s/t been resisted?
26....has there been a failure?
27....has s/o or s/t been rejected?
28....has s/t been helped

Write down DEEP elements as they turn up. If obvious material turns up, go into DEEP mode right away. Otherwise, look through your notes for the button just completed. Then you take up the charged DEEP elements, be it self-limiting thoughts, emotional content, or physical content (action, impulse). Charged persons can be taken up as well. But make sure the client is interested.

If an emotional charge, an effort or thought turns up you use Repeat and Tell. If fixed ideas turn up use the Fixed Ideas Tool. This may go into Repeat and Tell. Charged persons from the past are routinely addressed with the Dialogue Tool.

Deep Incident Clearing, Short Form

Check for interest!

"Are you interested in running...?"
1A. Incident Complaint: Locate the incident when (you fell off the bicycle.)
1B. or Thematic Complaint: Locate an incident that contains (the chosen theme.)
2. Where was it?
3. When did it happen?
4. Go to that incident.
5. How long does it last?
6. Go to the start of the incident and tell me when you have done so.
7. (Close your eyes) what are you perceiving (in the incident)?
8. Go through the incident (silently) to the end.
9. Tell me what happened.
   A. Go to the start of the incident and tell me when you have done so.
   B. Go through the incident to the end.
   C. Tell me what happened.

DEEP Mode
D1. Go to the start of the incident and tell me when you have done so.
D2.-EF. Go forward in the incident, and look for the first moment of emotion, reaction or charge. Then:
D4. Continue forward through the incident, and look for the next moment of emotion, reaction or charge.

Other Points of View (POVs)
P1 Assume the viewpoint (VP) of (opponent.)
P2 From that VP, go to the start of the incident.
P3 From that VP, what do you see or perceive?
P4 From that VP, go through the incident to the end.
P5 From that VP, what happened?

Earlier/other similar. Earlier starting point.
1A-ES. Is there an earlier similar incident? (if not, ask 1A-O)
1A-O. Is there another similar incident? (if not, ask 1A-EB)
1A-EB Does the incident we are running start earlier? (If not, do D1-D4 again)
1A-ES. Is there an earlier incident that contains (item)?
1A-O. Is there another incident that contains (item)?
1A-EB Does the incident we are running start earlier?

DIC Light – Deep Incident Clearing, Light

We find an incident from the person's past that the person obviously has charge on. We check that the person is interested in taking it up, and then we start to run it.

0. "Are you interested in running...?"
1. Locate the incident when (you fell off the bicycle.)
2. Where was it?
3. When did it happen?
4. Go to that incident.
5. How long does it last?
6. Go to the start of the incident and tell me when you have done so.
7. (Close your eyes) what are you perceiving (in the incident)?
8. Go through the incident to the end and tell me what happens.
9. Tell me what happened? (Ask only, if not already told.)
    A. Go to the start of the incident and tell me when you have done so.
    B. Go through the incident to the end.
    C. Tell me what happened.

We run A,B,C, one or more times until the story has settled. Now we go into DEEP mode:

DEEP Mode (Subjective experience)

D1. Go to the start of the incident and tell me when you have done so.
D2. Go forward in the incident, and find the first moment of emotion, reaction or charge.
(We handle the DEEP package per below.) Then:
D4. Go forward from there, and find the next moment of emotion, reaction or charge.

For each Moment (DEEP package), we have the person tell about the *subjective content*, question by question.

"At that moment, are there any: 1.emotions? 2. feelings? 3. body sensations? 4. body language or posture? 5. actions or reactions? 6. impulses? 7. thoughts?"

Keep it light; just ask one after the other and have the person tell about it. For a charged category we can make a list and ask the person to sort out the dominant elements. We can ask the person to assign a number value to each (0-10). Just take what the person gives. Allow the person to look, experience and feel – and to talk. In this fashion the person reviews and sorts out the subjective elements of that DEEP package.

    Then we use the D4 instruction and find the next DEEP package. In this way we cover the whole incident. When that is done, we may use D1 and make a second – and maybe additional passes the same way until it is free of charge.

    We can then use "Other Points of View" below. In conflicts it handles the counter-force, a common cause of hang-ups. In DIC Light we do not always do so.

Other Points of View (POVs)

P1 Assume the viewpoint (VP) of (opponent.)
P2 From that VP, go to his/her start of the incident.
P3 From that VP, what do you see or perceive?
P4 From that VP, go through the incident to the end.
P5 From that VP, what happened?

We can also use DEEP mode on the other viewpoint. It runs much lighter.

    When all is done, we can ask for another traumatic or stressful incident.

DEEP Body Clearing, Short Form

We use 'bad back' as an example below.

1. The clearer asks the introspector: "Is there any part of your body that is ailing, bothering you or has been acting up from time to time?"
The answer here is 'lower back'.

2. Tune in to the (lower back). "Do you get any messages or flows from there?"

3. If you do, clarify it and use Repeat and Tell on it.

4. If no response, but there seems to be some kind of problem with the back, you use Hello/OK on it.

"Say 'Hello' to your lower back."
"Have the lower back say 'OK' to that hello."
"Have the lower back say 'Hello' to you."
"You say 'OK' to that hello."

This may turn into a conversation or exchange. It can be in words or in flows, such as certain sensations and pains turning on. The clearer would try for getting it expressed in words but shouldn't insist on this.

"Is there something your lower back wants to say to you?"
"Acknowledge that."
"Is there something you want to say (in response to that) to the lower back?"
"Have the lower back acknowledge that."

5. If something now gets stirred up it is handled with Repeat and Tell and other tools from the DEEP tool box. This step may lead to painful and traumatic incidents that may have to be taken up with DEEP Incident Clearing or DEEP Viewpoint Clearing. In general, if a DEEP package turns up, all the tools and actions of DEEP may be considered.

6. Once the trouble area has been handled, we do an additional step. "Feel the aliveness of the lower back." This is asked repeatedly to its end point.

7. When lower back is handled, we ask for another trouble spot. The procedure 1-5 is then repeated on that body part.

8. Once all the trouble spots of the introspector's body have been addressed this way, we add this wellness step, going from toe to top of the person.

A. "Feel the aliveness of your right foot" to an end point.

B. Then "Feel the aliveness of your left foot," etc., taking all the main areas and body parts of the person. Skip body parts that may embarrass the introspector.

C. This is kept up until the whole body has been worked over, from feet to top of the head.

DEEP Viewpoint Clearing, Short Form

We find a person with whom the client repeatedly has conflicts and problems. We typically use a list of possible persons, collected from earlier sessions or we can ask the client directly:
"Is there a person with whom you have had repeated conflicts or problems?"

Can you find a specific situation or problem with (the other person) where you ran into trouble?
2. Get a short description, time, place, what happened, persons, etc.
3. What was your feeling or state of mind? (Repeat and Tell = R & T)
4. How did it feel in the body? (R & T)
5. What was your body language? (Show it)
6. Were there motions or actions you carried out or wanted to do? (Show it)
7. Was there a thought, decision or idea buried somewhere in that condition?
8. Repeat that thought aloud whilst you show the attitude and the condition as it was (R&T)
9. If the thought found in (7) seems negative or irrational, ask:
A. How has (the thought) helped you?
B. How has (the thought) harmed you?
10. Can you think of a better idea you could use in the same or a similar situation?
10 A. Imagine the situation we just looked at - using (the better idea)
10 B. How does it feel?
10 C. How does it feel in the body?
10 D. Say the statement and experience the entire package. (Give the client the time needed.)

THE COUNTERPART OR ANOTHER (A=another)
'A' (another) could be a direct opponent, but could also be another character appearing in the situation – or even a person in the clients thoughts ("what would your mother think?")
a 1. Take (A's) viewpoint
a 2. (As A) Describe the situation.
a 3. (As A) What was your feeling or state of mind? (R & T)
a 4. (As A) How did it feel in the body? (R & T)
a 5. (As A) What was your body language? (Show it)
a 6. (As A) Were there motions or actions you carried out or wanted to do? (Show it)
a 7. (As A) Was there a thought, decision or idea buried somewhere in that condition?
a 8. (As A) Repeat that thought aloud whilst you show the attitude and the condition as it was (R & T)
a 9. If the thought found in (7) seems negative or irrational, ask:
A...(As A), How has (the thought) helped you?
B. (As A), How has (the thought) harmed you?
a 10. (As A) Can you think of a better idea you could use in the same or a similar situation?
a 10 A. (As A) Imagine the situation we just looked at - using (the better idea)
(as help, ask: "You may be able to find a similar situation you have experienced yourself")
a 10 B. (As A) How does it feel?
a 10 C. (As A) How does it feel in the body?
a 10 D. (As A) Say the statement and experience the entire package. (Give the time needed)
Dialogue: If the situation and the relationship are still charged, use the Dialogue Tool from the Toolbox.
11. Get the client to imagine the other person in question and ask:
11 A.   Is there anything you would like to communicate to (A)?
11 B.   Get (A) to receive (acknowledge) the communication.
11 C.   Is there anything (A) would like to communicate to you?
11 D.   Receive (acknowledge) that communication.

New vitality lists

Each list deals with a specific area. First the clearer finds what area is of interest to the client. In what area does the client have problems and issues? Then you assess the list. Each 'button' is called directly to the client as a question and it is expected that the client answers with whatever comes to mind. The clearer keeps an eye on the client's emotional reactions, etc. The client is asked how much charge there is on the subject on a scale from 0 to 10. If it is charged, the client is asked if she is interested in looking at the item. We usually use DVC to discharge the item. Let's say the item is 'scared of the police'. Client is asked for an incident where she was scared of the police and now the DVC steps are used to handle both sides and end off with a dialogue.

If the client gives an 'illogic' or 'irrelevant' answer it is assessed for charge. If charged, it is picked up. The list should be seen as portholes to the repressed mind and we pick up what we find. If the client can't find an incident and the item is still charged, it can be taken up with DEEP Subject Clearing (DSC). "Regarding the police, has anything been suppressed?" etc. down the buttons. DSC will quickly uncover situations that can be picked up with DVC. Now you may ask the next DSC button and change to DVC on the next conflict uncovered.

The lists given here are not given as the final or best version. When a clearer knows his client well, he is the right person to put together a tailor made list. It should cover a wide spectrum – but still with the client's special difficulties at the center.

The lists are well suited for finding new material that, as a rule, is less charged—but still important for the person's ability to permanently put challenges and problems from the past behind him/her—not just expect that the same issues will return in new disguises. With the New Vitality Lists the client can expect to find subconscious self-limiting beliefs, preconceptions, dictates and thought- and action patterns that now can be inspected and released. This will open the gates to finding new possibilities and opportunities in life.

Work, career (Employees)	Work, Career (Executives)	Health
1. Colleagues 2. Bosses 3. Subordinates 4. Deadlines 5. Unreasonable demands 6. Lack of information 7. Gossip at work 8. Hostile colleagues 9. Costumers 10. Clients 11. No respect 12. Overtime 13. Too busy 14. Career 15. Promotion 16. Engagement 17. Rivals 18. Lack of interest 19. Long work days 20. Exhaustion 21. Long commuting time 22. Can't make it 23. Can't be bothered 24. Forced to work 25. Disloyal colleagues 26. Unpleasant boss 27. Underpaid 28. Mobbing 29. Backstabbing 30. Competing colleagues 31. Bad/Outdated/Missing Equipment 32. Mismanagement 33. Sexual harassment 34. Gender/Religious/Race …discrimination	1. Marketing 2. Competing …companies 3. Budget 4. Banks 5. Mutiny 6. Unions 7. Sabotage 8. Taxes 9. Regulations 10. Government 11. Bad publicity 12. Political problems 13. Environmental …problems	1. Doctors 2. Bad medical training 3. Hospitals 4. Medical drugs 5. Operations 6. Accidents 7. Infections 8. Broken bones 9. Wounds 10. Blood 11. Diabetes 12. Cancer 13. Dementia 14. Epidemics 15. Food sensitivities 16. Allergies 17. Sexually transmitted …diseases 18. AIDS 19. Genetic diseases 20. Medical error 21. Pregnancy 22. Birth control 23. Childbirth 24. Vaccinations 25. Menopause 26. Andropause 27. Old age 28. Dying 29. Nutrition 30. Missing know-how 31. Wrong know-how 32. Alcohol 33. Cigarettes 34. Recreational drugs 35. Bad examples 36. Subject illiterate Pparents 37. Unhealthy traditions

Environmental Stress Factors	Family
1. Droughts 2. Flooding 3. Storms 4. Extreme temperatures 5. Chemical pollution 6. Radioactive pollution 7. Noise pollution 8. Traffic 9. Overpopulation 10. Genetically modified plants 11. Pests 12. Parasites 13. Chem trails (from jet planes) 14. Natural disasters 15. War 16. The News 17. Social media	1. Noisy children 2. Sour spouse 3. We need money 4. Poor housing 5. Sick spouse 6. Sick child 7. Difficult kids 8. Uncontrollable children 9. Handicapped child 10. Dominating spouse 11. It is all routine 12. No love 13. Something just missing 14. Secrets 15. No confidentiality 16. Lies 17. White lies 18. Accident in the family 19. Death in the family 20. Intolerable in-laws 21. Intolerable relatives 22. Criminality in the family 23. I never see my children 24. Alienated children 25. No privacy 26. Violence 27. Sexual Abuse

Sexual Health	Sex in Relationships	Sex and Society

1. Birth control
2. Family planning
3. Disease prevention
4. Libido
5. Potency
6. Erectile dysfunction
7. Female sexual
   …dysfunction
8. Frigidity
9. Hormonal
   …imbalance
10. Sexual orientation
11. Homosexuality
12. Bisexuality
13. Straight
14. Gay
15. Lesbian
16. Transgender
17. Sexual identity
18. Sexual self-
   …expression
19. Sexual freedom
20. Authenticity
	1. It is all about sex
	2. Infidelity
	3. Flirting with another
	4. Do not want sex
	5. Want strange sex
	6. Never want sex
	7. Want sex all the time
	8. Fetish sex
	9. Too rough sexually
	10. Can't get sexually satisfied
	11. Pretend orgasms
	12. Masturbation
	13. Pornography
	14. Scared of sex
	15. Suppressing sex drive out of
	   …"respect"
	16. No interest in partner's sexual needs
	17. Does not listen to partner's
	   …wishes
	18. Lack of sexual skills
	19. Does not want to learn/practice sex
	20. Too lazy to take care of partner
	21. Too impatient to take care of
	   …partner
	22. Partner needs to much time to climax
	23. Bad hygiene
	24. Aversion against overweight
	   …partner
	25. Aversion against partner getting older
	26. Aversion against bodily smells
	27. Aversion against bodily fluids
	28. Aversion against wife after childbirth
	29. Can't have sex with "Madonna" wife
	30. Prudish
	31. Denying sex as a punishment
	32. Enforcing sex
	33. Date-Rape
	34. Rape in relationship/marriage
		1. Bonding type
		2. Relationship rules copied
		   …from Church
		3. Relationship rules
		   …copied from others
		4. Never Discussed Relationship
		   …Rules
		5. Rel. Rules in conflict
		   …with bonding type
		6. Monogamy
		7. Enforced monogamy
		8. Polygamy
		9. Enforced polygamy
		10. Arranged marriage
		11. Marriage of convenience
		12. Marriage contract
		13. No Marriage contract
		14. Platonic relationship
		15. Celibacy
		16. Enforced celibacy
		17. Polyamory
		18. Promiscuity
		19. Swingers
		20. "Sex is dirty"
		21. "Sex is a sin"
		22. "Sex is not honorable"
		23. "Sex is not spiritual"
		24. "Body is Inferior"
		25. Parents hostile towards sex
		26. Larger family hostile towards
		   …sex
		27. Culture hostile towards sex
		28. Church hostile towards sex
		29. Taboos
		30. Guilt
		31. Punishment
		32. Ostracism
		33. Firmly hooked into
		   …a group mind
		34. Can't detach from group
		   …agreements
		35. Overwhelmed by negative
		   …group energy
		36. Sexual revolution
		37. Sexual liberation

Relationships	Fear of People	Money and Finance
1. First date		1. Money
2. The only one	1. Bullies	2. Bankers
3. Being in love	2. Men	3. Loans
4. Fights	3. Sinister men	4. Debts
5. Conflicts	4. Angry men	5. Deposits
6. Secrets	5. Women	6. Interest
7. Going out	6. Tough women	7. Bills
8. Mutual interests	7. Provoking women	8. Outstanding bills
9. No mutual interests	8. Sexy women	9. Cheaters
10. Marriage	9. Gang member	10. Money fraud
11. Will not marry	10. Police	11. False claims
12. Date cancelled	11. VIP	12. Valid claims
13. Stood up on date	12. Politician	13. Taxes
14. Prevented from seeing each …other	13. Important person	14. Money collectors
15. Other more important things	14. Sexy men	15. Public funding
16. Engulfed in work	15. Smart types	16. No funding
17. Only talks about one thing	16. Dominating men	17. Loan applications
18. Engulfed in computer and …internet	17. Salesman	18. Bankruptcy
19. Will not talk about the future	18. Civil servant	19. Overcharging
20. Will not talk about self	19. Authority	20. Free of charge
21. Will not listen to problems	20. Public employee	21. Financial contracts
22. Will not change anything	21. Activist	22. Instalment plans
23. Bad taste	22. Terrorist	23. Can't afford it
24. Will not spend money on …relationship	23. Foreigner	24. Loans to friends
25. Forgot the birthday	24. Mexican	25. Borrowing from friends
26. Shy	25. Muslim	26. Co-signing
27. Scared of the opposite sex	26. Negro	27. Rent-to-own
28. Obsessed with the mobile … phone	27. Asian	28. Rental contracts
29. Obsessed with social media	28. Hindu	29. Quick loans
30. Jealousy	29. Fanatic	30 Investments
31. Possessiveness	30. Telephone salesman	31. Shares
32. Physical violence	31. Teacher	32. Bonds
33. No admiration	32. Headmaster	33. Stock market
34. No dedication	33. Priest	34. Bad accounting
35. No passion	34. Imam	35. No accounting
36. No desire	35. Criminal	36. False accounting
37. Heartbreaks	36. Murderer	37. Bad financial advice
38. Compersion ("Opposite of Jealousy")		38. Scarcity
		39. Miser
		40. Big spender
		41. Gamble with money
		42. Foreclosure
		43. Ruined
		44. Refuse to spend money
		45. Refuse to pay

Polarities		Spirituality, religion
Ask: Is _____ an identity you would detest or definitely would not be? 1. AIDS patient 2. Gang member 3. Cancer patient 4. Drug pusher 5. Crippled 6. Homeless person 7. A fraud 8. Gang member 9. Human wreck 10. Saboteur 11. Alcoholic 12. Drug addict 13. Victim 14. Hippie 15. Anarchist 16. Runaway driver 17. Criminal 18. Illegal alien 19. Thief 20. Spendthrift 21. Fraudulent person 22. Ruined 23. Tax evader 24. Bureaucrat 25. Social fraud person 26. Robot 27. Vagrant person 28. Invisible 29. Parasite 30. Follower 31. Scavenger 32. Party soldier 33. Beggar 34. Fanatic 35. Foreign worker 36. Insane 37. Refugee	38. Fruitcake 39. Negro 40. Neurotic 41. Sex fixated 42. "Saved" 43. Murderer 44. Helpless 45. Killer 46. Tormentor 47. Hit man 48. Battered victim 49. Sniper 50. Idiot 51. Terrorist 52. Oddball 53. Member of Islamic State 54. Sacrificial Lamb 55. Member of Alkaida 56. Buck 57. Combat soldier 58. Target 59. Bailiff 60. Scolded 61. Spy 62. Lost 63. Micro manager 64. Stickler to detail 65. Tyrannical person 66. Smear campaign victim	1. Telepathy 2. Ghosts 3. Dead people 4. Life after death 5. Life before birth 6. Heaven 7. Hell 8. Dreams 9. Nightmares 10. Psychic abilities 11. Love 12. Thoughts 13. Intuition 14. Spiritual abilities 15. Guardian angel 16. Angels 17. The Devil 18. Alternative therapies 19. Spiritism 20. Yoga 21. Theosophy 22. Catholicism 23. Protestantism 24. Buddhism 25. The almighty God 26. Providence 27. Astrology 28. Atheism 29. Shaman 30. Rituals 31. Poltergeist 32. Vampire 33. Soul mate 34. Eternal love 35. "Love they neighbor" 36. God's punishment 37. God's love 38. Destiny 39. Karma law 40. The spiritual universe

Dreams and DEEP

Dreams have been fascinating us humans for thousands of years. They can be very vivid, real and dramatic; very fantastic and supernatural. What is it that these very personal adventures and dramas try to tell us?

The clearer's professional code states that it is not the clearer's job to tell the client what to think. This includes what the client's dreams mean. And that is fine, because different dream interpreters can arrive at very different interpretations for the same dream. In the worst cases these interpretations can act as self-fulfilling prophecies. But is there another possibility of using dreams in self-development?

We can use dreams in a new way with DEEP. Dreams can be a new entrance to the client's situation and case. If the client is engaged in his dreams or comes in with one fresh one in mind, we discharge what the dream has triggered with DEEP. Our approach to dreams is based on Fritz Perls' use of dreams (Fritz Perls is the founder of Gestalt Therapy).

This approach means that in practice we will not try to interpret dreams. Instead we let the client live the dream out fully with its different aspects. We can do this with DEEP tools, especially different versions of Repeat and Tell. But Dialogue is often a good tool to use as well. A dialogue can be established between the different characters appearing in the dream. In addition to running every present person and being's DEEP package, we will include important objects, like a train, a mountain, a building, a location, etc. We find that objects and locations often are loaded with significance for the client but also with charge.

We see the different persons, objects and places appearing in the dream as aspects or fragments of the client's personality or situation. That the psyche is fragmented is an intricate part of any person's case and something we continuously work on to heal in all our session work. Fragmentation is a condition we all have and experience in different ways. When we talk about fragmentation we talk about polarization as each different fragment makes a pole in the mind.

When we run DEEP on all these aspects and characters the polarization will discharge to a point where it all is integrated. The person may not understand what the dream "means" even though such realizations do happen quite often. And realizations and new insights are of course the best end points for this type of clearing work. To facilitate that the Clearer can ask, when appropriate, "Do you see any similarity or parallel of this [dream element] with your current situation?" and handle anything that comes up with the appropriate tools.

The clearer holds a neutral position regarding interpretation of the dream. We are only there in order to keep the client going by asking the correct questions and giving the right instructions. We get the best results when we keep the clearer's professional code to the hilt. We run the person's reactions to the different aspects. And, if possible, we also get the person to "be" the things, objects and elements and run them from their perspective, including the energy (effort), atmosphere ("state of mind") and purpose/function ("thought") they contain—and possibly their physical impact on the person or the help they give. A building for example, can have a gloomy atmosphere in a dream, and contain some kind of hidden message. It could be "I will hurt you", or "I love you, come into my arms", etc. By going into all these emotions, thoughts and energetic aspects of the dream, the client has a chance to re-experience this very incredible and personal history and draw his own conclusions that only the client can reach.

Making Programs for DEEP Clearing Work

It is very individual how a DEEP series of sessions is planned or programmed. When professionally done, other modalities and techniques are often used. In the following, however, we give some guidelines that work very well and stay within the techniques and materials given in this book.

Start with an intake interview: The clearer prepares a number of interview questions to get a good overview of the client's background and situation in order to determine where to start. The interview should cover the following:

1. Client's name; address: phone number: e-mail; age; employment; education. 2. Family situation: is the client married/unmarried? Children. Siblings. Parents. 3. With whom does the client live? 4. Client's health and short health history, including illnesses the client may not need to see a doctor for. 5. Client's relationship to own body and illness. 6. Ask the client how daily life is going and get him/her to talk about it. 7. Ask into the client's relationships to family. 8. Ask about the relationship to work. 9. Ask about which groups and associations the client is a member of and the relationships to these. 10. Ask if the client has any experience with self-development or therapy, and what the client wanted to improve by help from those; also the outcome. 11. Ask for any accidents or serious illness the client has had. 12. Ask which problems and issues are the biggest in the client's life. 13. Ask what the client wants to gain from the present clearing work.

12 and 13 are essential questions as the answers can be used in the coming sessions directly.

14. End off by asking if there is anything the client would like to add or ask.

Several Layers of Case

You could say that the case has several layers. There is thinking and telling. The client simply tells what happened and which thoughts were present. This is the top layer and easiest available. Feelings and efforts (movements/action) can compete for the second place. There are people who feel and people who act. A "man of action" is probably better at explaining what was done and the efforts that went into it, than telling what the emotional content of an incident was. A woman engulfed in the emotions, on the other hand, is very aware of her feelings and maybe less aware of actions and consequences. This can be important and significant to take into account with new clients. There are specifically clients where emotions/feelings are a closed area. When you ask about feelings they have no answers. Therefore it is not a good idea to insist on getting what they felt. As a clearer you still ask, but not so insistently as to make the client embarrassed because of lack of answers. In this very short description we describe the level of difficulty of the different techniques first.

As clearer you first of all have to ensure that you choose a technique the client actually can do – maybe with a little effort in the beginning. Avoid techniques that are too difficult for the client as this can give the person a feeling of lacking ability, a feeling of loss which isn't productive. In the Toolbox we mentioned moving forward with the correct pace. This also goes for choice of the technique. We choose a technique that challenges the client sufficiently and achieves a gain—and not just bores the client.

Not all new clients are ready for DEEP. Therefore it is mentioned again that the techniques in the book can be used without the DEEP steps. The list below runs from the easiest techniques to the most demanding. But it shall be mentioned that the easier a technique is, the more superficial it is too. With some clients we ran some traumatic incidents first without DEEP steps which gave the client enough to do. Later we went back and ran the same incidents using DEEP Incident Clearing. This time we got the feelings, actions and thoughts fully discharged. In both the first and second run the client had plenty to do. We moved forward with the correct pace.

Interview: Using interview is mandatory. The purpose is to get enough data for use in further programming. The clearer has a list of prepared questions (like above) that helps decide where the client is at in his/her life and what he/she would like to change. The clearer can write a program based on the answers. Interviews are also used if the clearer has a lack of data in the middle of a series of sessions. The idea is to change gear and get the needed data for further effective programming. As a follow-up on an interview the clearer collects a list of items and issues from the answers and have the client assess them for charge and interest on a scale from 0 to 10.

Exploring: Consists of getting the client to tell about a specific problem or subject. The clearer is sticking to the professional code. His most important task is to get the client to keep talking and explaining by using light questions. He can ask for time, place, event, circumstances, thoughts, feelings etc. in connection with the subject. The clearer does not dive deep in Exploring and never gives his own opinion. It is the client's story and considerations that need to be brought forward. Using Exploring on a hot subject is a good starting point before using more formal techniques.

Unblocking: If you have a hot subject but it isn't quite clear how to size it up, it's a good plan to do Exploring first and then Unblocking on the subject. With experienced clients one would use the DEEP version, DSC. But with new clients this can be far too difficult and time consuming. You can return to the subject later using DEEP techniques and get all the layers of case handled. Unblocking will typically reveal stressed incidents and trauma that can be handled using Incident Clearing and DEEP Incident Clearing. The author learned Unblocking as part of his TIR education, but in the book we use our own version of the 'buttons'.

Incident Clearing, without DEEP: This technique is especially well suited for traumatic incidents, meaning incidents the client remembers with horror. You run the steps 1 – 9 and thereafter A, B, C again and again until the client feels released and freed. In USA we learned the technique as TIR (Traumatic Incident Reduction). It is a good idea to start out with Exploring as this gives the needed information in order to limit the traumatic event. We need a clear starting point and end. At a later point one should run the same incident with DEEP Incident Clearing in order to remove all the charged elements and layers in the incident.

DEEP Body Clearing (DBC): Can normally be used early in a program. If the client has bodily problems this technique helps the client to establish better contact and communication to the body and thereby a loosening up of the situation. For clients with bodily problems but only some understanding of DEEP we can recommend Bruce Lipton's book "Biology of Belief" that will open the door to understanding the biology and physiology involved.

DEEP Subject Clearing (DSC): This is the DEEP version of Unblocking. It is used the same way as described in the Unblocking chapter. When running the DEEP packages, you will sometimes end up in traumatic incidents that are handled to complete that button. They are taken up with DEEP Incident Clearing. When finished with the incident, you can return to use of the buttons if the subject is still charged and only partly solved. This approach can be rather time consuming with new clients, but it is still a good use of the session time if you are on a major issue.

DEEP Incident Clearing (DIC): If the client can run DEEP we use DIC for all major incidents showing up. At an early point you can collect all the traumatic and stressed incidents the client told about in the intake interview and run them with DIC. Likewise, a list of complaints can be made (as described in Chapter 19) and they are handled one by one. If new traumatic incidents come up, or new subject complaints do, then at a proper time you can add a new section of DIC to the major program.

DEEP Viewpoint Clearing (DVC): Our subconscious and repressed mind is filled with "negative inner dialogue" and self-limiting beliefs, dogma and judgements. All these fixed ideas control, for large parts, our behavior and destiny. DVC brings these into the light of consciousness and makes it possible to inspect and revise them.

The technique is best suited for clients who have already gotten all the stressful and traumatic material handled. We do not look for trauma primarily, but for stressful situations where the client fell short. Therefore we recommend saving this technique until a later point in a

DEEP Clearing

program.

DVC can be used with experienced clients instead of DIC. It might still happen that traumatic incidents show up which can then be handled with DIC.

DEEP Character Clearing (DCC): This is a professional technique and is not included here. It is designed to dissolve what we call 'archetypal conflicts'; i.e. super problems and conflicts that seem to repeat themselves again and again – even over several lifetimes. See chapter 21 for further information. Within the framework of this book, DVC can be applied on the same situations with some success. If that does not handle the situation one should consult a professional DEEP Clearer.

Model Programs for DEEP Clearing Work

The following can help get new clients started on DEEP Clearing.

Inexperienced clients:

Model 1: Inexperienced and new client	Model 2: Body problems	Model 3: Relationships
1. Do an intake interview
2. From 1. Make a list of issues
3. Evaluation of issues, 0 – 10.
4. Take the hottest issue
5. Do Exploring on the issue
6. Unblocking of the issue
7. Use Incident Clearing on stressful incidents (no/DEEP)
8. Interview: "How is it going now?" Get new evaluation, (0-10) of new and old issues.
9. Exploring on hottest issue.
10. DSC Light on the issue.
11. Use DIC Light on charged incidents
12. New interview
13. End or extend the program. | 1. Do an intake interview with emphasis on body problems
2. Exploring on biggest problem
3. Unblocking or DSC of the area
4. Run incidents that might have caused the problem. Use DIC Light.
5. Run DBC on the area and entire body
6. New interview
7. End or extend the program
8. Use 'Transparent Body' as needed | 1. Do an intake interview with emphasis on relationship problems
2. Exploring regarding the core challenge
3. Unblocking or DSC of the area
4. Run charged incidents from the client's relationship history. Use DIC Light.
5. Interview regarding how the relationship is now
6. End or extend the program

Note: Bad communication skills are the most common cause of relationship problems. Get both the partners to do the communication exercises for a more stable result. |

More experienced clients:

Model 4: Lack of self-worth	Model 5: Job, career	Model 6: Relationships
1. Do an interview
2. Exploring on the subject
3. Possibly DSC on same
4. Run larger defeats with DIC
5. Run situations with lack of self-worth with DVC
6. Run appropriate New Vitality Lists with DVC	1. Do an interview
2. Exploring on the subject
3. DSC on charged jobs
4. DIC on firings, if any
5. DVC on aspects of working life, relationship to colleagues and bosses.
6. Run appropriate New Vitality Lists with DVC	(Is combined with model 3)
1. Do an interview
2. Run break-ups with DIC, if any.
3. DVC on difficult situations in the relationship
4. Run appropriate New Vitality Lists with DVC

It is of course not possible to give final programs without knowing the content of the interview and the client's situation and ability to run the various techniques. But the clearer can use the above suggestions as inspiration when he has the results from the interview.

Glossary for DEEP

A

Area Complaint: see Complaint.

B

Being: 1. the consciousness; the part of us that is aware of being aware. 2. The spiritual self. 3. By the Being we mean the core personality. Not the body, not the mind, not the energy body. But the spiritual Being who is the person now and always has been the person. The Being is the same through countless incarnations.

Bypass Reaction: An Automatic reaction that bypasses the person's volition and control.

Bypass mechanism: The trigger mechanism. When the repressed mind is reactivated (triggered) outside our control and awareness and the rational mind has been bypassed, the Bypass mechanism is in play. It seems to be a warning system against danger. But the many triggers easily become a burden. They need to be inspected and cleaned up.

Body Memories: 1. the recordings of the person's dealings with force, objects and bodies. We find recordings of the person's own movements, body postures and actions. And we find recordings of the movements of other bodies and of physical objects around the person. Body memories record and map where bodies and things are, how they move and what forces are in play. It is a recording of what happens in the frequency band of effort. 2. Body memories, as we use it, cover recordings of impulses and motions, body language, and body sensations. 3. Body Memories include recordings of what is called Kinesthesia in medicine (British Dictionary, Kinesthesia: a. the sense that detects bodily position, weight, or movement of the muscles, tendons, and joints; b. the sensation of moving in space). It does however also include recordings of sensations.

Body sensations: 1. Feelings and sensory signals from the body. 2. Body sensations are comprised of various feelings stemming from the body, such as ache, soreness, itch, thirst, full stomach and dozens of other signals and impulses, good and bad. The body is trying to tell us about its condition. By perceiving the range of body sensations we are aware of and in contact with the body. Sometimes these signals stem from past situations that should be located and reviewed. They are unpleasant and distracting "noise" related to the past. Sometimes these signals should be cause to alarm and immediate action. Sometimes one needs to change habits or diet or seek medical help immediately as a consequence of these signals.

C

Character: 1. Identity; persona. 2. Character is used as a synonym for identity. The word Character originally means imprint, as on the surface of a coin. In DEEP Character Clearing we address such Characters that are artificial or temporary imprints on the Being, and may be acted out unknowingly. By doing the clearing work, they get dissolved and the person recaptures the life force tied up in them. When these artificial Characters are dissolved, the person experiences the word in its more noble meaning: getting in character, being whole and of high integrity and trustworthiness. 3. Role in movie. See also Identity*.

Charge: 1. Disturbing or harmful mental energy generated in mind and body. 2. Mental charge is generated between conflicting viewpoints, ideas and mental objects in the mind. Charge is electrical in nature as it is generated between two poles—like between the plus and minus pole of an electrical battery. 3. Repressed, unfulfilled decision, emotion or effort. If a decision, emotion or effort becomes a completed cycle, the tension or charge ceases. If it is held back (repressed) or is stopped due to opposition, it still seeks to complete the cycle on a subconscious or unconscious level. This is what we call charge. When we in DEEP contact the DEEP elements and embrace and release them, the cycles are allowed to complete and the charge ceases to exist.

Clearer: the practitioner in DEEP; DEEP practitioner, sometimes called Life Coach.

Complaint (a technical term in DIC)

Area Complaint: 1. An area or subject of difficulty caused by irrational factors. 2. The complaint can be about the person's feelings and reactions towards a certain subject or an area of difficulty or inability. One would find a general complaint's pains, emotions, feelings, attitudes, etc. connected to that subject or area and address them as general complaints. Examples of area complaints could be "feeling bad about one's time in middle school," "having troubles with study," "having difficulties in one's marriage," etc. Each general complaint can be taken up with DEEP Incident Clearing or with DEEP Subject Clearing.

General Complaint, Theme: 1. Unwanted emotions, sensations, feelings, pains, etc. stemming from the repressed mind. 2. The person can have a general complaint of unpleasant emotion and reaction to certain things or an inexplicable physical ailment, such as a pain, a soreness, itch, etc. with no immediate or medical explanation. One starts out by asking for incidents containing this theme: be it a negative emotion, unpleasant feeling, a pain, odd body sensation, etc. An incident containing this theme is found and reviewed. Then another incident is taken up, etc. until the complaint is gone or no more incidents can be found.

Incident Complaint: 1. A known traumatic or stressful incident. 2. The person can have a complaint about a certain and known traumatic incident. The incident will be addressed as a known event of the personal history. It can be loss of a loved one, an accident, an assault, an operation, a severe illness in the past, a period or situation of extreme stress, etc. It can be loss of any kind; emotional or physical trauma of any kind. Such incidents can be addressed directly.

Confidence: a positive quality of trusting oneself and others; a sign of a high mood and energy level. It has been said "the difference between self-confidence and arrogance is compassion!" It is important to understand the difference between confidence and self-righteousness*, which actually *is* arrogant and comes at the expense of others.

Counter-efforts, Counter-emotions, Counter-thoughts: 1. efforts, emotions, feelings, sensations and thoughts that work against the person or against the person's original vectors. The way we take up these counter-vectors is to find the viewpoint that holds them as their own. When viewing them from that perspective they are normal efforts, emotions and thoughts and are easy to duplicate and dissolve. These counter-vectors impeded or stopped discharge or completion of cycles in the first place. 2. The repression factor that stops a DEEP element from completing its cycle.

D

Decisions: are causative thoughts. They can be rational thoughts or bypass reactions. Bypass reactions as Thoughts are also called Dictates. Decisions set a course for the future or they can be causative or final conclusions about the past. A decision has a subjective and final quality to it. There may be hundreds of thoughts, for and against, before a decision is arrived at. The decision finalizes matters even when it is wrong.

Decision or Thought: A DEEP package is primarily held in place by a central decision or a dictate. The clearer asks for decisions and thoughts to get the introspector to talk about it. The objective is to find a causative thought that holds a condition in place. The team may take up several thoughts and decisions for each package. But finding and releasing the central decision is what really loosens up the charge contained in the package.

DEEP Clearing: D.E.E.P. is an acronym that stands for 1. Decisions, dictates; 2. Emotions, feelings; 3. Efforts, energies; 4. Polarity, points of view. DEEP is the self-development system or therapy presented in this book. Any issue or area that seems charged, blocked or riddled with irrationality is examined for *DEEP packages**. Once a DEEP package is found in the area, it is resolved using the DEEP techniques and tools. Several packages per issue are often dealt with. When the issue is cleared for the charge found in the DEEP packages, sanity, rationality and free life-force is restored to the area.

DEEP Body Clearing: a DEEP action where the body is being looked over for any weak spots that are bothering the person. Such spots are then examined, using various DEEP tools. It results in freeing up the life force in the body and the person being in better communication with the area and body in general.

DEEP Character Clearing (DCC): an advanced main action in DEEP. It addresses identities (called characters) the person has fought and own identities the person has been while fighting these opponents (counter-poles). DCC is also effective in dissolving unwanted identities the person is prone to slip into. In DCC we are dealing with archetypes, characters that have iconic status and long histories.

DEEP Double Package: we have the person's own decision, emotion, and effort. This is typically held in place due to opposition, the other pole. The person's side was met by someone else's counter-decision, counter-emotion and counter-effort and the two sides collided and locked up against each other. This becomes stored as emotional charge.

DEEP Element (DEEP Item): it can be a decision or thought, an emotion or feeling, an effort or impulse, a body sensation or perception. Each DEEP element exists as a recording that can be contacted and released by repeated mindful perception and talking about it.

DEEP Incident Clearing (DIC): a main DEEP action where traumatic or stressful incidents are contacted and discharged. The story line of the incident is first sorted out. This may take several passes. Then we find and discharge the DEEP packages that are at the core of the traumatic or stressful content.

DEEP Package: A DEEP package is one set of decision, emotion, sensation and effort. They were formed at the same time. The elements comprise the four layers of the package. The DEEP package imposes a certain way of thinking, feeling and acting in an area. By clearing the package charge is removed – free life force is restored. Once you find one of the elements the other three can usually be gotten by asking for them. The decision is the most important element to find; but all four layers should be contacted and discharged if available.

DEEP Subject Clearing (DSC): this action is used to discharge just about any subject the client can think of. "Fear of spiders", "being harassed at work", "trouble with the children", etc.—issues we also have described as *Area Complaints**. We use a series of button questions to uncover DEEP packages related to the subject. Once they are in view, we use the DEEP tools to get all the charge off. DSC is often used as an exploratory action. Incidents, identities, etc. may be uncovered that can be further worked on using other DEEP actions.

DEEP Toolbox: a collection of simple techniques that are used as part of a main action. The clearer who knows his/her business knows when to use a certain tool. Each tool has a special function and is used to accomplish one little step in a main action.

DEEP Viewpoint Clearing (DVC): a DEEP technique where charged incidents or relationships are handled by in turn viewing the matter from the viewpoints involved. Each viewpoint is handled as a DEEP package. Sometimes there are several packages related to one viewpoint. All packages found are handled with DEEP tools. DVC is especially suited for advanced clients where DEEP Incident Clearing may seem too tedious.

Dictate: 1. an automatic, uninspected thought that has command value. 2. A thought or decision coming from the repressed mind that has command value. It can be a self-limiting thought, an automatic response or other type of fixed idea. It fits under the category of thought and decision, but the word Dictate underlines that it has command value over the person – since a person's decisions about self are the "law of the land".

Duplication: 1. Perceiving exactly what is there in a focused and mindful manner. 2. This is the core activity of clearing. By recognizing the exact sources of charge and mindfully perceiving them for what they are, one is duplicating and releasing these sources and they will dissolve.

All the techniques of DEEP are designed to guide the client to locate these sources of charge in order to duplicate them. It is important that the clearer does not interfere with the introspector's endeavors to mindfully duplicate. The clearer guides skillfully the person to the sources; but it is the person's action of recognizing and mindfully perceiving and duplicating the original sources that has the therapeutic effect.

E

Effort: 1. Effort has to do with energy, motion, resistance, force and physical location. While emotions, feelings, thoughts and decisions are subjective mental phenomena, efforts have to do with motion and action and have a physical universe quality to them. Efforts can be traced and mapped in space.

2. Effort is directed force. To deal with the physical world, including our own body, other people's bodies and with physical objects, we have to use and direct physical energy and force. By using effort we try to control motion and action. We use effort to resist something or to hold a position. Effort is about causing and directing force and about dealing with forces coming from the outside. We talk about two kinds of efforts A. Physical efforts and B. Mental (energetic) efforts—as explained below.

Physical Effort: is used when a person does physical work. The person moves physical objects. This would include moving the body or parts of the body, such as arms and legs. Muscles are used. Examples of physical efforts are walking, gesturing, doing the dishes, using a hammer, typing, etc.

Body Language is part of the frequency band of Effort in DEEP. In body language, emotions and thoughts are translated into physical expressions. Again, muscles are used. The charge contained in body language can be released by showing the bodily expression or fully acting it out. Body language may be as subtle as tensing up muscles in the face, bending slightly, lifting an eyebrow or smiling. *Physical objects in motion* also exert efforts. That is by the physics books (Newton's Laws of motion). In traffic accidents we have the efforts of two cars colliding. Also a parked car or a tree along the road exerts effort—the effort to resist, to remain at rest. They contain force and physical location.

Mental Effort (energetic effort, impulse): the person is trying to cause a physical effect by willing something or by having a strong wish. This causes a change in the physical body and the energy body. It may take special instruments to measure the physical side of this but it is there.

Subjectively it is usually obvious to the person that he/she made an effort in a certain direction in order to cause a physical effect. The energy body of the person can push away, pull in, hold off or make itself more solid, etc. See also Energetic Efforts*.

An *Impulse* is the beginning of an effort. An impulse starts of course as a mental thing. The person starts activating the body with a certain action in mind. It could also be called a strong wish.

Effort Band: 1) The frequency band of energy where the person deals with the real world, including own body. 2) The band of physicality where the Being deals with controlling its own body, the bodies of others and the physical world. It's all about motion, physical position, resistance and impact.

Examples of phenomena in this band: motion, action, physical work, pushing, pulling, holding off, resisting, transporting, collision, explosion, implosion, holding onto, holding and defending a position. The list goes on.

3) In the materials it is also called Body Memories and Energies. We have not always pointed out that the Effort Band also includes body language and sometimes body sensations. But the Effort Band is "anything physical" plus Impulses where physical actions are formed in the mind.

Effort Point: that area of the body or in the energy body from where the person exerts effort; also, the area where the person receives effort. In running a non-physical action, it is essential to establish the two effort points involved, since they are not visually obvious – like they are in a physical effort.

Emergency Decision: a sudden adverse decision or thought made at the instant of great stress or danger, which holds the intensity or violence of the incident. Such a decision may become a dictate and a self-limiting thought. It can have great power to disturb future thinking. When reviewed in clearing it will soon lose its charge and power and sink back into its historical context. Examples: "O my God, I'm going to die!" or "I will never get into a car again!" They can be especially harmful when the Emergency Decision contains generalities, such as 'Never', 'Always', 'Everybody' and the like. One way to deal with this is to find out when the decision was made and when it should have ended to be in force.

Emotion: 1. an affective state of being; a spontaneous state of mind that affects physiology and body language. 2. Emotion is a type of mental energy closely related to being alive. In a healthy state the emotions flow freely. They energize us and help us respond well to the environment and energize us to act or get others to act. They are an important part of our communication and interaction with others. What we do in DEEP is to restore this natural state. Our focus is therefore on emotions and feelings that are not flowing naturally but have been locked up in past incidents and situations. By unlocking these emotions we restore vital energy to the person. We restore a healthier and more balanced life where the person acts and reacts on what *is*, rather than on what *was*. A healthy emotional life works as a compass that can guide our behavior, preferences, and reactions.

Emotional Charge: see Charge.

Emotions and Feelings: in DEEP we are not only interested in the classic emotions that can be found on the affinity scale. There are a lot of additional emotional nuances and states of mind that can be felt and experienced. Those we classify as Feelings. Examples of Emotions: apathy, grief, fear, resentment, anger, antagonism, boredom, complacency, interest, enthusiasm. Examples of feelings: surprised, disgusted, feeling energetic, feeling like dancing, revengeful, disorientated, hesitant, cautious, like laughing, mischievous, sneaky, distracted, ready to pounce, etc.

Emotional Marker: an emotional reaction to a certain thing or situation. The reaction time is short so we don't have to think about how to react – it's automatic. It can be self-installed or stem from the subconscious mind. We love certain things and hate others, be it foods, types of persons, or situations.

End Point: 1. The positive conclusion of a DEEP action. The client is happy and the difficulty being addressed has been resolved. 2. The main actions of DEEP are always carried to an End Point. This is a point where a major positive change has occurred in the client regarding the subject being worked on. It is typically a point where the subject does not bother the client anymore. There are Action End Points where the client is happy and released from the whole subject. There are also Session End Points where the client had a good win regarding the subject. It may not be completely handled but the client is in a good state and extroverted and to continue introspection at that point just isn't called for. Let the client enjoy the release point and come back another day to continue.

Energy Body: the energy field that pervades and surrounds the body and the Being; the aura (also called bio-field.) The aura or energy body has been recognized for millennia in Eastern spiritual practices. Also Christian saints are always depicted with a halo or aura. In Clearing we call this energy field *the Energy Body*. It is a product of the spirit and body rather than being the spirit itself. The energy body can exert energetic efforts*.

Energetic Efforts: are efforts executed by the energy body. They parallel physical efforts. They are perceived in the energy body as pushing away, pulling close, holding off, making self more solid, etc. Sensitive people can feel "energy beams" at work. It can be an outward urge or pushing away. It can be wanting, desiring or craving something or somebody. (pulling effort). The perception of a pulling effort can be that of pulling at a rope, sucking at a straw or taking a deep breath. The energetic "cords" connecting people are pulling efforts that are created and held in place from both sides.

F

Feeling: 1. An emotional state of mind that is more complex than simply a pure emotion. 2. Any given feeling is a complex combination of thoughts, emotions and sensations. It cannot be categorized into the well-known clean emotions, such as apathy, grief, fear, anger, etc. It can be a "gut feeling" or "feeling sort of happy but still not sure of the outcome." It is a way of "thinking" about one's situation, about other people, a project, etc. It is a clear manifestation of awareness and a way of knowing. It is thinking with one's heart—some say with their gut. Intuition falls in this category,

Flat point: 1. The used technique or tool has finished producing change to a good point. 2. When an action produces no more change and there is no remaining discomfort it is said to have reached a flat point. When using the many tools of DEEP there may be many small flat points. If something feels uncomfortable but apparently doesn't change much it is not flat. When the action is continued the uncomfortable part should recede and disappear. If it doesn't, one should consider another tool. Sometimes the counter-pole has to be addressed, since it is the opposing force that holds the charge in place.

G – General Complaint: see Complaint

I

Identity: 1. The beingness of a person, persona, character. 2. An Identity is a package of traits that make up a certain way of being of a person. 3. A role that a person is playing in one of his/her life's "movies". 4. Any person has, besides their main identity (such as profession and an agreed upon personality), a long series of junior identities that come into play in special situations. We have formed each of these identities as a special solution to a life situation, a life problem. An identity can be seen as being composed of thought patterns, emotional patterns and habits or action patterns (efforts) and body sensations. So we have thought emotion sensation and effort as the basic elements that make up an identity. (See also Character.)

Impulse: 1. An impulse is the beginning of an effort. An impulse starts of course as a mental thing. The person starts activating the body with a certain action in mind. 2. Impulses are defined as forming efforts or not executed efforts. They have a subjective existence but they haven't been acted out. The mind can record and play back impulses.

Impulse or Effort: 1. When we ask for Impulse or Effort in DEEP we are asking for the motion or action side of the DEEP package. It can be as subtle as frowning one's eyebrows, tensing a muscle, leaning against a wall, etc. (body language). It can be the body's motions, such as doing physical work, fighting, falling, running, etc. We are also interested in the motion or no motion (resistance) of physical objects we are dealing with or colliding with. 2. By Effort we mean physical force and muscle force in one form or another. By impulse we mean forming efforts or not executed efforts. Impulses have a subjective existence but they haven't been acted out. 3. There is often a "secondary effort" to stop a certain impulse to act, when it is socially unacceptable or would have dire consequences. In such cases it is essential to run both of them, but especially the first or "primary" (stopped) impulse, since that typically has a lot of destructive energy that can wreak havoc in the client's energy system.

Incident Complaint: see Complaint.

Introspector: 1. The person receiving DEEP clearing; client. 2. To introspect means to look inward. The introspector is continuously guided to look into his/her own mind, body and energy body in order to find the root causes to personal issues or difficulties.

M

Main Action: these are the principal techniques we use in DEEP. At this time we have 5 main actions: 1. DEEP Subject Clearing; 2. DEEP Incident Clearing; 3. DEEP Body Clearing; 4. DEEP Viewpoint Clearing; and 5. DEEP Character Clearing. Besides the Main Actions we also have DEEP Programs. These are series of main actions put together in a certain way in order to handle specific difficulties or areas of a person's life. It can be to overcome addictions, develop abilities (known as Ability Clearing), and more.

Mental Mass: see Ridge.

Moment of Overwhelm: The moment where a person is overwhelmed by another person or the environment. He can have resisted this effort or not. In the moment of overwhelm, or shortly before or after, we will find the most charged and negative thoughts and decisions. The outside force is also called a pressor effort (pushing effort). A similar thing can happen with a tractor effort (pulling force). See Snap Moment*.

P

Permeation, Pervasion: is the ultimate form of duplication. Permeation takes place when the person can fully *BE* something or recreate something in the mind. It could be a scene, an identity, an opponent, etc. When the person can fully be an opponent character, for instance, she can recreate, neutralize and dissolve that character in her own mind and is thus no longer the adverse effect of that character. The polarity that existed between the two sides has been eliminated. The person has taken full control over the area.

Point of view: the position from where something or someone is viewed. It usually includes the subjective experience of the person that holds that viewpoint. A person always occupies a point of view and that determines, of course, what he/she can see and not see. Point of view also covers the set of opinions, emotions and habits a person lives by and views the world from. Finally social position or job also determines a person's point of view.

Polarity: when we have two persons on opposite sides of a situation we have a polarity. The vectors they express are on a collision course. A man against a physical barrier or problem would also be the one side of a polarity where the physical obstacle is the other. What we address in DEEP are all the polarities of life. By addressing the two conflicting points of view, we can resolve such polarities and arrive at a more inclusive point of view. As a result the person gets more flexible and understanding and more capable of dealing with life with all its diversities.

Pop-up: 1) any stray thought, association, incident, comment, etc. that pops up in the introspector's mind while reviewing something else in DEEP. Usually the clearer simply listens, understands and acknowledges and returns to the action in progress. It is important to allow the introspector to talk freely about what pops up as it helps in dealing with the charge. 2) Sometimes the Pop-up reveals an incident or situation that is basic to the subject at hand. In running incidents, it may reveal a more basic and more charged incident. If so, it is taken up as next incident.

Pressor Effort: an energetic effort to push something away from self, or to put distance between oneself and an object or person. A pressor effort can turn into an energetic "weapon" resembling a laser beam or lightning flash if it has high speed and intensity. The popular expression "if glances could kill..." is a reminder of that. See also the definitions of Ridge* and Moment of Overwhelm*.

R

Repeat and Tell: is a central tool in DEEP. In the *Repeat* part the introspector tunes into and experiences the original recording of the DEEP item. It can be an effort or impulse; an emotion or feeling; a body sensation or perception; or a decision or thought. The original item is mindfully reviewed and experienced repeatedly until it has disappeared or has gone flat (no more change and not active). *The Tell part* consists of the introspector telling about the item, the circumstances, any thoughts popping up, etc. It is quite common that other incidents containing the same item pop up and the introspector is encouraged to tell about them without much comment or action from the clearer's side. Once the introspector has finished telling, the clearer simply acknowledges and asks the introspector to again experience the original DEEP item. In this way the original DEEP item flattens quickly and no pop up thoughts are left untold.

Repressed Mind: 1. The Repressed Mind is the repressed or never viewed part of the subconscious mind. It seems to have a will of its own. 2. That part of the subconscious mind that contains emotionally charged material and bypass reactions. It tends to bypass the rational mind and react directly to factors in the environment that are perceived as dangers. It is a collection of conditioned reflexes, of primitive survival patterns, that were "learned" during stressful and life threatening situations. It can be triggered by the same or similar elements in the environment. It seems to have a will of its own in the form of out of control thoughts (dictates), emotions and impulses that are in conflict with the rational mind. Part of this mind is also own misdeeds and failures that we repress, deny, alter or "try to forget".

Ridge: a mental mass. Inside a ridge you will find a confusion of vectors consisting of colliding DEEP elements and DEEP packages. All these vectors and polarities are what make up the ridge or mental mass. Ridges can be formed either by colliding pressor efforts, in which case they feel heavy and massy; or by tractor efforts pulling away from each other, in which case they feel tense or in extreme cases like a vacuum.

S-T-V

Self-limiting Thoughts: 1. Automatic thoughts running in a person's head that tells him/her negative things about his/her capabilities, worth, status, etc. It can be generalities ("I never succeed"), self-destructive ("I am no good"); destructive ("beat up the bastards!"), etc., etc. They can usually be traced back to incidents and DEEP packages. 2. If generalities, destructive, self-destructive, or self-limiting decisions or conclusions are made during a traumatic incident, they can have a very negative effect on one's thinking and behavior. Since a person's decisions about self act as the "Law of the Land", they become self-limiting thoughts and self-fulfilling prophecies. They are also called Dictates and Fixed Ideas.

Self-righteous Idea: A type of fixed idea where the person stubbornly insists on being right and others wrong. It may show up under an arrogant or mocking attitude. It comes in many variations. One way to address such ideas is to ask: "How has it helped you?" "How has it harmed you?" back and forth until a new insight is obtained. For comparison see the definition of Confidence*, which is a sign of strength and sees no need to make others wrong.

Self-Serving Computation: A self-righteous idea* that elevates oneself at the expense of others. See the definition of Confidence* for comparison.

Sensation: see body sensation.

Session End Point: 1. A positive, happy outcome of a session is expected. When reached, the session can be ended. 2. A Session End Point is when the client had a good win regarding the subject at hand. The item or subject may not be completely handled but the client is at a good point and extroverted and continuing introspection at that point just isn't possible. If ignored, there is a risk that charge that still exists, but is out of reach at the moment, will not be addressed in future sessions. Therefore the clearer should end the session and let the client enjoy the win.

Shock Moment: 1. A moment of defeat, despair or overwhelm. 2. A Shock Moment is a moment of overwhelm and defeat. This is at the core of trauma or extreme stress. Of special interest in DEEP are decisions and thoughts made during shock moments. Any thought content has been locked up in the incident together with emotions, sensations and other body memories. It is likely to react on the person rather than be part of rational thinking.

Snap Moment: 1. The moment where a person cannot uphold a tractor effort anymore; his pulling gets more and more intense and then suddenly "snaps".. In the snap moment, or shortly before or after, we will find the most charged and negative thoughts and decisions. 2. In the moments before the actual snap there will be a sharp feeling of tension that resembles a vacuum. This is the similar to the moment of overwhelm caused by a pressor effort. The other party can have resisted this effort, typically by pulling against it, as it often happens in break-ups between lovers

Theme: See Complaint (General Complaint).

Thought: thought is mental activity dealing in ideas and concepts. Thought can usually be verbalized. There is A. Repressed thoughts with its bypass reactions; and B. Rational thoughts (reason). Re A: Repressed thoughts and bypass reactions are described as self-limiting thoughts, dictates, and emergency decisions in this glossary. They are negative automatic thoughts without inspection or rational analysis. In DEEP we are very interested in locating these, inspecting and reevaluating them in order to dissolve the ones that make us smaller and less able. Re B: Rational thoughts are correct estimations and representations of what we observe and how things work and interact. They are modified by a person's point of view.

Tractor Effort: an energetic effort to pull something closer by contraction of an energetic beam; a pulling effort. See also the definitions of Ridge* and Snap Moment*.

Trigger: Something in the environment that causes the person to act or feel irrationally. The trigger has some similarity with an element in a trauma. Perceiving this object or circumstance reactivates the trauma and its negative content.

Vector: 1. Used as the common denominator for all the DEEP elements. 2. In mathematics a vector is an arrow where its length stands for the magnitude of force; the direction shows where it is going. We use the word Vector as the in-common word for efforts, emotions, sensations, thoughts; and counter-efforts, counter-emotions, counter-sensations and counter-thoughts. Each of these elements has a direction or target and a magnitude or intensity.

Viewpoint: see Point of View.